Resilience and Urban Disasters

NEW HORIZONS IN REGIONAL SCIENCE

Series Editor: Philip McCann, *Professor of Urban and Regional Economics, University of Sheffield, UK*

Regional science analyses important issues surrounding the growth and development of urban and regional systems and is emerging as a major social science discipline. This series provides an invaluable forum for the publication of high quality scholarly work on urban and regional studies, industrial location economics, transport systems, economic geography and networks.

New Horizons in Regional Science aims to publish the best work by economists, geographers, urban and regional planners and other researchers from throughout the world. It is intended to serve a wide readership including academics, students and policymakers.

Titles in the series include:

Resilience and Urban Disasters

Surviving Cities

Edited by

Kamila Borsekova

Faculty of Economics, Matej Bel University, Banska Bystrica, Slovakia

Peter Nijkamp

Adam Mickiewicz University, Poznan, Poland, Jheronimus Academy of Data Science (JADS), 's-Hertogenbosch, the Netherlands and Universitatea Alexandru Ioan Cuza din Iasi, Iasi, Romania

NEW HORIZONS IN REGIONAL SCIENCE

Edward Elgar
PUBLISHING

Cheltenham, UK • Northampton, MA, USA

Published by
Edward Elgar Publishing Limited
The Lypiatts
15 Lansdown Road
Cheltenham
Glos GL50 2JA
UK

Edward Elgar Publishing, Inc.
William Pratt House
9 Dewey Court
Northampton
Massachusetts 01060
USA

A catalogue record for this book
is available from the British Library

Library of Congress Control Number: 2018959301

This book is available electronically in the **Elgar**online
Economics subject collection
DOI 10.4337/9781788970105

ISBN 978 1 78897 009 9 (cased)
ISBN 978 1 78897 010 5 (eBook)

Typeset by Servis Filmsetting Ltd, Stockport, Cheshire
Printed and bound in Great Britain by TJ International Ltd, Padstow

Contents

Contributors

Kamila Borsekova, PhD, is Coordinator of Research at Matej Bel University, Slovakia, and Head of the Research and Innovation Centre at the Faculty of Economics. She has extensive project experience. She was the project and mobility manager of the successfully implemented 7th FP project FOLPSEC. Currently, she is the principal investigator and coordinator of various national and international projects as well as team member in several domestic and foreign projects related to smart and creative cities, urban and regional development and policy. She has authored and co-authored more than 80 scientific publications. She is a member of The Regional Science Academy (TRSA), the university representative in the UNESCO Slovak Committee MOST, and member of the International Association on Public and Nonprofit Marketing (IAPNM) and the Slovak Section of the Regional Science Association International (RSAI).

Tuba İnal Çekiç is Research Associate at Hafencity University of Hamburg, Department of Planning and Regional Development, Germany. She received her BSci in Urban and Regional Planning from Istanbul Technical University, doctorate in Regional Planning in 2009 and became Associate Professor at Yıldız Technical University, Turkey in 2015.

Michal Dobrík, PhD, graduated at the Faculty of Political Science and International Relations of Matej Bel University, Slovakia. He is a scientist and lecturer in International Relations, particularly on international security and security policy, focusing on civil crisis management. He is a former coordinator of Center of Excellence projects – scientific priority no. 9 Security and Defense (co-financed by Operational Program Research and Development and ERDF). He is a Director of the Crisis Management Center, Matej Bel University (CEKR UMB) and his scientific work is on usage of simulation technologies in crisis management and modelling and simulation in crisis management.

Karol Fabián, doc. Ing., CSc, is a senior lecturer and scientist at the Crisis Management Center, Matej Bel University (CEKR UMB), Slovakia. From 1974 to 1993 he was a researcher at the CTU in Prague, ETH Zurich, TH Eindhoven Holland and the Slovak Academy of Sciences in Bratislava. Since 2013, he has worked as a senior lecturer in Security Policy, particularly on information security and computer science. As a researcher, he is engaged in the research of crisis management scenarios. He is also a principal investigator of the project entitled 'Cognitive Analytics of Real World Security Threats', supported and financed by IBM Global University Programs and the Ministry of Education, Science, Research and Sport of the Slovak Republic. He is the author and co-author of several monographs, academic papers and presentations presented at domestic and foreign academic conferences.

Richard Fabling is an empirical microeconomist specializing in business and labour economics, with a particular interest in understanding New Zealand workers, firms and jobs. He is an independent researcher, having previously held senior research positions at Motu Economic and Public Policy Research, the Reserve Bank of New Zealand and the Ministry of Economic Development. He was instrumental in the development of the Business Operations Survey, the Longitudinal Business Database (LBD), and the labour and productivity datasets within the LBD, and has co-authored over 40 papers using these data. He has a PhD in Applied Mathematics (Magnetohydrodynamics) from the University of Waikato, where his thesis entailed modelling solar flares.

Daniel Felsenstein is Professor and Chair of the Department of Geography at the Hebrew University of Jerusalem. His work uses the tools of dynamic simulation modelling and spatial econometrics. Current research projects relate to simulating urban resilience to large-scale shocks, dynamics of change in housing markets and estimating a spatial general equilibrium model for Israel. He has worked in the areas of local economic development, land use-transportation modelling, measuring regional income disparities, local labour market processes and dynamics of regional housing markets. He has published over 130 papers as well as six books on these and related topics. He served as Chair of the National Committee for Geography, Ministry of Education, 2012–16, and is currently consultant/national expert on the OECD Programme on Local Economic and Employment Development (LEED).

Ruslan Goncharov is Associate Professor at the Vysokovsky Graduate School of Urbanism, National Research University, Higher School of Economics, Russia, with a PhD in Geography (2016). A specialist in data analysis and visualization, he is the author of a course of lectures and seminars on methods of spatial analysis and urban informatics at HSE, and the author of more than 15 scientific publications and conference proceedings.

Arthur Grimes holds the Chair of Wellbeing and Public Policy at Victoria University of Wellington's School of Government, New Zealand. He is a senior Fellow at Motu Economic and Public Policy Research, and a member of the World Wellbeing Panel. His current research focuses on the economics of wellbeing and public policy and on urban economics. With respect to the latter, his work covers issues of infrastructure, housing and urban renewal. Prior positions include Chairman and Chief Economist of the Reserve Bank of New Zealand. He has a PhD in Economics from the London School of Economics and a BSocSc (Hons) from the University of Waikato.

A. Yair Grinberger is a postdoctoral researcher and Alexander von Humboldt Fellow at the GIScience Research Group, Institute of Geography, Heidelberg University, Germany. His work centres on developing geographical tools for knowledge production in various fields such as mobility analysis, volunteered geographical information (VGI), urban planning and the dynamics of real-estate markets. His current research projects include simulating urban dynamics in the wake of large-scale disasters, developing tools for analysing geographical effects on VGI and social media data, and identifying cognitive effects on spatio-temporal behaviour using mobility traces. His work on these subjects has been published in leading journals such as the *International Journal of Geographical Information Science, Professional Geographer, Computers, Environments and Urban Systems* and *Journal of Travel Research.*

Yoshifumi Ishikawa is Professor at the Faculty of Policy Studies at Nanzan University, Japan. In 1992, he joined Tokai Research Institute as a researcher. He received his PhD from Gifu University, Japan, with a dissertation on regional input-output analysis in 2000. He joined the Faculty of Policy Studies, Nanzan University, in 2004 as Associate Professor and became Professor in 2011. From 2016 he has been Head of the Graduate School of Social Sciences. His research focuses on the economic impacts of urban policy and structural analysis of the regional economy. He is currently a member of the Committee for Promoting the Integrated Economic and Fiscal Reforms, Government of Japan. He was the recipient of the Association Awards of the Japan Section of the Regional Science Association International (JSRSAI) in 2015.

Masafumi Morisugi is Professor at Meijo University, Japan, with a PhD in Engineering. He holds a Master of Economics degree from Nagoya University and was a visiting scholar at Wuppertal Institute for Climate, Environment and Energy, Germany, in 2017. His research interests are on various activities around environmental economics and policies and currently focus on evaluation of economic damage due to global warming, sand beach erosion, flood increases, effects on skiing sites and damage to health caused by heat stress and stroke. These topics have been conducted in such research projects as 'The Social Implementation Program on Climate Change Adaptation Technology' (SI-CAT) and 'Grant-in-Aid for Scientific Research (B), 2017–2019 (17H01938, Masafumi MORISUGI)', Japanese Ministry of Education, Culture, Sports, Science and Technology (MEXT).

Kazunori Nakajima is Associate Professor at the University of Hyogo, Japan, with a PhD in Economics from Tohoku University, Japan. He was a visiting scholar at SOAS, University of London, UK, from 2016 to 2017. His main research interests are on environmental economics and policy assessment (cost-benefit analysis of climate change strategies and environmental valuation), and health economics (benefit evaluation of emergency medical service in Japan) by using computable general equilibrium modelling, dynamic optimization modelling and applied econometrics. His research in these areas has been supported by grants from the Japan Society for the Promotion of Sciences (JSPS), the Ministry of the Environment (MOE), and the Japanese Ministry of Education, Culture, Sports, Science and Technology (MEXT).

Peter Nijkamp is Emeritus Professor in Regional and Urban Economics and in Economic Geography. He is currently affiliated with Adam Mickiewicz University, Poznan, Poland, the Jheronimus Academy of Data Science (JADS) in 's-Hertogenbosch, the Netherlands and Universitatea Alexandru Ioan Cuza din Iasi, Iasi, Romania. He is a member of the editorial/advisory boards of more than 20 scientific journals. According to the RePec list, he belongs to the top-25 of well-known economists worldwide. He is also a Fellow of the Royal Netherlands Academy of Sciences, and past vice-president of this organization. He was awarded the most prestigious scientific prize in the Netherlands, the Spinoza award. His publication list comprises more than 2000 contributions (articles and books), while his H-index is around 90. In addition to his academic research, he has also been involved in many practical policy issues in the fields of decision-making, regional development, environmental management, governance of culture, transportation and communication, and advanced data analytics.

Mehmet Doruk Özügül is Associate Professor at Yıldız Technical University, Istanbul, Turkey, in the Faculty of Architecture, Department of Urban and Regional Planning, which he joined in 2000. His research interests span a variety of interconnected topics including sustainable urban development, ecological planning, and strategic environmental impact assessment and planning theories.

Francesco Pagliacci is a postdoctoral research Fellow at the University of Modena and Reggio Emilia, Italy. After having received his PhD in

Agricultural Economics and Statistics from the University of Bologna, he conducted research activities at the Università Politecnica delle Marche and the University of Modena and Reggio Emilia, focusing on the fields of regional economics and rural and local development, with particular attention to quantitative aspects. Recently, he contributed to the research project 'Energie Sisma Emilia' and is currently working on disaster risk reduction as well as vulnerability of local systems to natural hazards.

Margherita Russo is a Full Professor of Economic Policy at the University of Modena and Reggio Emilia, Italy. Her main research activities include analysis of innovation processes, competence networks, effects of innovation on the organization of labour, structure and change in local productive systems, and evaluation of innovation policies. She has been a member of international research projects on innovation, and coordinated research projects on the mechanical industry in Italy and on the assessment of innovation networks policies. Since 2015, she has coordinated the research project 'Energie Sisma Emilia' on the socio-economic effects of the 2012 earthquake in Emilia (Italy). She is the Representative of Italy in the OECD WPTIP (Working Party on Innovation and Technology Policy), and in the EUSALP (European Union Strategy for Alpine Regions).

Lucia Rýsová graduated from the Faculty of Political Sciences and International Relations, Matej Bel University, Slovakia, in 2001. In 2008, she earned a PhD in International Relations. She is a senior lecturer in International Relations, particularly on political geography, European integration theories, international economic integration and post-modern theories of international relations, and a member of the academic Center of Excellence in security research. Currently, she is a Vice-Dean for Student Affairs at the Faculty of Political Sciences and International Relations, Matej Bel University.

Naoki Sakamoto is Associate Professor at Yamagata University, Japan. He holds PhD in Economics from Tohoku University. He is involved with various activities around public and environmental economics. His current research interests include theoretical and empirical analysis of national and local public finance as well as cost-benefit evaluation of adaptation to the impacts of climate change, emergency transport and tourism policy.

Ebru Seçkin, PhD, is Associate Professor at the Faculty of Architecture, Department of Urban and Regional Planning at Yildiz Technical University, Turkey, where she has been working since 2002. Her research interests revolve around four core themes: tourism, social enterprise, regional planning and agri-food chains and networks.

Mojgan Taheri Tafti is Assistant Professor at the School of Urban Planning, University of Tehran, Iran. Her PhD is from the Melbourne School of Design, University of Melbourne. She has worked in a number of teaching, research and operational roles in the areas of resilience, post-disaster reconstruction and housing projects for disadvantaged households in different countries. In 2015–16, she was a postdoctoral Fellow at Melbourne Social Equity Institute, University of Melbourne. Her main research interests are policy analysis, justice, vulnerability and political ecology. Her work has appeared in peer-reviewed journals and edited volumes such as *Urban Planning for Disaster Recovery* (2017) and *The Routledge Companion to Architecture and Social Engagement* (2018).

Levente Timar is a Fellow at Motu Economic and Public Policy Research in Wellington, New Zealand. His research areas include the economics of natural hazards and environmental economics, with a particular interest in responses to extreme events and environmental policies. A native of Hungary, he has a PhD in Economics from North Carolina State University.

Nadezhda Zamyatina is a leading research Fellow at the Faculty of Geography in Moscow State University, Russia. She obtained her PhD in Geography in 2001. She is the author of a course of lectures on the development of the Arctic, on the geography of Canada, demography, amongst others. In combination, she cooperates as an expert in regional development with the Council for the Study of Productive Forces under the Ministry of Economic Development of the Russian Federation (2010–16), and as Deputy Director of the Institute of Regional Consulting (since 2017). She is the author of more than 100 scientific publications.

Preface

Man-made, biological and physical systems have never been static, but always in a state of flux, be it in the short term or in the long term. Such changes may sometimes take the form of gradual or incremental transitions, but sometimes they reflect also abrupt transformations with structural dynamics, often in a non-linear form. Depending inter alia on the specification of the system's border, such drastic changes may be caused by internal forces or by external stimuli. The questions addressed in system dynamics are not only related to the causes of such changes in systemic patterns, but also to the implications and the recovery potential of such multi-faceted dynamic systems. In recent decades, the scientific study of such dynamic evolutionary patterns has received much attention, for example, in bifurcation theory, catastrophe theory, synergetics, chaos theory, tensor analysis and complexity theory. Applications of this new strand of thinking are not only found in the natural sciences, but also in the social sciences (e.g., demography, sociology, geography, economics, neural sciences and so on). Against this background, the present volume is focussed on the relevance of systemic perturbances in cities or urban agglomerations.

Nowadays, we observe an increasing scientific interest in urban and spatial evolution, with a particular view to the analysis of causal mechanisms and recovery patterns after a disruption of a stable urban system. Such disruptions may inter alia be caused by catastrophes (e.g., earthquakes, storms, floods, fires), political turbulence (e.g., revolutions, political turmoil), economic shocks (e.g., recession or crises), and the like. Modern resilience analysis aims to trace the pathway towards recovery after an initial disaster or jump happening in an urban system. In many cases, it appears that the transition path of 'back to normal' contradicts the initial – often pessimistic – catastrophic forecasts on the future of the city concerned. In reality, the recovery rate is sometimes much faster and more efficient than anticipated during or right after the occurrence of the abrupt event. From a scientific perspective, there is thus, alongside a descriptive event history investigation, also a clear need for a more strategically oriented and quantitative analysis of urban resilience patterns, with a view to a dynamic analysis of the recovery trajectory of a city after an initial disruption.

In urban history, we find numerous illustrations of negative catastrophe events, such as a destruction of cities during a war situation, a total collapse of a city after an industrial crisis, a disastrous decay as a result of political unrest, or a sudden turndown caused by natural catastrophes. Such events prompt of course questions on the severity and financial costs of such dramatic changes in relation to the systemic structure and organization of the city, as well as questions on recovery strategies in relation to institutional support systems and financial means needed. Urban disaster impact studies have indeed gained much popularity over the past years. In general, urban disaster impact assessment forms a systematic and measurable scientific approach to assessing the order of magnitude – in terms of costs and impacts on citizens – and the restoration capability and operational recovery strategy for a city, after it has been dramatically affected by an external rather abrupt change.

This volume aims to provide an original contribution to urban disaster analysis, with a focus on the quantitative analysis of urban recovery patterns after an initial disruption or catastrophe. The various chapters provide novel contributions of an analytical nature on urban evolution and adjustment patterns based on studies from all over the world. Both causal mechanisms and policy responses to the high social costs of a disaster are addressed in the volume. The volume addresses in particular issues concerning the long-term survival pathway of cities.

A prominent question that often shows up in the general disaster management literature – and hence also in urban disaster management studies – is the degree of vulnerability of an urban system vis-à-vis external shocks. Vulnerability refers to the potential weakness of a system against drastic influences from the outer world. It describes the shock resistance of cities, which may mean that, in our case, a shock may be mitigated or aggravated depending on the system's structure and the nature or direction of motion. Urban disaster management always has a preventive component and thus building up a priori resistance measures or programmes before a disastrous event takes place is a critical component of policy. For example, early warning systems, building dikes or good medical care may provide the means to safeguard the sustainability of cities.

On the effect side, there is a need for a solid impact analysis on urban disaster management. In particular, the socio-economic (including human) impacts on urban systems or cities subjected to disasters need a careful evidence-based investigation. Methods used can comprise input-output analysis, partial or general equilibrium modelling, bifurcation analysis and so on. This type of system impact analysis reflects a rather common trend, with one exception: there is a shock effect and no gradual effect on the urban system. Thus, there is a need for 'jump' effects in urban disaster management analysis and this is a great challenge. The present volume contains several interesting evidence-based applications in this field.

Finally, any urban disaster management problem is faced with the task to explore recovery options, in particular, in the context of abatement policy and the recovery potential in cities. Sometimes a return to the original system or position may be strived for, while in other cases a transformation of the city or its morphology may be seen as a smart urban policy. In this context, scenario building techniques regarding urban design and future may provide useful strategic information, while simulation methods on urban recovery processes may also offer meaningful decision support.

In conclusion, this volume aims to offer a broad panorama of studies on urban shocks and disasters, in which quantitative management techniques play a crucial role. The studies included in this volume are systematically organized (see Contents) and have different features: they may be analytical or policy-oriented, they may be conceptual or applied in nature. But in all cases they reflect the new trend in urban management analysis that urban contingency and disaster management belongs to the toolbox of modern urban planners and policy-makers seeking for sustainable development of cities.

Kamila Borsekova and Peter Nijkamp

PART I

Methodology and disaster impact analysis

1. Blessing in disguise: long-run benefits of urban disasters

Kamila Borsekova and Peter Nijkamp

1.1 CITIES IN MOTION

The Saint-Elisabeth's Flood (19 November 1421) was one of the most dev-astating flood disasters in Dutch history. Dozens of cities and villages in the south-western part of the country were swept away due to an unprecedented heavy storm, with a death toll of thousands of people. It is noteworthy that several cities which were completely destroyed (e.g., Dordrecht) later on played an important role as economic, cultural and political centres in the Netherlands. Apparently, urban recovery after disaster is by no means an exception and may even be a more universal phenomenon.

It is a well-known fact from ecology that forest fires may strengthen the long-run stability and diversity of woods and ecosystems. Apparently, an environmental disaster may lead to a better and more sustainable outcome for an ecosystem in the long term. Similar positive findings may be recorded on external shocks in human-made or social systems. For example, the large influx of refugees (Huguenots, Jews) to the Low Countries in the sixteenth and seventeenth centuries prompted the rise of flourishing cities (e.g., Antwerp, Amsterdam). Countries in a war may sometimes be better off in the long run than countries without a war, as witnessed by the post-World War II *Wirtschaftswunder* of Germany. Social systems apparently comprise an abundance of responsive or creative talent which makes these systems highly resilient and adaptive. In human history it appears that disasters may create challenges or threats which may be turned into new opportunities. This 'challenge and response' mechanism of human societies (see Toynbee 1934–61) provides an unprecedented degree of learning and adaptation behaviour which may lead to relatively stable social systems. Economies and societies in motion may be more resilient and robust than others in a static standstill position. Coping with dynamics is also the core message of a Schumpeterian 'creative destruction' conceptualization of the evolution of human-made systems.

Dynamics not only refers to a simple time-varying trajectory, but may also encapsulate non-linear dynamic behaviour in space and time (see for an exposition Reggiani and Nijkamp 2006). This phenomenon has prompted an avalanche of studies on non-linear dynamics in complex spaces (see Reggiani and Nijkamp 2009), which may exhibit various dynamic evolutionary pathways (e.g., a cusp catastrophe), depending on initial conditions and transition dynamics. Sometimes, very complicated – even fractal – movements in spatial systems may occur in complex multi-agent systems (see, e.g., Banaszak et al. 2015). Clearly, both natural and human-made systems may exhibit a wealth of dynamic behaviour, especially in those cases where human responses intervene with natural systems (e.g., in the case of climate change). This observation has prompted a great variety of studies on resilient spatial systems and adaptive behaviour of agents (see Reggiani et al. 2015). For example, in the literature on flood management the notions of flood hazard (the probability of the occurrence of extreme events) and flood effects or damage in catastrophic events often show up. Such damage is contingent on the range of exposure (people, resources) and the areal vulnerability (or lack of resistance in case of a flood) in the area concerned. For more details and applications in the domain of climate change we refer to van der Pol (2015).

Clearly, besides flood disasters, there are many other types of disasters which may adversely and dramatically affect a spatial system. For example, an urban system may be exposed to a great variety of external shocks, such as fires (e.g., Lisbon), earthquakes (e.g., Kobe), wars (e.g., Mombasa), famine (e.g., Calcutta), social unrest (e.g., Tripoli), environmental disasters (e.g., Bhopal), volcanos (e.g., Pompei/Napoli), economic collapse (e.g., Detroit), or several planning disasters (see, e.g., Hall 1982). A prominent question is of course whether human response (e.g., adaptation, abatement measures) may lead to a more favourable and stable long-run outcome, and if so, under which conditions.

In this context, various policy responses may be distinguished, such as anticipatory adaptation, mitigation measures, or *ex ante* control or preventive measures, which all aim to transform a system out of equilibrium back into a stable – sometimes initial – state. Disaster management is usually geared towards achieving the original equilibrium situation. In all such cases, solid empirical and scientific information is needed. Van der Pol (2015) makes a distinction here into three sources: scientific information for policy, evidence-based learning, and incident-based learning. Clearly, information, learning and adjustment are critical parameters in uncertainty management. It is increasingly recognized that governing a balanced future of urban systems is an unprecedented challenge that requires novel, contemporaneous decision support tools (e.g., imagineering methods, dashboard techniques, scenario experiments) (see Kourtit 2015).

The main proposition put forward and tested in the present study is whether, how and why an organized type of dynamic spatial system, that is, a city, once it is dramatically affected by an external shock or disaster, is able to recover. In particular, we want to investigate whether – as a result of dedicated recovery and rehabilitation strategies after a shock or disaster has occurred – the city concerned may operate at a higher achievement level compared to the 'without' effect ('dead weight'). Our study is organized as follows. Section 1.2 provides a concise description on the dynamics of urban systems and outlines the problems addressed in the chapter in greater detail. Section 1.3 gives a review of the database used to collect information about various types of disasters. Section 1.4 provides a comprehensive overview of the world evidence of natural disasters, including distribution of different types of natural disasters across the world and a comparison of the total number of disasters and the total number of deaths and people affected by natural disasters between 1974 and 2003. In the second part of this section we discuss the resilience of countries all over the world against natural disasters by using the inspirational example of Japan and its cities. Section 1.5 is devoted to the implications for urban disaster management based on statistical evidence. The chapter concludes with general policy lessons.

1.2   THE DYNAMICS OF CITIES

Cities – and urban agglomerations – are complex and interrelated spatial entities that include a wide variety of dynamic trajectories over time (see, e.g., Taylor 2007; Kourtit et al. 2014; Kourtit 2015). Despite the worldwide urbanization mega-trend, not all cities have the same growth pace; some may show an unprecedented growth rate, while others may even exhibit a decline (see Haase 2015). Urban growth and urban shrinkage in the world are often taking place at the same time. Urban areas are usually showing a life cycle pattern with upturns and downturns, sometimes similar to business life cycles in industry. There is a wealth of studies that document these dynamic urban trajectories (see, e.g., an early seminal study on the life course of cities by van den Berg et al. 1982). In recent years, we have witnessed an avalanche of studies on urban growth and decline under different economic and political regimes (see, e.g., Couch et al. 2005; Nuissl and Rink 2005; Cheshire 2006; Haase et al. 2009; Kabisch et al. 2010, 2012). An interesting overview of various trends in urban dynamics can be found in Haase (2015).

Interesting contributions to a further understanding of resilience mechanisms and vulnerability analysis can be found inter alia in Alexander

(2000), Richardson et al. (2008) and Rose (2007). Urban evolution is the result of a complex internal, external and policy force field. In contrast to a regular life cycle pattern of urban agglomerations caused by endogenous forces of a city or urban system (as studied in the earlier urban dynamic systems literature; see Forrester 1969), our chapter aims to focus attention on the external shocks that impact the urban economy and that lead to disequilibrating forces, without any prior guarantee of a stable outcome or a return to the original position.

The analysis of external shocks to an urban system prompts two types of methodological research challenges:

- What are the intermediate and long-term effects of such a shock on the urban economy? Such effects may show up in various urban sectors, such as tourism, the retail sector, public services or the business sector at large. This leads to the need for a systematic and comprehensive urban disaster impact assessment (UDIA).
- Under which conditions is the urban system able to return to its initial position or to a new equilibrium? This question is often addressed in the context of resilience and vulnerability analysis. The conceptual framework and operational meaning of resilience and vulnerability – with a distinct reference to the transportation sector – have been presented in recent articles by Kim and Marcouiller (2015) and Reggiani et al. (2015).

Resilience refers in general to the ability of actors to develop and implement adaptation mechanisms to external perturbations that mitigate the long-run effects of such shocks and that might lead to a restoration of the original equilibrium or to the realization of a new equilibrium state. Resilience may thus be considered as 'the capacity of a system to absorb disturbance and reorganize while undergoing change so as to still retain essentially the same function, structure, identity and feedbacks' (Walker et al. 2004, p. 8). Vulnerability is related to the robustness of a man-made system to cope with the emergence of external shocks and to combat their negative consequences; it is a shock absorption ability that reflects to some extent a risk-persistence of a system in a timely and effective manner. Reduction of vulnerability through deliberate actions may increase the resilience of the system concerned.

In the past decades, there has also been a permanent interest in a related phenomenon, viz. hysteresis. This is a particular type of systematic singularity that leads to out-of-equilibrium situations as a result of a delayed response to shocks. Depending on initial conditions, different types of asymmetric behaviour of a complex system may be observed (known as a cusp in the catastrophe theory literature). Such inert response mechanisms may find their origin in historical and cultural attitudes in some regions or cities or in ineffective and low-responsive management and policy systems in cities. In other words, even though disasters or shocks are often not forecastable, the response system (in terms of local attitudes and effective counter-measures) is critical in coping with jumps in a system and hence in paving a road to a new balance (also see for a recent study Tubadji et al. 2016).

In recent years, much interest has arisen in disaster impact assessment. Methods employed in such an assessment comprise inter alia: input-output analyses, shift-share analysis, general equilibrium modelling and so forth (see, e.g., Rodriguez et al. 2007; Cuaresma et al. 2008; Cavallo et al. 2013; Okuyama and Santos 2014). The geographical scale level of a disaster impact assessment may range from a macro perspective (see, e.g., Skidmore and Toya 2002) to a local (regional and urban) angle (see, e.g., Baade et al. 2007; Chang 2010; Coffman and Noy 2011; Okuyama 2015). It is also noteworthy that a need for a more systematic impact assessment has emerged, as reflected in some recent meta-analytical studies (see, e.g., Lazzaroni and van Bergeijk 2014; van Bergeijk and Lazzaroni 2015).

The history of spatial and urban dynamics over many centuries prompts intriguing questions on the 'why' and 'how' of urban evolution. In this context, Tellier (2009) adopts a long-run perspective on urban development patterns and concludes that the force field of the spatial development of our world has to be found in hyper-dynamic corridors in our urban world which spur economic development in these areas. Cities on these corridors have more favourable seedbed conditions and are able to recover more swiftly from decay and destruction. The broader literature on regional resilience, especially the literature on resilience to natural disasters, offers new insights that may be relevant to a better understanding of regional-economic resilience. A common finding in this literature is that access to economic resources promotes regional or community resilience in the face of natural disasters (Morrow 2008; Pastor and Benner 2008). This observation suggests that regions with higher average incomes or wages (independent of human capital) may recover more quickly from external shocks (Hill et al. 2012). Consequently, urban resilience may be income-dependent.

In the current age of local and global uncertainty, we are continually facing new and unforeseen threats at all levels – international, national, regional and local. Natural disasters, technological catastrophes and terrorist attacks beset the world of today. Cities and their urban structures are positioned in the first line of attack, while they have to be able to satisfy the needs and expectations of society in the event of disasters – and to cope with the fear of future disasters.

1.3 DATA AND METHODOLOGY

There is a great deal of evidence on urban disasters, but often on an anecdotal basis, so that a systematic comparison is often problematic. For our purposes we have resorted to an extensive disaster database. Data inspection and mining have been undertaken through the Emergency Events Database (EM-DAT).[1] EM-DAT uses a classification that was initiated by the Centre for Research on the Epidemiology of Disasters (CRED) with the aim to create – and agree – on a common hierarchy and terminology for all global and regional databases on natural disasters and to establish a common and agreed upon definition of sub-events that is simple and self-explanatory. In this context, CRED defines a disaster as 'a situation or event that overwhelms local capacity, necessitating a request at the national or international level for external assistance; an unforeseen and often sudden event that causes great damage, destruction and human suffering' (Guha-Sapir et al. 2016, p. 7). For a disaster to be entered into the database, at least one of the following criteria should be fulfilled:

- ten or more people reported killed
- 100 or more people reported affected
- declaration of a state of emergency
- call for international assistance.

CRED distinguishes two generic categories for disasters, natural disasters and technological catastrophes.

The natural disasters category is divided into five sub-groups, which in turn cover 12 disaster types and more than 32 sub-types. The five sub-groups and 12 types are:

- biological disasters (insect infestations, epidemics and animal attacks – the last two categories are not included in the dataset)
- geophysical disasters (earthquakes and tsunamis, volcanic eruptions, dry mass movements)
- climatological disasters (droughts with associated food insecurities, extreme temperatures and wildfires)

---

[1] Since 1988, the Centre for Research on the Epidemiology of Disasters, located in the School of Public Health at the Université catholique de Louvain, has been developing and maintaining an Emergency Events Database, EM-DAT. EM-DAT was created with the initial support of the World Health Organization (WHO) and the Belgian government. The main objective of the database is to serve the purposes of humanitarian action at national and international levels. It is an initiative aimed to rationalize decision-making for disaster preparedness and prevention, as well as to provide an objective base for vulnerability assessment and priority setting.

● hydrological disasters (floods including waves and surges, wet mass movements)
● meteorological disasters (storms divided into nine sub-categories).

The technological catastrophes comprise three groups:

● industrial accidents (chemical spills, collapse of industrial infrastructure, explosions, fires, gas leaks, poisoning, radiation)
● transport accidents (transportation by air, rail, road or water)
● miscellaneous accidents (collapse of domestic/non-industrial structures, explosions, fires).

EM-DAT contains essential core data on the occurrence and effects of over 18,000 mass disasters in the world from the year 1900 to the present. The database is compiled from various sources, including United Nations (UN) agencies, non-governmental organizations (NGOs), insurance companies, research institutes and press agencies. EM-DAT provides an objective base for vulnerability assessment and rational decision-making in disaster situations. For example, it helps policy- and decision-makers identify disaster types that are the most common in a given country and have had significant historical impacts on a specific human population.

The following three figures summarize, compile and show the development of the occurrence of disasters from 1900 to 2015 in relation to death tolls caused by disasters, total affected people by disasters and total economic damage.

Figure 1.1 shows the total death toll caused by disasters from 1900 to 2015 and the occurrence of disasters from 1900 to 2015. While the disaster occurrence has an increasing trend, the number of deaths is decreasing. Figure 1.2 demonstrates total affected people by disasters.

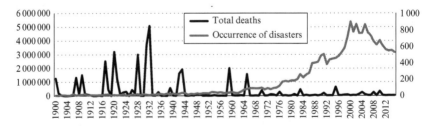

Source: http://www.emdat.be/advanced_search/index.html

Figure 1.1   Total deaths caused by disasters from 1900 to 2015

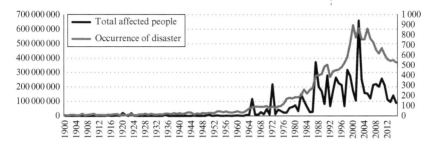

Source: http://www.emdat.be/advanced_search/index.html

Figure 1.2   Total affected people by disasters from 1900 to 2015

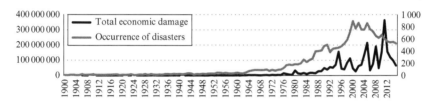

Source: http://www.emdat.be/advanced_search/index.html

Figure 1.3   Total economic damage caused by disasters from 1900 to 2015 in thousands of US$

The data show an increasing trend of people affected by disasters from 1900 to 2015. They correspond to the trend of the increasing world population. Figure 1.3 provides an overview of the total economic damage caused by the disasters.

Figure 1.3 shows that the economic damage caused by disasters has a similar trajectory as the occurrence of disasters during the period concerned. The total economic damage as well as the total affected number of people essentially mirrors the increasing occurrence of disasters. The occurrence of disasters forms a clear contrast with the total number of deaths (Figure 1.1), which is decreasing during the reporting period.

As reported by EM-DAT, it turns out that from 1993 to 2014, 56.27 per cent of all disasters occurred in high-income and upper-middle-income countries, where the share in the number of deaths is 32.17 per cent, in contrast to lower-middle-income and low-income countries with 67.83 per cent of total deaths, corresponding to 43.73 per cent of the total number of disasters. While the economic losses from disasters tend to be greater in high-income countries due to higher value of properties, infrastructure and assets, low- and middle-income countries tend to face higher fatalities and disruptions to hard-earned development gains. On average, around 82,000 people are killed annually by disasters, with most fatalities concentrated in low- and middle-income countries (Dickson et al. 2012).

1.4   SUCCESS AND FAILURE IN CASE OF DISASTERS

Success and failure of cities and countries exposed to and coping with disasters depend on many place-based 'specific features'. In the distant past, disasters usually had far-reaching consequences. Historical evidence can, for instance, be found in devastating fires common in big cities, inter alia, London in 1666, Chicago in 1871 and Thessaloniki in 1917. Large fires are nowadays no longer devastating major cities in high-income nations.

> In high-income nations, the concentration of people, buildings, motor vehicles and industries (and their wastes) in cities is not generally associated with higher disaster risks because this same concentration also means many economies of scale and proximity for the comprehensive web of infrastructure and services that reduce disaster risks and disaster impacts. Urban populations in these nations take it for granted that they will be protected from disasters, including extreme weather, floods, fires and technological accidents. (World Disaster Report 2010, p. 16)

It is noteworthy that several high-income countries are very often facing natural disasters. Let us take a look at the distribution of different types of natural disasters across the world. In Figure 1.4, there are four maps of the world with occurrences of different types of natural disasters from 1974 to 2003. Severity of disasters reported on maps is evaluated according to the CRED methodology as indicated in Section 1.3. Of course, we may assume that a large country (by area) will tend to have a higher number of occurrences than a small country. But as seen from the maps, this is not always the case. Very often, the location in areas where tectonic plates are meeting (Japan, Italy) or in hurricane areas (Caribbean) is a crucial factor for the higher occurrence of disasters.

Map 1 shows the number of occurrences of earthquake disasters in the world from 1974 to 2003. A light colour means occurrence of an earthquake frequency from 0 to 5, the grey colour represents the occurrence from 5 to 10, and the black colour means more than 10 earthquakes during the investigation period. Map 2 shows the number of occurrences

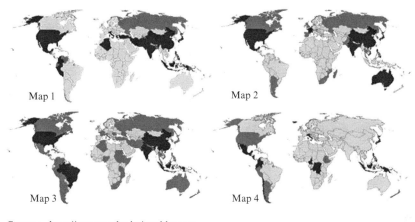

Source: http://www.emdat.be/world-maps

*Figure 1.4   Occurrence of different types of natural disasters in the world
from 1974 to 2003*

of windstorm disasters in the world from 1974 to 2003. The light colour
means a frequency from 0 to 10 windstorms, the grey colour represents the
interval from 11 to 30 windstorms and the black colour means more than
30 windstorms. Map 3 shows the number of occurrences of flood disasters
in the world from 1974 to 2003. The light colour means a frequency of
occurrence from 0 to 15, the grey colour represents an interval from 15 to
60 floods and the black colour means countries are affected by more than
60 floods within the relevant period. Finally, map 4 shows the number of
occurrences of volcano disasters in the world from 1974 to 2003. The light
colour means countries have a zero number of volcano disasters, the grey
colour indicates countries have 1 to 2 occurrences of volcano disasters, and
the black colour means countries have more than 2 occurrences of volcano
disasters in the period concerned.

It is evident that some geographical localities in the world are more
affected by the occurrence of disasters than others. As mentioned before,
higher occurrence of different types of disasters (e.g., earthquakes or hurricanes) is often place-specific. Different countries have different severities of
natural disasters. This can also be caused by a higher density of population
(e.g., India) or a well-built and complicated infrastructure (e.g., United
States, Japan). Countries most affected by the occurrence of all types of
natural disasters are Japan, the United States, Mexico and the Philippines
that are fighting with the high occurrence of all types of disasters, followed
by China, India, Indonesia and Italy.

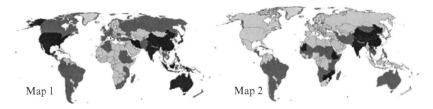

Source: http://www.emdat.be/world-maps

Figure 1.5   *The total number of disasters occurrence (map no. 1) and the*
total number of deaths and people affected (map no. 2) by
natural disasters between 1974 and 2003

Figure 1.5 provides a comparison of the total number of disasters occurring (countries shown in light colour represent 0 to 30 natural disasters occurrence, countries shown in grey represent the interval from 31 to 120 natural disasters, and countries shown in black represent 121 to 506 natural disasters) and the total number of deaths and people affected by natural disasters (countries in light colour from 0 to 1 million, countries in grey colour from 1 million to 5 million, and countries in black from 5 million) between 1974 and 2003.[2]

Figure 1.5 evidences that several countries, despite the enormous occurrence of natural disasters, are able to deal better with catastrophes and to develop more preventive measures for the protection of their inhabitants. Countries in the group with the highest occurrence of natural disasters that belong to the group of countries with the lowest number of people affected or the lowest death tolls are the United States, Mexico, Japan and Indonesia. In contrast, there are several other countries, especially in the African continent, that despite the lower occurrence of natural disasters belong to the most affected countries in the world. The worst situation is in the Islamic Republic of Mauritania with an occurrence of less than 31 natural disasters, while the total number of deaths or people affected by natural disasters within the investigated period is more than 5 million. With the current population of 3.6 million people this number is more than alarming.

The world evidence of natural disasters brings us to the question, why and how some countries and cities are able to cope with natural disasters, to protect inhabitants and to rise from the ashes like a phoenix relatively fast and to return in an even more favourable position than before?

---

[2] Occurrences of disasters are in total numbers, not standardized for the size of the country.

According to the World Disaster Report (2010), the reason for this is found in the solid built environment and urban management:

> in a well-governed city, much of the disaster risk in terms of death and serious injury is enormously reduced by good-quality buildings and infrastructure. If these interventions do not prevent disasters, they can dramatically cut the death and injury tolls and should limit the economic impacts. This applies not just in cases of extreme weather or earthquakes but also for industrial accidents and fires. (p. 140)

To support the evidence of this statement, we will use here the example of Japan and its cities. Japan with more than 120 million inhabitants is one of the most densely populated countries in the world. The census in 2010 shows that more than 90 per cent of the Japanese population lives in cities (Ministry of Internal Affairs and Communications Statistics Bureau 2015). Table 1.1 shows the occurrence of all types of natural disaster in

Table 1.1   Occurrence of natural disasters and its consequences in Japan from 1900 to 2016

Disaster type	Disaster sub-type	Events count	Total deaths	Total affected	Total damage (thousands of US$)
Earthquake	Ground movement	47	161 835	963 619	146 841 400
Earthquake	Tsunami	14	32 576	436 947	212 821 000
Epidemic	Viral disease	1	0	2 000 000	0
Epidemic	Bacterial disease	2	1	534	0
Extreme temperature	Heat wave	7	675	122 487	0
Extreme temperature	Cold wave	1	6	0	0
Flood	Flash flood	1	21	25 807	1 950 000
Flood	–	56	14 685	7 210 152	721 800
Flood	Coastal flood	2	34	384 143	7 440 000
Flood	Riverine flood	15	253	196 080	4 614 000
Landslide	Landslide	21	1071	25 773	248 000
Landslide	Avalanche	1	13	0	0
Storm	Convective storm	17	280	118 517	6 670 200
Storm	Tropical cyclone	128	32 673	7 713 297	56 356 100
Volcanic activity	Ash fall	15	515	99 979	132 000
Wildfire	Forest fire	1	0	222	0
Total		329	244 638	19 297 557	437 794 500

Source: http://www.emdat.be/country_profile/index.html

Japan from 1900 to 2016 including total deaths, total people affected and total economic damage.

Table 1.1 shows that in Japan from 1900 to 2016 a total of 329 different types of natural disasters occurred, with a total death toll of 244,638 people. Although this number is high, in comparison with the total number of almost 20 million people affected, as noticed by Davis and Weinstein (2002), evidence from Japan has shown that temporary shocks, even of a frightening magnitude, appear to have little long-run impact on the spatial structure of the economy. In addition, empirical results from Japan strongly confirm that there is a great deal of persistence across time, especially in the densely settled regions.

The data in the table show that natural disasters caused gigantic economic damage over time. It is noteworthy however, that despite all the destructive consequences of natural disasters in Japan, the country is still one of the most competitive countries in the world and obtained the 6th highest ranking according to the Global Competitiveness Index in 2015–16. Similarly, Japanese cities are among the most beautiful and flourishing ones in the world, with the highest standards of living, even though several of them are located in an area with a high seismic activity.

1.5   THE URBAN DIMENSION OF DISASTERS

As shown in the previous sections of the chapter, disaster occurrence impacts all parts of our world, and all countries in the world have experienced some kind of natural disasters. When we look at the spatial dimension of natural disasters, cities and urban areas concentrate higher disaster risk than rural areas due to the density of people, infrastructure and assets. Clearly, uncontrolled urban explosion and inefficient urban management may affect the level of disaster impact on urban development.

Extremely stressful experiences regarding natural disasters are mainly associated with significant physical damage and human suffering. In the short run, there is obviously an expectation of a significant negative impact of natural disasters on economic growth and activity in the area concerned. However, as mentioned by Cole et al. (2016), the results of the existing empirical studies on such areas are mixed among authors finding negative, positive or no effect at all of a natural disaster on economic growth. The absence of a consensus on the average effects of natural disasters is illustrated by the results of two recent studies by Cuaresma et al. (2008) and Cavallo and Noy (2010) who argue that on average natural disasters have a positive and negative impact, respectively. Negative effects of disasters are undisputable and are often very devastating in terms of death tolls, economic damage and total number of people affected by disasters.

The UN reports a steady increase of disasters across the globe (UNISDR 2004). If comparing disasters in developed and developing countries, it becomes evident that the effects of disaster are not uniform. Developing countries affected by natural disasters have usually experienced the highest numbers of people both affected and killed. Mileti et al. (1995) and Aleskerov et al. (2005) perceived this as a consequence of unsustainable development, lack of land use planning, and absence of interest and resources to solve issues concerning disaster preparedness. Developing countries mostly deal with disasters after they are hit. Disaster prevention is often weakly developed. Loayza et al. (2009) support this argument and conclude that developing countries are more sensitive to natural disasters. Expectedly, negative effects of natural disasters have been researched and highlighted in many books, articles and reports. Despite the considerable economic damage caused by natural disasters, only little research has been undertaken on the long-range effect of such disasters on economic activity. Several studies are dealing with short-term impacts of natural disasters (Cole et al. 2016). Noy (2009) finds a significant short-run effect of natural disasters, concentrated in developing countries only, but almost no long-term impact. In growth models with increasing returns to technology in production, theory says any destruction of capital can lead to a longer-term negative impact. Likewise, the destruction of infrastructure lowers returns to all factors of production (Cole et al. 2016). A similar result is provided by Rasmussen (2004) who finds that natural disasters lead to a reduction in same-year growth of more than 2 per cent and an increase in the current account deficit and public debt, while Fisker (2012) finds that an earthquake does have a negative impact on five-year growth at the local level. In this context, Ahlerup (2013) argues that if the only negative effects are found for disasters, then the intuitive assumption of a negative impact lacks robustness. Cole et al. (2016, p. 5) conclude then that the

> type of disaster has an important influence on the magnitude and sign of the growth effect. The main negative impact tends to come from damage to essential intermediates such as the effect of drought on agriculture. The positive impact is more prevalent in those cases where there is a physical damage to buildings and infrastructure and the reconstruction leads to positive returns.

In this context, Davis and Weinstein (2002, p. 1271) argue:

> the pure random growth theory predicts that growth follows a random walk – all shocks have permanent effects. By contrast, the locational fundamentals story holds that so long as the shock is purely temporary, even strong shocks should

shortly be reversed, as the advantages of the particular locations reassert
themselves in relatively rapid growth rates on the path to recovery.

Beside many negative effects of natural disasters, there are several
reasons why we might expect natural disasters to have a positive economic
impact on the short-run or long-run growth path. Several empirical studies deal with short-run positive effects of natural disasters on economic
growth. The most visible one is an endogenous reaction of an affected
country or city (or an international organization) to the disaster in the
form of a fiscal stimulus (multiplier effect) and related foreign (financial
and non-financial) aid stimulating the locally affected area (Albala-
Bertrand 1993; Cole et al. 2016). Generally, we can say the gross domestic
product (GDP) is increasing in periods immediately following a natural
disaster (Dacy and Kunreuther 1969; Albala-Bertrand 1993; Otero and
Marti 1995). This is often caused by the increased direct production and
activities connected with repairing of infrastructure or its overall rebuilding or revitalization of cities, very often in a more efficient form. The same
effect can be observed on employment. Leiter et al. (2009) focused on the
impact of selected natural disasters on employment in developed countries.
He examined European firms that have been affected by floods and found
that employment growth is higher in regions that experienced major floods.

A positive long-run effect of natural disasters on growth can be found in
the work of Skidmore and Toya (2002) based on the Schumpeterian notion
of creative destruction. Disaster risk may reduce tangible asset investments,
but at the same time disasters provide an opportunity to update the capital
stock through invention or adoption of new technologies. While adopting
endogenous growth theory, disaster risk could potentially lead to higher
rates of growth. Individuals and institutions invest in physical but also
human capital which prompts and supports positive externality associated
with human capital accumulation. If disasters reduce the expected return
to tangible assets, then there is a correspondingly higher relative return to
intangible assets, which may have a positive effect on growth.

While disasters are considered to be external shocks that may destroy
urban development gains, disaster risk is internal to the development
process of cities. The rapid and often unplanned expansion of cities is
exposing a greater number of people and economic assets to the risk of
disasters and related risks, such as the effects of climate change. For city
governments, increased climate variability imposes additional challenges
to effective urban management and the delivery of key services, while for
residents it increasingly affects their lives and livelihoods due to a greater
frequency of natural disasters. There is an urgent need for cities to consider
the issues of disaster and climate change by streamlining assessments of

related risks in their planning and management processes and delivery of services (Dickson et al. 2012).

A disaster response can result in the development of more effective infrastructure and increased productive effort in affected – but also in unaffected – areas of a country. Likewise, when more capital is destroyed than labour, the return to capital increases resulting in short-term growth, while local workers may also be incentivized to work harder so as to compensate for inter-temporal losses (Melecky and Raddatz 2011). According to the World Disaster Report (2010),

> the quality and capacity of local government in a city have an enormous influence on the level of risk that its population faces from disasters and, in particular, on whether risk-reducing infrastructure serves everyone including those living in low-income areas. Local or municipal governments also influence whether provision has been made to remove or reduce disaster risk from events such as floods and large-scale fires or to build into the city the capacity to withstand potential disaster events such as earthquakes. The quality and capacity of local government also have an enormous influence on the levels of risk from everyday hazards that can contribute much to mortality, injury or illness but that are not considered disasters, such as vector-borne diseases and traffic accidents. These risks are not an inherent characteristic of cities but the result of the limitations of their governments in meeting their responsibilities and, more broadly, of limitations of governance including the quality of their relations with the inhabitants and civil society organizations. (p. 139)

According to the World Bank (Guigale 2017), one source of disaster risk management usually remains under-exploited: insurance. Data from Geo Risks Research for 2006 indicate that very few developing countries have appropriate property insurance in comparison to developed countries (Wirtz 2008). The seriousness of the post-disaster capital gap and the emergence of novel insurance instruments for pricing and transferring catastrophe risks to global financial markets have motivated many developing country governments, as well as development institutions, NGOs and other donor organizations, to consider pre-disaster financial instruments as a component of disaster risk management (Linnerooth-Bayer et al. 2005). Insurance instruments are only one of many options in managing risks of natural hazards (Linnerooth-Bayer et al. 2007), but they can significantly influence the path of recovery.

Ahlerup (2013), who pays attention to controlling carefully the endogenous nature of natural disaster losses and controlling for unobserved heterogeneity, finds a clearly positive effect on the subsequent economic performance in the short, medium and long term.

Urban agglomerations have an expensive and vulnerable infrastructure and a massive concentration of humans, businesses, houses and offices.

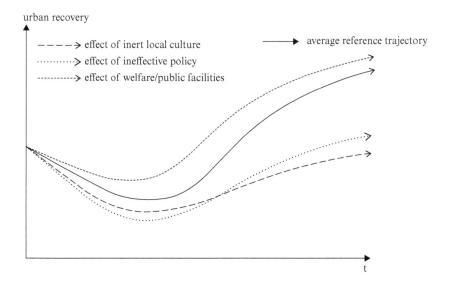

urban recovery

- $----\to$ effect of inert local culture
- $\cdots\cdots\to$ effect of ineffective policy
- $-------\to$ effect of welfare/public facilities
- $\longrightarrow$ average reference trajectory

t

Figure 1.6   Urban resilience trajectory after an external shock

Consequently, any disaster will have a dramatic effect on the socioeconomic position of an agglomeration, if affected by an external shock. The
long-run consequences are likely also determined by local cultural attitudes
and effective policy responses. But it is also important to realize that the
contribution of a modern and up-to-date urban infrastructure – in combination with external economies of density, proximity and connectivity –
may reinforce the long-range socioeconomic progress potential of a city.
We may therefore, hypothesize that the urban resilience trajectory – after
an external shock – may have the following shape outlined in Figure 1.6,
which is influenced by various moderator variables, viz.: (i) current level
of high welfare and appropriate public facilities; (ii) inert local cultural
attitudes on urban management; (iii) ineffective or delayed policy response
after a shock.

Testing the validity of the constituents of the urban resilience curve
would need extensive panel data – on a cross-comparative base – over a
long time period. This may be difficult to achieve, although in several cases
basic data (such as population numbers, migrants, infrastructure, public
expenditure, employment, houses, buildings and so on) may exist, which
might be suitable for a solid validation of our propositions. If not, we
have to resort to case study research, which may be insightful regarding
the drivers and effects of urban catastrophic events, but often offer only
anecdotal evidence.

Cities can plan and respond better if the location and nature of risk is known and clearly mapped out, and also if risk assessment and management is mainstreamed in urban development and management programmes. Therefore, the database like that for UDIA mentioned above should contain at least the following information ingredients:

- institutional assessment
- hazard impact assessment
- social assessment.

According to the methodology of the World Bank (Dickson et al. 2012, pp. 24–61), the assessment should be based upon three principal assessment pillars (institutional, hazard impact and socioeconomic), each of them associated with three levels of complexity (primary, secondary and tertiary). This framework is built around a central pillar for assessing the impact of hazards, aimed at identifying the type, intensity and locations of potential changes and losses resulting from future hazards and climate change scenarios. Given that risk is a function of hazards, the relative vulnerability of people and economic assets, and the capacity to respond, an operational urban risk assessment should take into account the role of institutions and the socioeconomic conditions of city residents in order to understand and enhance the competence of agencies that are responsible for managing the risks arising from disasters and climate change, and identify the most vulnerable populations likely to be adversely affected, as well as understanding their adaptive capacity. We briefly summarize here the most important lessons.

1.5.1 Institutional Assessment

The bases for institutional assessment are: legal foundations, national and regional frameworks. At the primary level, institutional assessment is oriented towards an institutional mapping of disaster risks and climate change. The first step in institutional assessment is the identification of institutions and organizations explicitly responsible for addressing climate change and natural hazards, and those that have a more indirect impact. It is followed by undertaking an institutional mapping exercise that includes government agencies within the city and a description of their specific competences before, during and after disasters. At the secondary level, interventional analysis is realized with the aim to identify key resources, policies, tools, programmes and coordination tools and approaches. It creates an inventory of relevant planning instruments, including existing policies, programmes, plans and projects. The secondary and tertiary levels overlap with intervention gap analysis. This identifies shortcomings in current city management tools and policy programmes, and provides preliminary recommendations to mainstream risk reduction including adaptive capacity assessment and identification of possible fiscal transfers for risk financing.

1.5.2   Hazard Impact Assessment

The main pillar of urban disaster impact assessment is oriented towards understanding hazard trends, identifying relevant populations and tangible assets at risk of hazards and climate change in a city, and quantifying potential impacts of future hazards. The primary level assessment is focused on geospatial analysis of historical incidence through secondary data collection and stakeholder consultations to develop simple maps of hazard impacts showing where hazards have historically affected a city. At a secondary level, hazard mapping, exposure mapping and vulnerability studies are the basis for development of more detailed risk maps. Risk modelling for natural hazards and climate changes, scenarios of economic and social loss are defined based on impact modelling. The tertiary level involves modelling probabilistic risk through using different hazard scenarios to approximate economic loss for exposed tangible assets. Modern approaches and tools are used through the design of concrete and specific probabilistic risk assessment tools. Well-developed planning tools can enhance the capacity of city managers or project developers to understand and integrate climate change into future planning. The most effective risk planning tools encourage users to focus on the conditions, assumptions and uncertainties underlying the results of climate models to enable them to estimate the robustness of the information, make an informed assessment of current and future risks, and evaluate the appropriateness of response options.

1.5.3   Social Assessment

Social assessment is mainly based on demographic information that is very important for efficient and robust risk assessment. Socioeconomic assessment focuses on identification of demographic, housing, welfare, human development and investment variables. It develops a comparative ranking of specific areas based on simple qualitative codification. The primary level of social assessment is based on a socioeconomic analysis of city residents. Understanding urban risk at this level can contribute to reducing vulnerability at the level of citizens or households. The secondary level of social assessment is focused on the identification of vulnerable areas and community profiles and slum mapping, while the tertiary level of social assessment focuses on household hazards and vulnerability surveys. Socioeconomic assessment incorporates community-based approaches. Combination of bottom-up and top-down approaches creates more robust tools for urban risk assessment but also for disaster response. Community participation can empower local residents, build social capital and establish a common foundation for neighbourhood level risk assessments. Participatory approaches enable communities to have greater control over information and interventions, thereby enhancing their resilience.

> One of the most important responses after disaster is to support people affected to meet, network and often share their grief and, in their own time, begin to participate in creating solutions. This means involving local people from the start in any discussion of rebuilding and in managing the shift from relief to reconstruction. Well organized, representative, community organizations are also valuable allies for agencies supporting reconstructions as they can provide much of the information base for rebuilding, contribute to the rebuilding and supervise local builders and contractors. (World Disaster Report 2010, p. 55)

In developed countries, there is a strong effort of citizens, different organizations (NGOs, community centres, alliances and so on), but also local municipalities and authorities to empower community life in urban areas. Thus, community participation has a positive impact due to elimination of the consequences of natural disasters as well as prevention and assessment of natural hazards.

The same positive effect can be observed in developing countries. As an example we mention here the work of Shelter Associates (SA) from Pune in India using very high resolution images for slum surveys and poverty mapping at the city level. Their work in close collaboration with residents of slum communities helped them to achieve information about households, their dwellings and the overall site characteristics. Slum settlements were mapped by professional agencies using plane table methods to produce large-scale slum maps showing plot and building boundaries, while residents engaged in household surveys, gaining knowledge and skills on data collection and a better understanding of their community's problems, their opportunities and the planning process. The spatial and socioeconomic data are entered into a geographic information system (GIS) database and analysed for direct use by the communities to prepare upgrading plans and to negotiate with local government authorities on policy and developmental issues. The process therefore contributes to community empowerment by enabling them to be full partners in settlement upgrading and in the subsequent management of their community. As a result of these community-based approaches, many slums have been mapped, while plans for their improvement have been produced (UN-HABITAT

2008). All these data and surveys are at the same time usable for urban risk assessment and disaster response. Engaging urban poor in a direct dialogue regarding risk and vulnerability and having them involved in risk mapping have led to favourable experiences. This is in addition to creating critical spatial data about low-income urban areas that would assist in more inclusive city planning and analysing urban risk. It is important that city governments recognize the value of raising public awareness of climate change and the need for disaster mitigation. Engagement of community groups and NGOs provides necessary inputs to urban risk assessment and has significant importance not only for the data and maps used for risk assessment, but also for the support provided in identifying and acting on risk and vulnerability (Dickson et al. 2012).

There is a clear need for a systematic urban disaster/resilience impact assessment, in which the most crucial aspects of decline and recovery are mapped out in a relevant time frame. Figure 1.7 presents a cascade model from urban downturn back to urban upturn. It comprises a suitable and focused combination of various urban community assessment tools:

- a well-working urban risk assessment mechanism
- well-prepared disaster response tools and policies

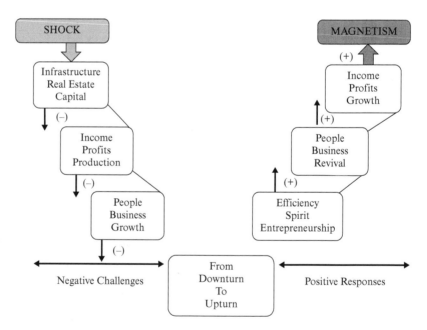

Figure 1.7   A cascade presentation of the urban 'phoenix' mechanism

- a deliberate attitude of competent urban authorities
- a smart engagement of local communities.

It should be noted that testing this cascade model requires panel data on several relevant variables over a long time period, from the first shock to final recovery and beyond.

1.6   CHALLENGES IN URBAN RISK ASSESSMENT AND DISASTER RESPONSE

Urban resilience after an external shock is influenced by many factors, including geographic location, the social and economic situation, level of infrastructure, density of population, culture habits, environmental conditions and many others. Although there may be different levels of suffering from and impacts by the natural disasters in different countries and parts of the world, it is clear that the issue is global. The solution of this issue, including decreasing the risk of natural disasters and their impact on urban areas, takes place at national, mostly regional, or even local scales. So far, there is no generally valid mechanism for disaster and hazard assessment as well as no well-functioning tool or system for revitalization and restoration of urban areas. On the other hand, there is an infinite creativity, smartness and ingenuity of humans that bring much hope regarding disaster prevention and abatement.

Urban risk assessment and appropriate disaster response are real challenges of the world today. One of the biggest challenges is to enhance the quality of urban risk assessment and to mitigate the impact of natural disasters worldwide. Our overview shows that mitigation of disaster impact on cities in low- and middle-income countries and their disaster response urgently need improvement. In Figure 1.8 we present a comprehensive approach for risk assessment, identification and management leading to a desirable urban resilience pattern based on methodology for the risk assessment produced by the World Bank (see Dickson et al. 2012), the adaptive capacity index approach (for more information see Pelling and Zaidi 2013; Zaidi and Pelling 2015) and the risk management methodology based on the adaptive capacity approach (for more information see Paterson et al. 2017).

Urban risk assessment is mainly based on accessible and operational data to be used by competent authorities. Furthermore, the collection of needed data, their integrity and the capacity of exploitation and interpretation of data in different formats seem to be problematic in many cities. The collection of information relevant to urban planning and management

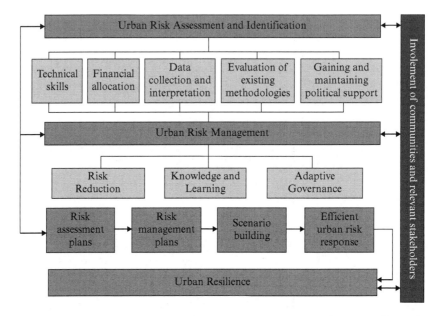

Source: Own processing based on Dickson et al. (2012), Paterson et al. (2017), Pelling and Zaidi (2013) and Zaidi and Pelling (2015).

Figure 1.8   Urban resilience based on urban risk assessment, identification and management

is one of the core tasks of the urban public sector. This involves producing credible information on hazard risk and making it easily available to all stakeholders (Deichmann et al. 2011). Better data leads to better tools and analytics and thus to better decisions (World Bank 2012).

The crucial issues for urban risk assessment are shown in Figure 1.8.

Specialized technical skills are a first challenge. Although existing technical capacity can be used for undertaking a primary level of urban risk assessment (with adequate training), specialized technical skills are required for elements of higher level risk assessments such as flood or seismic risk assessment. A proper financial allocation for risk assessments is needed. While the primary level of urban risk assessment would require modest financial resources, the associated costs of the tertiary level may exceed a city's budget for developing urban management tools. Specific resources will have to be generated to initiate and sustain efforts towards risk assessment and risk reduction. Data collection and interpretation are also necessary. Collecting reliable, accurate and timely data remains a daunting task in many cities. Even if the data are available, problems may arise due to different organizations or agencies using different data formats. The extent to which assessment methodologies represent the actual situation needs attention. Community consultation-based assessment (primary level risk assessment) is important, but while more cost-effective may not be accurate enough to plan for structural reduction of disaster risk. Available risk modelling and climate change projections also have large uncertainties associated with them. Gaining and maintaining political support is another task. It may be difficult to gain necessary political support to initiate and mainstream urban risk assessment. Priorities may change with a change of leadership, leaders may focus more on other pressing issues or there may be vested interests in delaying dissemination of the results of a risk assessment to a city's population (Dickson et al. 2012, p. 34).

Risk management needs adaptive governance which might be understood as an ability to reflect on practical outcomes, flexibility in organizational structures and management and support for practical experiments. Risk management needs to reflect local knowledge (Aitsi-Selmi et al. 2016) and requires relevant knowledge and training in terms of risk reduction training, identification of barriers to adaptation and incremental improvement mechanisms. Consequently, risk reduction should be based on risk consideration and land use planning, policy and financial support for alleviating risk, public education on risk reductions and ability to access and influence risk knowledge (Pelling and Zaidi 2013; Zaidi and Pelling 2015; Paterson et al. 2017). Involvement of communities and all relevant stakeholders is a crucial issue in urban risk assessment. Communities and relevant stakeholders may fill the gap in data gathering. They should be involved through the preparation of plans for urban risk assessment and reduction as well as in scenario building. Communities also play a very important role in terms of disaster response.

Appropriate and smart disaster response mechanisms – and not disasters themselves – may be a blessing in disguise and may result in long-term urban resilience. A suitable and focused combination of well-working urban risk assessment mechanisms, well-prepared disaster response tools and policies, a deliberate proactive attitude of competent urban authorities, and a smart engagement of local communities may lead to a rebirth of cities and urban areas from the dust of disasters – like the phoenix – in a new and brighter shape. The comprehensive approach to risk assessment, identification and management proposed in the chapter serves to depict a desirable urban resilience pattern after an external shock.

REFERENCES

Ahlerup, P. (2013) Are Natural Disasters Good for Economic Growth. University of Gothenburg. Working Paper No. 553.
Aitsi-Selmi, A., Murray, V., Wannous et al. (2016) Reflections on a Science and Technology Agenda for 21st Century Disaster Risk Reduction. *International Journal of Disaster Risk Science* **7**(1), 1–29.
Albala-Bertrand, J.M. (1993) *Political Economy of Large Natural Disasters with Special Reference to Developing Countries.* Oxford and Princeton, NJ: Clarendon Press and Princeton University Press.
Aleskerov, F., Say, A.I., Toker, A., Akin, H. and Altay, G. (2005) A Cluster Based Decision Support System for Estimating Earthquake Damage and Casualties. *Journal of Disaster Studies and Policy Management* **29**, 255–76.
Alexander, D. (2000) *Confronting Catastrophe: New Perspectives on Natural Disasters.* New York: Oxford University Press.
Baade, R.A., Baumann, R. and Matheson, V. (2007) Estimating the Economic Impact of Natural and Social Disasters, with an Application to Hurricane Katrina. *Urban Studies* **44**(11), 2061–76.
Banaszak, M., Dziecielski, M., Nijkamp, P. and Ratajczak, W. (2015) Self-organisation in Spatial Systems – From Fractal Chaos to Regular Patterns and Vice Versa. *PLoS One* **10**(9), e0136248.
Cavallo, E. and Noy, I. (2010) The Economics of Natural Disasters – a Survey. IDB Working Paper No. 124, Inter-American Development Bank.
Cavallo, E., Galiani, S., Noy, I., and Pantano, J. (2013) Catastrophic Natural Disasters and Economic Growth. *Review of Economics and Statistics* **95**(5), 1549–61.
Chang, S.E. (2010) Urban Disaster Recovery. *Disasters* **34**(2), 302–27.
Cheshire, P. (2006) Resurgent Cities, Urban Myths and Policy Hubris: What We Need to Know. *Urban Studies* **43**, 1231–46.
Coffman, N. and Noy, I. (2011) Hurricane Iniki. *Environment and Development Economies* **17**, 187–205.
Cole, M.A., Elliott, R.J.R., Okubo, T. and Strobl, E. (2016) Natural Disasters and Plant Survival: The Impact of the Kobe Earthquake. RIETI Discussion Paper Series 13-E-063.
Couch, C., Karecha, J., Nuissl, H. and Rink, D. (2005) Decline and Sprawl: An Evolving Type of Urban Development – Observed in Liverpool and Leipzig. *European Planning Studies* **13**(1), 117–36.
Cuaresma, J.C., Hlouskova, J. and Obersteiner, M. (2008) Natural Disasters as Creative Destruction? Evidence from Developing Countries. *Economic Inquiry* **46**(2), 214–26.
Dacy, D.C. and H.C. Kunreuther (1969) *The Economics of Natural Disasters: Implications for Federal Policy.* New York: The Free Press.
Davis, D.R. and Weinstein, D.E. (2002) Bones, Bombs, and Break Points: The Geography of Economic Activity. *American Economic Review* **92**(5), 1269–89.
Deichmann, U., Ehrlich, D., Small, C. and Zeug, U. (2011) *Using High Resolution Satellite Information for Urban Risk Assessment.* Washington, DC: European Union and World Bank.
Dickson, E., Baker, J.L, Hoornweg, D. and Tiwari, A. (2012) *Urban Risk Assessments: Understanding Disaster and Climate Risk in Cities.* Washington, DC: World Bank.

Fisker, P.S. (2012) Earthquakes and Economic Growth. Working Paper No. 01/2012, Development Research Working Paper Series, Institute for Advanced Development Studies (INESAD), La Paz.

Forrester, J.W. (1969) *Urban Dynamics*. Cambridge, MA: MIT Press.

Guha-Sapir, D., Hoyois, P. and Below, R. (2016) *Annual Disaster Statistical Review 2015: The Numbers and Trends*. Brussels: CRED.

Guigale, M. (2017) *Time to Insure Developing Countries Against Natural Disasters*. Washington, DC: World Bank.

Haase, A. (2015) Urban Development in Europe Beyond Growth, Demography and Climate Change. In F. Prettenhaber, L. Meyer and J.W. Polt (eds), *Demography and Climate Change*. Vienna: Joanneum Research, pp. 149–72.

Haase, A., Kabisch, S., Steinführer, A. and Ogden, P.E. (2009) Emergent Spaces of Reurbanisation: Exploring the Demographic Dimension of Inner-city Residential Change in a European Setting. *Population, Space and Place* **16**(5), 443–63.

Hall, P. (1982) *The Great Planning Disasters*. Berkeley, CA: University of California Press.

Hill, E., St. Clair, T., Wial, H. et al. (2012) Economic Shocks and Regional Economic Resilience. In M. Wier, N. Pindus, H. Wial and H. Wolman (eds), *Urban and Regional Policy and Its Effects: Building Resilient Regions*. Washington, DC: Brookings Institution Press, pp. 193–274.

Kabisch, N., Haase, D. and Haase, A. (2010) Evolving Reurbanisation? Spatio-temporal Dynamics as Exemplified by the East German City of Leipzig. *Urban Studies* **47**(5), 967–90.

Kabisch, N., Haase, D. and Haase, A. (2012) Urban Population Development in Europe, 1991–2008: The Examples of Poland and the UK. *International Journal of Urban and Regional Research* **36**(6), 1326–48.

Kim, H. and Marcouiller, D.W. (2015) Considering Disaster Vulnerability and Resilience. *Annals of Regional Science* **54**(3), 945–71.

Kourtit, K. (2015) The New Urban World. PhD Dissertation, Mickiewicz University, Poznan.

Kourtit, K., Nijkamp, P. and Reid, N. (2014) The New Urban World: Challenges and Policy. *Applied Geography* **49**, 1–3.

Lazzaroni, S. and van Bergeijk, P.A.G. (2014) Natural Disasters Impact, Factors of Resilience and Development: A Meta-analysis of the Macroeconomic Literature. *Ecological Economics* **107**(11), 333–46.

Leiter, A.M., Oberhofer, H. and Raschky, P.A. (2009) Creative Disasters? Flooding Effects on Capital, Labor and Productivity Within European Firms. *Environmental and Resource Economics* **43**, 333–50.

Linnerooth-Bayer, J., Mechler, R. and Pflug, G. (2005) Refocusing Disaster Aid. *Science* **309**, 1044–6.

Linnerooth-Bayer, J., Hoeppe, P., Petersen, L. and Gurenko, E. (2007) Summary: Expert Workshop on Insurance Instruments for Adaptation to Climate Risks: Linking Policy Agendas. IIASA, Laxenburg, Austria, 24–25 September.

Loayza, N. Olaberria, E. Rigolini, J. and Christiaensen, L. (2009) Natural Disasters and Growth – Going Beyond the Averages. Policy Research Working Paper Series, World Bank.

Melecky, M. and Raddatz, C. (2011) How do Governments Respond After Catastrophes? Natural-disaster Shocks and the Fiscal Stance. Policy Research Working Paper No. WPS 5564, World Bank.

Mileti, D.S., Darlington, J.D., Passaini, E., Forest, B.C, and Myers, M.F. (1995) Toward an Integration of Natural Hazards and Sustainability. *Environmental Professional* **17**, 117–26.

Ministry of Internal Affairs and Communications Statistics Bureau (2015) http://www.stat.go.jp/data/kokusei/2010/final/pdf/01-02.pdf (accessed 27 July 2016).

Morrow, B.H. (2008) *Community Resilience: A Social Justice Perspective*. CARRI Research Report 4, Florida International University.

Noy, I. (2009) The Macroeconomic Consequences of Disasters. *Journal of Development Economics* **88**, 221–31.

Nuissl, H. and Rink, D. (2005) The Production of Urban Sprawl in Eastern Germany as a Phenomenon of Post-socialist Transformation. *Cities* **22**(2), 123–34.

Okuyama, Y. (2015) How Shaky was the Regional Economy After the 1995 Kobe Earthquake? *Annals of Regional Science* **55**, 289–312.

Okuyama, Y. and Santos, J.R. (2014) Disaster Impact and Input-Output Analysis. *Economic Systems Research* **26**(1), 1–12.

Otero, R. and Marti, R. (1995) The Impacts of Natural Disasters on National Economics and the Implications for the International Development and Disasters Community. In M. Munasinghe and C. Clarke (eds), *Disaster Prevention for Sustainable Development: Economic and Policy Issues*. Geneva and New York: International Decade for Natural Disaster Reduction and World Bank, pp. 11–40.

Pastor, M. and Benner, Ch. (2008) Been Down So Long: Weak Market Cities and Regional Equity. In R.M. McGahey and J.S. Vey (eds), *Retooling for Growth: Building a 21st Century Economy in America's Older Industrial Areas*. Washington, DC: Brookings Institution Press, pp. 89–118.

Paterson, S.K, Pelling, M, Nunes, L.N., Moreira, F.A, Guida, K. and Marengo, J.A. (2017) Size Does Matter: City Scale and the Asymmetries of Climate Change Adaptation in Three Coastal Towns. *Geoforum* **81**, 109–19.

Pelling, M. and Zaidi, R.Z. (2013) Measuring Adaptive Capacity: Application of an Indexing Methodology in Guyana. EPD Working Paper No. 47, Department of Geography, King's College London.

Rasmussen, T.N. (2004) Macroeconomic Implications of Natural Disasters in the Caribbean. IMF Working paper WP/04/224.

Reggiani, A. and Nijkamp, P. (2006) *Spatial Dynamics, Networks and Modelling*. Cheltenham, UK and Northampton, MA, USA: Edward Elgar.

Reggiani, A. and Nijkamp, P. (eds) (2009) *Complexity and Spatial Networks*. Berlin: Springer.

Reggiani, A., Nijkamp, P. and Lanzi, D. (2015) Transport Resilience and Vulnerability. *Transport Research A: Policy and Practice* **81**, 4–15.

Richardson, H.W., Gordon, P. and Moore, J.E. (eds) (2008) *Natural Disaster Analysis After Hurricane Katrina: Risk Assessment, Economic Impacts and Social Implications*. Cheltenham, UK and Northampton, MA, USA: Edward Elgar.

Rodriguez, H., Quarantelli, E.-L. and Dynes, R.-R. (eds) (2007) *Handbook of Disaster Research*. Berlin: Springer.

Rose, A. (2007) Economic Resilience to Natural and Man-made Disasters: Multidisciplinary Origins and Contextual Dimensions. *Environmental Hazards* **7**(4), 383–98.

Skidmore, M. and Toya, H. (2002) Do Natural Disasters Promote Long-run Growth? *Economic Inquiry* **40**(4), 664–87.

Sliuzas, R.. Mboup, G. and Sherbinin, A. (2008) Expert Group Meeting on Slum Identification and Mapping. Netherlands Ministry of Spatial Planning, Housing and the Environment (VROM).

Taylor, P.J., Derudder, B., Saey, P. and Witlox, F. (eds) (2007) *Cities in Globalization: Practices, Policies and Theories*. London: Routledge.

Tellier, L.-N. (2009) *Urban World History: An Economic and Geographical Perspective*. Quebec: Presses du l'Universite du Quebec.

Toynbee, A. (1934–61) *A Study of History*. Oxford: Oxford University Press.

Tubadji, A., Nijkamp, P. and Angelis, V. (2016) Cultural Hysteresis, Entrepreneurship and Economic Crisis. *Cambridge Journal of Regions, Economy and Society* **9**, 103–36.

UN-HABITAT (2007) *Enhancing Urban Safety and Security: Global Report on Human Settlements 2007*. London: Earthscan.

UNISDR (United Nations Office for Disaster Risk Reduction) (2004) *Living with Risk: A Global Review of Disaster Reduction Initiatives*. Geneva: United Nations.

van Bergeijk, P.A.G. and Lazzaroni, S. (2015) Macroeconomics of Natural Disasters: Strengths and Weaknesses of Meta-analysis versus Review of the Literature. *Risk Analysis* **35**(6), 1050–72.

van den Berg, L., Drewett, R. and Klaassen, L.H. (1982) *Urban Europe: A Study of Growth and Decline*. Oxford: Pergamon.

van der Pol, Th.D. (2015) Climate Change, Uncertainty and Investment in Flood Risk Reduction. PhD Dissertation, Wageningen University.

Walker, B., Holling, C.S., Carpenter, S.R. and Kinzig, A. (2004) Resilience, Adaptability and Transformability in Social–Ecological Systems. *Ecology and Society* **9**(2). http://www.ecologyandsociety.org/vol9/iss2/art5/ (accessed August 2018).

Wirtz, A. (2008) Hitting the Poor: Impact of Natural Catastrophes in Economies at Various Stages of Development. Geo Risks Research, Munich Reinsurance, IDRC 2008, Davos.

World Bank (2012) *Building Urban Resilience: Principles, Tools and Practice*. Washington, DC: World Bank.

World Disaster Report (2010) *Focus on Urban Risk*. Imprimerie Chirat, Lyons: International Federation of Red Cross and Red Crescent Societies.

Zaidi, R.Z. and Pelling, M. (2015) Institutionally Configured Risk: Assessing Urban Resilience and Disaster Risk Reduction to Heat Wave Risk in London. *Urban Studies* **52**(7), 1218–33.

2. Natural selection: firm performance following a catastrophic earthquake

Richard Fabling, Arthur Grimes and Levente Timar*,**

2.1 MOTIVATION

The Canterbury earthquake sequence, beginning with an earthquake of 7.1 on the Richter scale in September 2010, was the most damaging natural hazard event in New Zealand's written history. The second major quake, in February 2011, was centered on the central business district (CBD) of the region's largest city, Christchurch, which in the 2006 census had an urban area population of 373,000. The February 2011 quake killed 185 people, forced many from their homes, and closed Christchurch's CBD which was legally cordoned off for over two years. Both the September 2010 and February 2011 earthquakes caused major damage to land, property and infrastructure. Census estimates show a declining population in Christchurch City after the earthquakes, dropping 4 percent in the two years to June 2012 (Statistics New Zealand 2014a), while the number of business locations dropped substantially in the year following February 2011 – down 2.5 percent overall, and down 34.6 percent in the CBD (Statistics New Zealand 2012).

*   Acknowledgements: We gratefully acknowledge funding from the Ministry of Business, Innovation & Employment (MBIE) Natural Hazards Research Platform. We also thank Lynda Sanderson for helpful feedback, and Statistics New Zealand for supplying and enabling access to the data.
**   Disclaimer: Access to the anonymized data used in this study was provided by Statistics New Zealand in accordance with security and confidentiality provisions of the Statistics Act 1975, and secrecy provisions of the Tax Administration Act 1994. The findings are not Official Statistics. The results in this chapter are the work of the authors, not Statistics New Zealand, MBIE, Motu or Victoria University of Wellington, and have been confidentialized to protect businesses from identification. See Fabling et al. (2014) for the full disclaimer.

The New Zealand Treasury (2013) estimated that total investment associated with the rebuild would be around NZ$40 billion.[1] The industry composition of the region's workforce changed markedly, with a large (59 percent) jump in the number of workers employed in the construction industry, making it the largest employing sector in Greater Christchurch (Statistics New Zealand 2014a).[2] Conversely, other industries, such as retail and hospitality, experienced an initial decline in sales (Statistics New Zealand 2014b). While these regional aggregates demonstrate the scale of change, they do not paint a detailed picture of the adjustments that have taken place following the disaster; we help to fill this gap.

The scope of the disaster presents an important opportunity for learning about the post-event responses and resilience of firms. We document the heterogeneity of the disaster's effects on firms which differed both spatially (as a result of the disaster's direct and indirect effects) and by industry. One sector in particular – construction – experienced buoyant economic success following the earthquakes, while others – notably hospitality – suffered disproportionately. In addition, we identify a key factor that contributed to firm resilience in the face of disaster: prior profitability.

There is now a body of microeconomic studies examining the effects of disasters on individuals' outcomes within an affected area.[3] To date, however, there is a much smaller group of microeconomic analyses that investigate the differential effects of disasters across firms.[4] Our work is most similar to Basker and Miranda (2014) in both intent and methodology. Both studies use a difference-in-difference estimation approach to understand heterogeneity in survival and growth outcomes based on prior firm performance. Basker and Miranda (2014) have the advantage of being able to consider the dynamics of recovery over a longer time frame. We have the advantage of access to financial data, allowing direct measurement of prior profitability, rather than relying on proxy measures (firm size and age) as in Basker and Miranda.

Access to financial data enables us to examine the extent to which firms' prior profitability enhances resilience in the face of a natural disaster.

---

[1] This investment is spread across residential property ($18 billion), commercial property ($9 billion) and infrastructure and social assets ($11 billion). In February 2011, 1 NZ$ = 0.76 US$; NZ$40 billion was 20 percent of New Zealand's 2010/11 gross domestic product (GDP).

[2] Greater Christchurch is taken here to include the Territorial Authorities of Christchurch City, Selwyn District and Waimakariri District. Greater Christchurch is treated as the affected area in this chapter; henceforth we use the name Christchurch for simplicity.

[3] For instance, see Belasen and Polachek (2008); Deryugina et al. (2014); Fabling et al. (2016); Fussell (2015); Groen et al. (2015); Mueller and Quisumbing (2011).

[4] This literature includes studies of Hurricane Katrina (e.g., Basker and Miranda 2014); the Kobe and Tohoku earthquakes (e.g., Cole et al. 2013; Uchida et al. 2013, respectively); and major flooding in European regions (e.g., Leiter et al. 2009).

Schumpeter's (1962) concept of 'creative destruction' sees firms (driven by entrepreneurs) opening up new markets and growing as their products rise in demand, but then declining as they can no longer compete with new entrepreneurial innovations. Frequently, however, declining firms do not exit the market completely as their owners strive to keep the firm alive. With uncertainty surrounding future opportunities, such behavior may be optimal for a time (Dixit and Pindyck 1994) but finally a large enough negative shock will make it optimal for the firm to exit. A natural disaster may provide that shock and so act as a 'cleansing agent', removing declining firms from the economy and freeing up resources for new firms to emerge. Some of these new firms may be critical to the recovery process.

In addition to building on recent international work, our analysis builds on that of New Zealand's Inland Revenue (Inland Revenue 2014) which used tax data to measure changes in sales post-quake using simple counter-factuals based on historical averages. We extend this preliminary work by matching Christchurch firms to similar 'control' firms in other cities within detailed firm cells, tracking a number of outcome variables, and examining heterogeneity of outcomes across a variety of dimensions. This more detailed work is enabled by the linking of tax data to firm characteristics held by Statistics New Zealand.

We quantify substantial heterogeneity in firm outcomes by industry and by location. Consistent with Schumpeterian creative destruction, we show that firms' prior financial viability materially influenced their chance of survival. However, conditional on continuing to operate, average profitability returned to pre-quake levels quickly. Taken together, these effects support economic models in which firm exit is at least partly driven by selection on profitability. Section 2.2 outlines the empirical method, while Section 2.3 describes the data that we use. Results are discussed in Section 2.4 before we summarize our findings in Section 2.5.

2.2   HYPOTHESES AND ESTIMATION APPROACH

Our empirical strategy triangulates two difference-in-difference (DID) approaches. The first DID approach compares outcomes (i.e., changes in performance pre- and post-quakes) of affected firms in Christchurch to 'similar' unaffected firms in two other cities, Auckland and Hamilton (the 'control' group). The second approach compares subgroups of Christchurch firms, demonstrating the heterogeneity of outcomes between firms directly affected by the earthquakes and those affected indirectly through, say, reduced demand or supply chain interruption. It also examines whether prior firm profitability affected subsequent firm outcomes.

The potential for marked heterogeneity in outcomes is a key motivating factor for this analysis, for two reasons. Firstly, to accurately estimate the potential impact of future disasters, we need to understand the heterogeneity in outcomes across businesses. If firm-level outcomes vary by activity and location, then insights for other regions must account for variations in industry structure and for the distribution of firms inside and outside natural hazard risk zones. For this reason, we consider the experienced intensity of the shock as an important dimension of the analysis. Whereas firms in less directly affected physical locations may experience disruption to supply chains, changes in demand and changes in staff turnover, firms in severely affected areas may also suffer from forced suspension of business. In Christchurch's case, the CBD was physically and legally cordoned off following the February 2011 earthquake, making such suspension of business a reality for many firms.

Secondly, heterogeneity across firms may give general insights into firm responses to shocks beyond the sphere of natural disasters. In particular, we test whether prior profitability affects the firm's exit decision, exploiting the fact that the quakes were an exogenous, unanticipated shock to performance.

Since the composition of firms within Christchurch may differ from the control regions (Auckland and Hamilton), we reweight control observations so that they reflect the distribution of Christchurch firms. Matching is exact within industry, firm size and prior employment growth cells. We also control directly for pre-existing firm characteristics, particularly at a detailed industry level, to eliminate the possible confounding effect of sector-specific macroeconomic shocks. The following section describes the outcome variables, controls and matching cells.

2.3 DATA

Aside from information about location-specific earthquake intensity, all data are obtained from New Zealand's Longitudinal Business Database (LBD) and Linked Employer-Employee Data (LEED), both maintained by Statistics New Zealand as part of the Integrated Data Infrastructure (IDI).[5]

Measured outcomes are restricted to those obtainable from timely full-coverage tax-based data on employment and wages (from Pay-As-You-Earn returns or PAYE) and sales and purchases (from Goods and Services Tax (GST) data). This data is linked within the LBD to the

---

[5] We use the December 2013 IDI Clean, together with the 2014 LBD. Fabling (2009) describes the LBD in more detail.

Longitudinal Business Frame, which identifies business locations, industry, group structure, ownership type and sector. Firms are tracked over time using Fabling's (2011) enhanced longitudinal identifiers.

Outcomes are measured at the aggregate firm level, rather than the plant level, because the former is the filing unit.[6] Denoting firm-level employment, sales and profitability[7] as L, Y and π, respectively, we focus primarily on the following outcomes:[8]

1. Employment status, $\Delta\delta(L > 0)$;
2. Sales status, $\Delta\delta(Y > 0)$;
3. Employment, $\Delta\ln L$;
4. Sales, $\Delta\ln Y$;
5. Break-even status, $\Delta\delta(\pi \geq 0)$ conditional on $L > 0$ and $Y > 0$;
6. Profitability, $\Delta\pi$ conditional on $L > 0$ and $Y > 0$.

We also report results for the worker retention rate (of initial 'pre-quake' workers).[9]

From the date of the first major quake (September 2010) onwards, effects are calculated and reported on a monthly basis. The pre-event time period ($t = 0$) against which outcome changes are measured is the average over the five months from April 2010 to August 2010 to align the period to the predominant start of the 2010/11 financial year.[10] The population is constrained to private-for-profit firms that are active, which is defined as employing and having sales at some point during $t = 0$.[11]

In matching Christchurch to Auckland/Hamilton firms we use industry matching at the one-digit level. We utilize six firm size groups, based on employment (with cutoffs for employment at 1, 3, 5, 10, 50), with the two largest groups ($L_0 > 10$) further distinguished by whether they have multiple employing locations. Historical employment growth is used as

---

[6]   We explicitly control for multi-location firms.

[7]   Profitability (π) is measured as the return on sales [$\pi = (Y - W - M)/Y$] where W and M respectively represent the total wage bill and purchases of intermediate goods. We normalize by sales, rather than capital, since it may be hard to value the latter after the quakes (and would require additional data linking, which would restrict the population of interest). π is naturally bounded above by one, and we impose a lower bound at minus one to truncate a small number of extreme values.

[8] $\delta(.)$ is an indicator function equal to one if the argument holds, and zero otherwise.

[9]   Fabling et al. (2014) report a range of additional outcome variables.

[10]   An exception is made for profitability. Since this measure is noisier, the pre-event measure is taken as the average over the (partial) $t = 0$ year and the two preceding financial years.

[11]   An exception is made for the 102 firms in Finance and Services to Finance, since financial services do not attract GST. These firms are included in the employment analysis if they employ in the pre-quake reference period. Working proprietors paid through the PAYE system are excluded from L.

Table 2.1   Distribution of Christchurch firms by industry and location

	Number of firms		
	Impact intensity area		Total
	Low	High	
Agriculture, forestry & fishing	723	81	804
Mining & manufacturing	627	732	1359
Construction	729	777	1506
Wholesale trade	483	579	1062
Retail trade	789	1239	2028
Accommodation, cafes & restaurants	399	480	879
Transport & storage	267	189	456
Communication, finance, insurance, property & business services	699	1377	2076
Education, health, community, cultural, recreational, personal & other services	699	759	1458
Total	5412	6210	11 622

Note: High impact intensity areas are meshblocks with at least half of eligible firms receiving the Earthquake Support Subsidy. Multi-location firms are assigned based on the maximal value of this share across their meshblock locations. All counts in the first two columns are random-rounded in accordance with Statistics New Zealand confidentiality rules; counts in the Total column are the sum of the values listed in the first two columns.

a matching variable, and this is calculated as the log change employment over the prior two years allocating entering firms to separate cells based on their start year. Matching on employment growth is done within employment-level cells, since small and large firms have quite different employment growth distributions. Industries are as shown in Table 2.1. Overall, our sample comprises approximately 11,622 Christchurch firms and 33,615 Auckland/Hamilton (control) firms.[12] Fabling et al. (2014) describe the composition and some limited restrictions on the sample (required to ensure comparability) in more detail.

Within Christchurch we wish to separately identify firms that are more heavily impacted by the effect of the quakes. To do this, we make use of the Earthquake Support Subsidy (ESS), which was established to assist firms that wished to continue employing, but which couldn't meet the wage bill

[12]   All firm counts in the chapter are random-rounded in accordance with Statistics New Zealand confidentiality rules.

because of the earthquakes. The subsidy ran from 22 February 2011 for up to six weeks, paying \$500 per week per full-time employee.[13]

The subsidy was limited to firms with fewer than 50 employees. Nevertheless, the geographic location of recipient firms should provide a good indicator of whether firms not receiving the subsidy were also heavily affected. We form two groups for much of the analysis: firms in locations where the majority of eligible firms received the ESS; and firms not in these areas.[14] We hypothesize that the effect of the quakes should be weaker for this latter group, while the effect on non-recipients in heavily affected areas may be stronger or weaker than that of recipients. Reflecting the geography of the February quake, many ESS recipients were clustered in and around the Christchurch CBD, but this was not the only area where the majority of businesses were hit hard.

Aside from the heterogeneity imposed by the quake's geography, we split the firms based on pre-existing industry and pre-existing profitability. All regressions include controls for pre-quake ($t = 0$): log employment, as a piecewise linear function for small ($L_0 \leq 10$), medium ($10 < L_0 < 50$) and large ($L_0 \geq 50$) firms; log average wage; multi-location status, as a binary dummy variable; employment growth, including a separate binary dummy variable for entrants; log firm age; profitability; business type, as a set of binary variables that account for business type, foreign ownership and domestic enterprise group membership; and industry, as a set of 146 (three-digit ANZSIC'96) dummy variables.[15]

2.4   RESULTS

A separate regression is used to estimate each outcome in each of 25 post-quake months to allow the effect of pre-quake firm characteristics on outcomes to vary over time.[16] Because of the volume of estimates this creates, our DID estimates are presented in graphical form. Interpretation of results focuses on effects significantly different from zero at the 5 percent level. Some additional results are discussed in the text but are not shown graphically to economize on space.

---

[13]   A disadvantage of using the subsidy data is that they do not give a complete picture of the most affected firms. In particular, a business owner may decide to immediately exit post-event and, therefore, be heavily affected but not be a subsidy recipient.

[14]   Location is measured at the meshblock level, which is the most detailed available, and approximately corresponds to a city block in dense urban areas. See Fabling et al. (2014) for maps of affected areas.

[15]   Since all regressions include three-digit industry dummies, these relationships can be interpreted as indicating relative performance within industry.

[16]   All regressions are Ordinary Least Squares (OLS) with robust standard errors.

2.4.1   Average Impact on Christchurch Firms

The paths of the effect of the earthquakes on each of employment and sales status (with 95 percent confidence intervals) are shown in Panels A and B of Figure 2.1. Employment and sales performance, conditional on survival, are shown in Figure 2.2, while break-even status and profitability are shown in Figure 2.3.

Panel A of Figure 2.1 shows that at the time of the first major quake (Sep-10), there is no difference between Christchurch and their control firms in terms of employment status. This is a picture we see with most results, consistent with the first major quake having little immediate impact on business outcomes. Importantly, if the initial impact was actually moderate, this result also implies that the matching and control process has achieved the desired outcome.

After the second major quake, in February 2011, Christchurch firms are initially 1.2 percent less likely to be employing (relative to matched control firms), and this falls further to –2.6 percent in September 2011, before recovering to 1 percent less likely in September 2012. Because these are DID results, the decline in effect could be due to the restarting of Christchurch firms that temporarily stopped employing and/or to a slower rate of firm exit (from employing) in the latter period, relative to the matched controls. A relatively low exit rate in the latter period might be expected if the earthquakes initially accelerated the exit of Christchurch firms that would have exited anyway at some later date – an idea to which we return when considering variation in survival rates by prior performance.

As with employment status, there is an immediate drop in the likelihood of having sales following the February earthquake with a subsequent recovery, resulting in the status of having sales being 1.2 percent less likely by September 2012.

Conditional on continuing to employ, average employment briefly dips below control levels, before ending 4.5 percent above the level of their matched control firms (Figure 2.2, Panel A). The recovery in employment is not achieved entirely through re-employing pre-quake staff; retention of initial employees is significantly, and seemingly permanently, 3 percent lower than control firms. Firms that survive the initial sharp negative output shock – an average 9 percent drop in sales – also experience a steady increase in sales relative to what might be expected in the absence of the quakes, ending at 7.2 percent above control (Figure 2.2, Panel B).

Partly as a consequence of the different dynamics of sales and employment, firms initially suffer a decline in profitability (Figure 2.3) but there is a rapid return of profitability to the status quo. In 11 of the 18 months

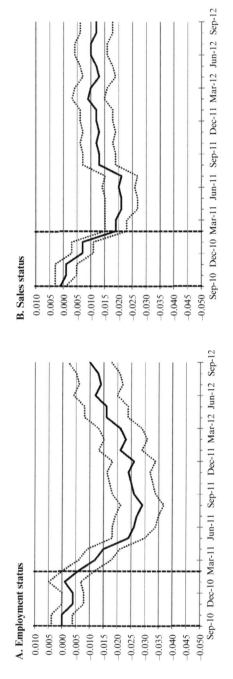

Figure 2.1   Average impact of earthquakes on survival

38

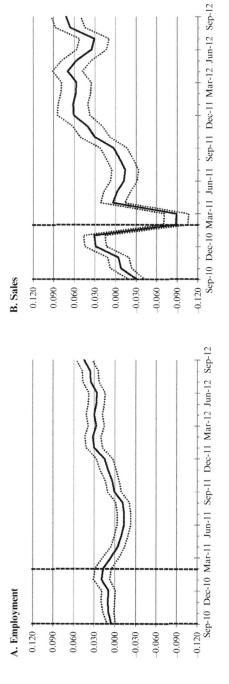

Figure 2.2   Average impact of earthquakes on employment and sales, conditional on survival

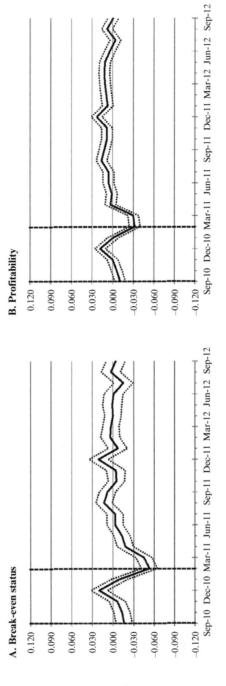

Figure 2.3 Average impact of earthquakes on profitability, conditional on survival

from April 2011, the effect on the profit rate is insignificantly different from zero.

These average effects conceal marked differences in outcomes across firms. The next subsection focuses on the effect that the geography of the February event had both on the intensity of the shock and on the subsequent outcomes experienced by firms.

2.4.2 Heterogeneity Across Christchurch Firms

Geography and the ESS
To understand the location-specific heterogeneity in firm outcomes with respect to the quake's intensity, we utilize the take-up by eligible firms of the ESS scheme. We define location-specific earthquake intensity using the share of eligible firms receiving the ESS. Specifically, locations with less than half of eligible firms receiving the ESS are deemed 'low' impact intensity areas, whereas locations with 50 percent or more of eligible firms receiving the ESS are in 'high' impact intensity areas. This distinction helps control for potential confounding factors between geography and industry, say, which may have a geographical dimension. (For example, the average effect of the quakes on farms may appear weak because they were not present in the CBD.) The following analyses of heterogeneity in outcomes across industries and prior profitability are each split according to these high and low impact intensity areas.

Industry
Industry is an important dimension over which outcomes may differ. Table 2.1 shows the distribution of industries by impact intensity area (where we have pooled some industries to maintain reasonable sub-population sizes). As expected, agriculture is under-represented in the high impact area, unlike retail trade and the business services group which are both over-represented in the heavily affected CBD. Because we have nine industry groupings, we choose not to report them all graphically, instead focusing on the two extreme cases – accommodation/cafes/restaurants and construction – and the two largest remaining industries – retail trade and business services – which are also the most concentrated in the CBD.

Figures 2.4 and 2.5 show effects on survival and performance respectively (each measured using employment) for the four selected industries. Comparison between the extremes – construction and accommodation/cafes/restaurants (which we refer to below as hospitality) – demonstrates the breadth of heterogeneity in outcomes. Regardless of location, construction firms have improved survival rates (8–10 percent for employment) and performance outcomes (25–30 percent for employment) at

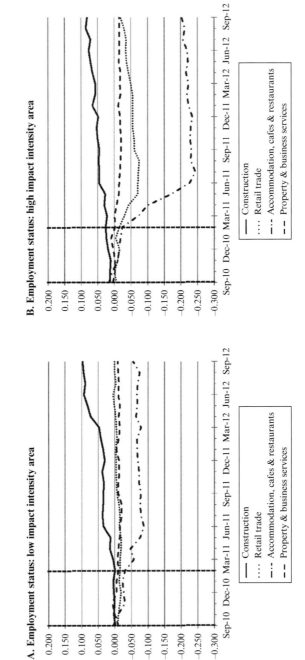

Figure 2.4 Impact of earthquakes on survival by industry

42

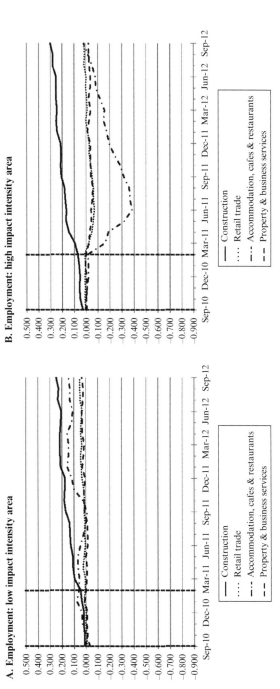

Figure 2.5 Impact of earthquakes on employment by industry, conditional on survival

September 2012. Unlike other subgroups, construction firms did not see any impact on the retention of initial staff which, presumably, helped mitigate problems associated with growing the workforce so rapidly. These results do not take into account the entry of new businesses, which further accelerated changes in the industry structure of the region (Statistics New Zealand 2014a).

At the other extreme, survival of hospitality firms is negatively affected both inside and outside the high impact area, with little sign of recovery over time. In the high impact intensity area, the probability of continuing to employ initially falls by 24 percent, recovering only slightly to end the period at 20 percent below control. In addition to large-scale exit from trading, surviving hospitality firms in the high impact area take a large hit to employment which halves almost immediately following the February quake. Those firms' loss of initial staff rises by 29 percent (over and above the traditionally high staff turnover rates in the industry), settling at 17 percent lower by the end of the period.

Surviving hospitality firms in high impact areas also suffered a major reduction in sales. In contrast, sales rose for surviving hospitality firms in the low impact area, presumably in part because these firms picked up customers that were formerly serviced by exiting firms or by firms in the high impact area.[17]

The large industry groupings – retail trade and business services – experience similar performance outcomes to each other, conditional on survival. However, in the high impact area, retail businesses have somewhat lower survival rates compared to business services firms. Several mechanisms might explain these differences: retail firms may be more exposed in the high impact area because of a dependence on walk-up trade, which may have been impacted by damage to transport infrastructure, the cordon and/or by the effect of the closure of other businesses on foot traffic.[18] In addition, business services may be easier to relocate and/or to continue operating with staff working from home; and/or demand may have been relatively weak for some retail goods following the second major quake. The results for the hospitality sector support the hypothesis that the geographic location of immobile capital had a large impact on relative outcomes.

Perhaps remarkably, given the marked disparity in industry dynamics, effects on profitability were muted. The profitability of all reported industries in the high impact area was negatively affected in February 2011, but this effect dissipated by April 2011. Hospitality firms in the low impact

---

[17]   See Fabling et al. (2014) for further details.
[18]   See Haltiwanger et al. (2010) for evidence on this spillover effect.

area had significantly higher measured profitability over February 2011 to May 2012 (peaking at 11 percent above control), consistent with increased demand for these services and, in the short term, significantly lower supply. Indeed, all industries, other than mining and manufacturing, saw surviving firms' profitability return to normal levels by September 2011. (Mining and manufacturing recorded a significant negative coefficient on profitability for September 2011 but the relevant coefficient is insignificantly different from zero for the three months either side of that date suggesting that this industry effect was, at best, marginal.) The general pattern of a rapid return to normal profitability, conditional on survival, is explored in more detail in the next subsection, where we consider the role of prior profitability in determining which firms survive.

Profitability
We separate firms based on whether they at least broke even over the three years prior to the first major earthquake and, for firms that did, we further divide the population into those firms with returns below 20 cents in the dollar, and those at or above that point. Eighteen percent of Christchurch firms with the relevant tax data are estimated to fall below the break-even point prior to the earthquakes, with a further 44 percent having positive returns less than 20 percent. There is no apparent sorting on profitability by location consistent with land prices having an equalizing effect on profits.

Figures 2.6 and 2.7 show effects on (employment-based) survival and performance, respectively, by prior average profitability. Focusing first on survival, and concentrating on high impact area results (Figure 2.6, Panel B), it is clear that longer-term survival effects as proxied by employment status are restricted to firms previously below the break-even point. Firms in the two positive profitability categories experience very similar survival effects. By contrast, low profitability firms are roughly 9 percent more likely to have ceased employing than their corresponding control firms. Firms may cease to operate if their profitability is shifted below a threshold at which their business is viable, with this threshold being closer for low profitability firms. Alternatively, the shift in profitability may be more substantial for low profitability firms. Another possibility may be that the ability to continue to operate is related to accumulated cash reserves and/ or the ability to raise external (debt or equity) capital, which may reflect prior profitability.

Conditional on survival, low prior profitability firms in high impact areas also have poor employment outcomes (Figure 2.7, Panel B). Employment bottoms out 10.8 percent lower before recovering to –3.5 percent by September 2012. In contrast, the earthquakes result in surviving

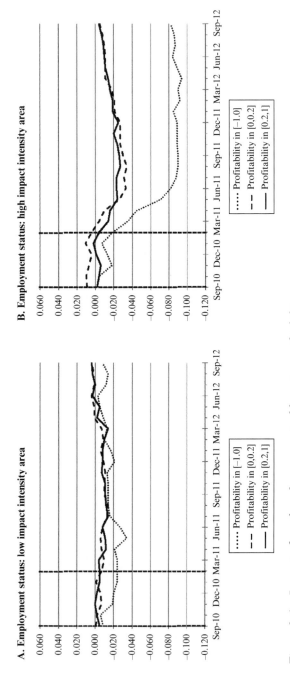

Figure 2.6 *Impact of earthquakes on survival by prior profitability*

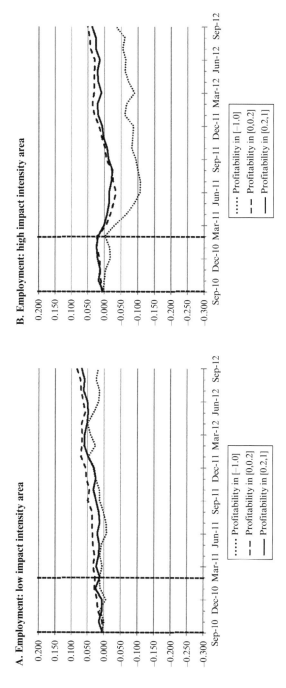

Figure 2.7   Impact of earthquakes on employment by prior profitability, conditional on survival

historically profitable firms being, on average, larger (by 4–8 percent) in terms of employment in September 2012. In low impact areas, the effects of prior profitability on employment are muted, albeit in the same direction as for the high impact areas.

These results are consistent with persistent differences in management capability. As Fabling and Grimes (2014) found for New Zealand businesses, management practices can have a material impact on relative firm performance. It is plausible that these practices – or the managers who put these practices in place – have a tangible effect on the ability of firms to be resilient and to recover after unexpected shocks.

In high impact areas, and directly after the second major quake, profitability was significantly lower for all firm types. By June 2011 the negative impact had fully dissipated, with the most profitable firms then significantly above their pre-quake average – an effect that persisted through to September 2012. Firms initially below the break-even point had a significantly positive profitability outcome in the low impact zone, perhaps reflecting a windfall gain to unaffected firms that had previously operated below capacity, though this effect eventually faded and was close to zero by September 2012.

2.5   CONCLUSIONS

We document wide variability in earthquake outcomes for pre-existing firms. Such results should lead to better estimates of the potential outcomes of natural disaster events in other locations, by allowing the distribution of firm characteristics in high impact zones to be accounted for.

In particular, we show that post-quake outcomes vary hugely for firms across different sectors. Not surprisingly, construction firms prosper following the quakes while hospitality firms – especially those in high impact areas – fare poorly. Thus, one cannot generalize about the effects of a disaster across private sector firms; some may do very well following a disaster, even one which has sizeable negative aggregate effects.

In a broader economic context, we show that initial profitability differences between firms led to different dynamics following the second major earthquake. Prior poor performers are disproportionately, and strongly, selected to exit. In contrast, surviving firms rapidly revert to status quo profitability levels. Both results are consistent with competition acting to prevent extreme profits, and to eliminate poorly performing firms. The latter process reflects a process of Schumpeterian creative destruction which we show is accelerated by the shock of the earthquakes.

These results indicate the complexity that policy-makers face following a disaster if they wish to cushion the disaster's effect on firms. Firms in some industries and some locations may require no assistance, while others will fail unless assisted. Amongst this latter group is likely to be a disproportionate number of firms with prior poor profitability. Their failure may be beneficial for the economy, freeing up resources that could move into the construction industry and into new entrepreneurial ventures. Preventing this process through policy actions designed to save firms may therefore reduce the potential for recovery of an area. At least in the case of Christchurch – a developed world city in a country with strong institutions – aggregate recovery was swift (Fabling et al. 2016) despite the firm failures documented here. An implication of our findings, therefore, is that following a disaster, governments may be well advised to concentrate on the broader recovery and reconstruction process and leave individual firm survival to the dictates of the market.

REFERENCES

Basker, E. and J. Miranda (2014). Taken by storm: business survival in the aftermath of Hurricane Katrina. Working Papers 14-20, Center for Economic Studies, US Census Bureau.

Belasen, A.R. and S.W. Polachek (2008). How hurricanes affect wages and employment in local labor markets. *American Economic Review*, **98**(2), 49–53.

Cole, M., R. Elliott, T. Okubo, and E. Strobl (2013). Natural disasters and plant survival: the impact of the Kobe earthquake. RIETI Discussion Paper Series 13-E-063, Research Institute of Economy, Trade and Industry, Tokyo.

Deryugina, T., L. Kawano, and S. Levitt (2014). The economic impact of Hurricane Katrina on its victims: evidence from individual tax returns (No. w20713). National Bureau of Economic Research. Washington, DC.

Dixit, A. and R. Pindyck (1994). *Investment Under Uncertainty*. Princeton, NJ: Princeton University Press.

Fabling, R. (2009). A rough guide to New Zealand's Longitudinal Business Database. Global COE Hi-Stat Discussion Papers No. 103, Institute of Economic Research, Hitotsubashi University, Tokyo.

Fabling, R. (2011). Keeping it together: tracking firms in New Zealand's Longitudinal Business Database. Working Paper 11-01, Motu Economic and Public Policy Research, Wellington.

Fabling, R. and A. Grimes (2014). The 'suite' smell of success: personnel practices and firm performance. *Industrial and Labor Relations Review*, **67**(4), 1095–126.

Fabling, R., A. Grimes, and L. Timar (2014). Natural selection: firm performance following the Canterbury earthquakes. Motu Working Paper 14-08, Wellington.

Fabling, R., A. Grimes, and L. Timar (2016). Labour market dynamics following a regional disaster. Working Paper 16-07, Motu Economic and Public Policy Research, Wellington.

Fussell, E. (2015). The long-term recovery of New Orleans' population after Hurricane Katrina. *American Behavioral Scientist*, **59**(10), 1231–45.

Groen, J.A., M.J. Kutzbach, and A.E. Polivka (2015). *Storms and Jobs: The Effect of Hurricane Katrina on Individuals' Employment and Earnings over the Long Term* (No. 15-21R). Center for Economic Studies, US Census Bureau.

Haltiwanger, J., R. Jarmin, and C. Krizan (2010). Mom-and-Pop meet Big Box: complements or substitutes? *Journal of Urban Economics*, **67** (1), 116–34.

Inland Revenue (2014). *The Impact of the Canterbury Earthquakes on Small and Medium Enterprises: Adverse Events Longitudinal Study – Administrative Data Analyses*. Research report, Inland Revenue, Wellington.

Leiter, A., H. Oberhofer, and P. Raschky (2009). Creative disasters? Flooding effects on capital, labour and productivity within European firms. *Environmental and Resource Economics*, **43** (3), 333–50.

Mueller, V. and A. Quisumbing (2011). How resilient are labour markets to natural disasters? The case of the 1998 Bangladesh flood. *Journal of Development Studies*, **47**(12), 1954–71.

New Zealand Treasury (2013). *Half Year Economic and Fiscal Update 2013*. Wellington: The New Zealand Treasury.

Schumpeter, J. (1962). *Capitalism, Socialism, and Democracy*. New York: Harper and Brothers.

Statistics New Zealand (2012). New Zealand business demography statistics: at February 2012. Statistics New Zealand, Wellington.

Statistics New Zealand (2014a). 2013 Census QuickStats about Christchurch. Statistics New Zealand, Wellington.

Statistics New Zealand (2014b). Christchurch retail trade indicator: December 2013 quarter. Statistics New Zealand, Wellington.

Uchida, H., D. Miyakawa, K. Hosono, A. Ono, T. Uchino, and I. Uesugi (2013). Natural disaster and natural selection. Research Center for Interfirm Network Working Paper 25, Institute of Economic Research, Hitotsubashi University, Tokyo.

3. What factors determine economic strength in the restoration process from extreme disasters?

Masafumi Morisugi, Kazunori Nakajima and Naoki Sakamoto*,**

3.1 INTRODUCTION

In the past three decades, Japan has experienced two extreme large-scale earthquakes, namely, the Great Hanshin Earthquake in 1995 and the Great East Japan Earthquake in 2011. Other than Hurricane Harvey in 2017, these two disasters have wreaked the maximum economic damage on society alongside Hurricane Katrina in 2005.

The earthquake of 1995 had a magnitude of 7.3; it was a type of inland shallow earthquake. The maximum seismic intensity 7 was seen in Kobe City, among other areas. The main damage came from landslides, fires, building-infrastructure collapse, and liquefaction of the soil. There were 6434 deaths, 43792 injured, and three people declared missing. The total economic damage was estimated by the Cabinet Office at about 9.9–10 trillion yen. The total official budget for restoration was estimated by the Ministry of Finance in 2013 at about 9.2 trillion yen at a minimum.

The earthquake of 2011 had a magnitude of 9.0–9.1; it was a type of inter-plate earthquake. The maximum seismic intensity of 7 was seen in Kurihara City of Miyagi Prefecture. The main damage came from the tsunami wave (up to 40.1 meters), causing flooding, landslides, fires, building-infrastructure collapse, and nuclear incidents including radiation

* The chapter is dedicated to Masafumi Morisugi's late father, Hisayoshi Morisugi.
** The authors would like to give special thanks to the following organizations for their financial support: Environment Research and Technology Development Fund (S-8-1) of the Ministry of the Environment, Japan, 2010–14; Social Implementation Program on Climate Change Adaptation Technology (SI-CAT), Ministry of Education, Culture, Sports, Science and Technology (MEXT), Japan; and Grant-in-Aid for Scientific Research (B), 2017–019 (17H01938, Masafumi Morisugi), Ministry of Education, Culture, Sports, Science and Technology (MEXT), Japan.

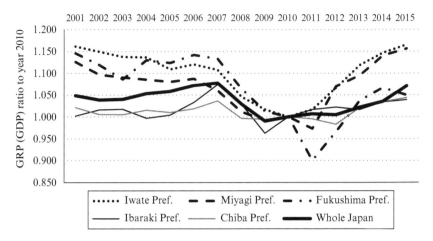

Figure 3.1   Nominal GDP and GRP transition (based on fiscal year 2010)

release. There were 15,893 deaths, 6152 injured, and 2553 people declared missing. The total economic damage (exclusive of the Fukushima nuclear accident) was estimated by the Cabinet Office at about 16–25 trillion yen. The total official budget for restoration was estimated by the Ministry of Finance in 2013 at about 19 trillion yen at a minimum.

While the region affected by the second extreme earthquake example is in the process of restoration even today, the period of annual real gross regional product (GRP) recovery in the disaster-stricken regions after the 1995 earthquake is much longer (Figure 3.1).

Figure 3.1 shows the transitions in the proportion of nominal gross domestic product (GDP) for each fiscal year, using 2010 as year one (the criteria year). These statistics are all available on the website of the Economic and Social Research Institute of the Cabinet Office of the Government of Japan. The economic damage cost may be the largest-ever in the world's history as an incidence of a single disaster.

The regions in Figure 3.1 represent some of the prefectures heavily affected by the Great East Japan Earthquake in 2011. In particular, the Miyagi, Iwate, and Fukushima Prefectures were the most damaged. Fukushima also suffered from a nuclear power plant accident and, because of restrictions in residential areas, fast and sufficient restoration may be much more difficult than in the other two regions. Miyagi Prefecture, although closest to the seismic center of the East Japan Earthquake, has seen extensive and high real economic growth rates in recent years, as high as 10.0 percent in 2012, 2.4 percent in 2013, 4.1 percent in 2014, and 1.4 percent in 2015 (nevertheless, the consumption tax rate was raised to

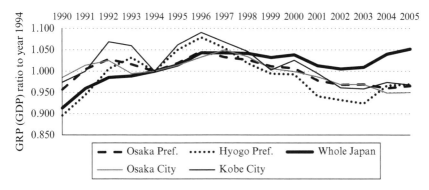

Figure 3.2   Nominal GDP and GRP transition (based on fiscal year 1994)

8 percent from 5 percent in 2014). In addition, the annual real GRP of Miyagi Prefecture exceeded 9 trillion yen, a number the region had never experienced before. These growth trends are very similar in the neighboring Iwate Prefecture.

It is noteworthy that such nominal GRP trends in Miyagi and Iwate Prefectures cannot be explained directly in terms of population transition. Throughout the periods shown in Figure 3.1, the resident population of Miyagi showed almost no change or a slight decrease. However, the population in Iwate showed a remarkable decline.

For the extreme earthquake of 1995, Figure 3.2 shows the transitions of the proportion of nominal GDP in each fiscal year based on 1994 as the criterion year. The regions in the figure represent some of the prefectures and capitals that were heavily affected by the Great Hanshin Earthquake.

Figure 3.2 shows that only Hyogo Prefecture and its capital city, Kobe City, enjoyed relatively higher economic growth for two to three years, at most, following the earthquake. As can be seen, in the following periods, Osaka Prefecture and its capital, Osaka City, suffered from unusually longer economic stagnation recessions. Compared to the GDP for all of Japan, the gap in regional growth seemed to continue to expand until around 2003.

The remarkable economic growth of Hyogo Prefecture and Kobe City from 1994 to 1996 was part of the restoration process and depended on financial aid and reconstruction support. Even today, the exact numbers for the cost of the damage in each region are not available. However, 99 percent of the human and building damage was in Kobe and the other cities in Hyogo. In addition, throughout the periods shown in Figure 3.2, the resident population of Hyogo was increasing, except for 1995 to 1996, until around 1999, when the population completely returned to the *ex ante* level of the earthquake. Therefore, the nominal GRP trends in Hyogo and Kobe cannot be explained directly by population transition. The question is then: where do such differences come from?

In terms of "resilience," the Construction Standard Act of Japan was revised in 2000 with the specific aim of addressing the seismic strengthening of wooden buildings and houses. As a result, the structural resilience of buildings in the twenty-first century is much higher than in the 1990s. Most damage in the 1995 earthquake was wrought by its main shockwaves, whereas it was the tsunami in the 2011 case. Hence, we do not think the difference in the economic recovery between the two earthquake areas was due to some kind of physical "resilience" to natural disasters.

In contrast to what many people often believe, the amount of financial aid or reconstruction support for a disaster-stricken region from a nation or other areas may not matter either. Such assistance almost always coincides with the value of the economic damage estimated by the asset valuation method (we call this economic damage value "the direct damage cost"). This is also true in the cases of the two largest earthquake examples discussed here.

In the next section, we introduce our analytical framework. It is a representative dynamic economic model, the so-called neoclassical growth model or Ramsey model. Although this model is simple and it cannot incorporate directly any factors of "resilience," the model structure seems to be adequate enough to represent the economic situation of Japan. As is well known, Japan is a highly seismic country. Fortunately, most regions in the country seem to have the power to recover from the severe damage created by a rare disaster. In this model, the economy is assumed to accumulate private capital again immediately after a region suffers a disaster as part of a "restoring process." Such recovery power may be considered one of "resilience."

In Section 3.3, in reference to our previous studies, we apply the Ramsey model to describe the situation of the restoration process from damage brought about by huge and rare disasters like the Great East Japan Earthquake. From the viewpoint of the utilitarian economist (that is, the standard way of thinking of a cost-benefit analysis), all benefits and costs should be measured by the change in consumption (or the equivalent of the expenditure change) as the crucial incidence form. Here, we make the point that the measurement of capital loss in its original form (that is, "the direct damage cost") is not a correct indicator to evaluate such disasters' economic damage because of the existence of the "dynamic effect." We provide the proof in this section, which shows that even Japanese regions with sufficient "resilience" to natural disasters need outside investment or financial assistance for recovery and reconstruction.

In Section 3.4, to answer the question why regional ability to recover after extreme disaster varied for each incidence, we develop "the restoration model" and "the steady state shifting model." While well-known earthquakes have occurred in Japan in the last 100 years, the Great Hanshin Earthquake seems to be the beginning of the latest intensive period of large earthquakes. In addition, under the hypothesis of rational expectation, this earthquake might have an impact on the regional macroeconomy not only in terms of capital destruction but also in terms of a shift in the steady state. Accordingly, the situation after the Great Hanshin Earthquake can be more likely explained.

Finally, in Section 3.5, we make brief concluding remarks and offer some political suggestions, in particular, for the time following the Great East Japan Earthquake.

3.2   THEORETICAL FRAMEWORK

In this section, according to Barro and Sala-i-Martin (2004), we introduce the so-called neoclassical growth model discussed by Ramsey (1928), Cass (1965), and Koopmans (1965). There is no shortage of examples of empirically and theoretically relevant extensions of the neoclassical growth model. In recent years, many precedent studies have attempted to estimate the effects of natural disasters on economic growth using various types of model building. Loayza et al. (2012) provided a good review of these in their empirical study. One large research stream is endogenous growth models. As highlighted by Acemoglu (2009), the neoclassical growth model does not, on the whole, generate new insights about the sources of cross-country income differences and economic growth relative to the Solow (1956) growth model. However, in studies with endogenous growth models of public capital, human capital, research and development, learning by doing, and so on, policies could influence the rate of economic growth as well as making the resource allocation the Pareto improvement. Here, we have no intention whatever of confirming or criticizing such approaches; however, adopting a new approach is not necessarily correct. We use only one model, the most fundamental and simplest dynamic equilibrium model. All of the content in the other sections of the chapter includes nothing more than an expansion of the Ramsey model. What we hope to show is that we can gain some new insights from this model even today and what we find relates in depth to policy making for disaster prevention.

In our model, we assume an aggregated closed economy with one sector consisting of a representative household and a firm.

First, we describe the behavior of the representative household. The household supplies the firm with one unit of labor annually. The laborer receives wages and interest on assets, consumes goods, and saves the rest of the income. The household maximizes the present value of lifetime utility, subject to a budget constraint per capita, as follows:

$$\max_{c_t} U = \int_0^\infty u(c_t)e^{nt} \cdot e^{-\rho t} dt \qquad u(c_t) = \frac{c_t^{1-\theta} - 1}{1 - \theta} \tag{3.1}$$

$$s.t. \ \dot{a}_t = w_t + r_t a_t - c_t - n a_t \tag{3.2}$$

where ρ is the rate of time preference, θ is the inverse of the elasticity of inter-temporal substitution, n is the labor growth rate, c is the consumption per capita, w is the wage rate, and r is the interest rate. The utility function is assumed to be CRRA, that is, the constant relative risk aversion of Arrow (1951) and Pratt (1964), or CIES, the constant inter-temporal elasticity of substitution.

The necessary condition and the transversality condition of Hamiltonian dynamics for this optimization problem are well known as follows:

$$\frac{\dot{c}}{c} = \frac{1}{\theta}(r - \rho) \tag{3.3}$$

$$\lim_{t \to \infty} \left[a(t)\exp\left\{ -\int_0^t [r(v) - n]dv \right\} \right] = $$
$$\lim_{t \to \infty} \left[k(t) \cdot \exp\left\{ -\int_0^t [f'(\hat{k}(v)) - \delta - x - n]dv \right\} \right] = 0 \tag{3.4}$$

Here, we also define $L(t) = L_0 e^{nt}$ as the population number or amount of labor supply in period t and $\hat{L}(t) = L(t)e^{xt}$ as the effective labor considering the Harrod (1942) neutral technology in which x indicates rate of exogenous technological progress. At the same time, capital stock $K(t)$ per effective labor can be represented as below.

$$k = \frac{K}{L} \quad \hat{k} = \frac{K}{\hat{L}} = \frac{K}{L \cdot e^{xt}} = ke^{-xt} \quad k = \hat{k}e^{xt} \tag{3.5}$$

Second, we describe a firm's behavior. In this economy, only one good is assumed to exist. In addition, only the representative firm can produce it. It also maximizes its annual profit π under constraint of production technology $F(\cdot)$ as follows:

$$\max_{\hat{k}} \pi = F(K,\hat{L}) - (r+\delta)K - w\hat{L} = \hat{L}[f(\hat{k} - (r+\delta)\hat{k} - we^{-xt})] \quad (3.6)$$

where $F(\cdot)$ is the neoclassical production function, which shows constant returns to scale with respect to inputs of capital and labor as well as positive and diminishing returns for these inputs, and also satisfies the Inada conditions and essentiality (see chapter 1 in Barro and Sala-i-Martin, 2004), and δ is the depreciation rate of capital stock.

The first-order condition in the firm's optimization problem is written as follows:

$$f'(\hat{k}) = r + \delta \qquad f'(\hat{k}) - (r+\delta)\hat{k} = we^{-xt} \quad (3.7)$$

Third, all variables are converted into the effective labor unit with the equilibrium condition $a = k$. Equations (3.2), (3.3), and (3.7) determine the equilibrium value of the variables such as c, k, w, and r. In order to express this economic system by only $\hat{c}$ and $\hat{k}$, substituting $\hat{k} = \hat{k}e^{xt} + x\hat{k}e^{xt}$ and equation (3.7) into equation (3.2) derives

$$\dot{\hat{k}} = f(\hat{k}) - \hat{c} - (n + x + \delta)\hat{k} \quad (3.8)$$

In addition, we substitute $c = \hat{c}e^{-xt}$ into equation (3.3).

$$\frac{\dot{\hat{c}}}{\hat{c}} = \frac{1}{\theta}(r - \rho - \theta x) = \frac{1}{\theta}[f'(\hat{k}) - \delta - \rho - \theta x] \quad (3.9)$$

Thus, two differential equations (3.8) and (3.9) determine the equilibrium path substantially.

Finally, with these equilibrium conditions, and assuming that $\dot{\hat{c}} = 0$ and $\dot{\hat{k}} = 0$, the steady state equilibrium conditions can be derived as below.

$$f(\hat{k}) - (n + x + \delta)\hat{k} = \hat{c} \quad (3.10)$$

$$f'(\hat{k}) - \delta = r = \rho + \theta x \quad (3.11)$$

Figure 3.3 shows the transitional dynamics of the original Ramsey model. By dividing the space into four regions, we can confirm that $\dot{\hat{c}} = 0$ and $\dot{\hat{k}} = 0$, The model has only one steady state equilibrium (**SS**) and exhibits saddle-path stability. The paths, other than the stable arm, in Figure 3.3 indicate that either consumption is 0 or it collapses to the transversality condition. Therefore, these are irrational alternatives for the representative principal of this economy. The stable arm is an upward-sloping curve that goes through the origin and the steady state. For details, see chapter 2 in Barro and Sala-i-Martin (2004).

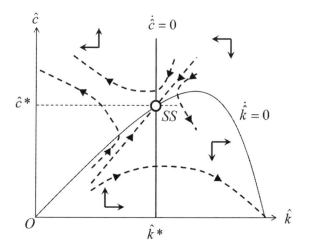

Figure 3.3   Phase diagram of the original Ramsey model and the steady state

3.3   RESTORATION PROCESS MODEL

In this section, with the foundation of the Ramsey growth model explained above, we develop a model that describes the restoration process of a disaster-stricken region. It supposes that the disaster is rare and large enough, such as the Great East Japan Earthquake, and that the main damage is due to building-infrastructure collapse. This is equivalent to losing a substantial amount of private and public capital at once here. As seen in the previous section, we do not treat the variable of public capital explicitly. Therefore, the impact of disaster on the society is described simply as $-\Delta K$.

Okuyama (2003) discussed that standard neoclassical growth theories predict that destruction of capital stock per worker temporarily accelerates growth in the aftermath of a disaster by increasing its marginal return (while a reduction in the number of effective workers would decelerate it). This logic is also true for our model.

There are differences to some extent about the kinds of disasters treated or analytical methodologies used in our precedent research (see Nakajima et al., 2015, 2017) and in this study. However, we develop a similar theoretical model to explain what "the dynamic effect" is and how the damage cost for a rare disaster should be calculated in terms of a utilitarian economist meaning (Figure 3.4).

Let us assume that the economy in the subject region has been on the

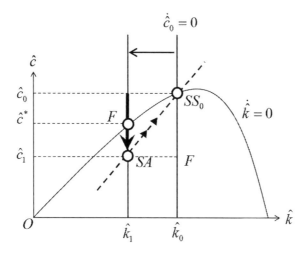

Figure 3.4   Phase diagram: restoration process from rare disaster damage

initial steady state equilibrium (SS_0) until the disaster strikes. The impact of the disaster is expressed as the drastic and instantaneous reduction of capital stock $\hat{k}_0$ to $\hat{k}_1 (< \hat{k}_0)$. Therefore, the left arrow represents the impact of the rare disaster. In addition, we set the variable of the depreciation rate as the δ_0 constant only in this section. It also assumes that there is no financial aid or fiscal support from outside regions. The disaster-stricken area should behave as an autarky economy and restore itself by investing and accumulating the amount of capital stock again. As for the phase diagram in Section 3.2, under the assumption of the principal's rationality and perfect foresight, the economy jumps to SA immediately by adjusting the level of consumption. The point SA is on the stable arm, that is, the upward-sloping curve going to the original steady state SS_0. From the point SA, the economy begins to restore itself by accumulating the amount of capital per effective labor and increasing the consumption level per effective labor. We express this in Discussion 1 below.

Discussion 1:
When the economy of the disaster-stricken region is on the restoration proc-ess trajectory from SA to SS_0, both the capital stock per effective labor $\hat{k}$ and the consumption level per effective labor $\hat{c}$ are increasing all the time. Such a situation continues until the economy reaches the steady state SS_0, but the rate of increase in these variables becomes gradually smaller. The reason for this is shown in equation (3.9). Immediately after the disaster occurs, the capital stock per effective labor $\hat{k}$ becomes substantially smaller compared

with the ex ante *level. Then, as the interest rate = marginal productivity of capital becomes large enough, the variables of ĉ increase in parallel. However, as k̂ becomes larger and nears the level of the previous steady state, the interest rate and the growth rate of consumption decrease and approach 0 ultimately. In addition, in Figure 3.4 and equations (3.9) and (3.10), as the vertical distance between the current consumption level on the saddle path and the curves of k̂ = 0 represent k̂, the growth rate of k̂ is positive and decreases gradually. At the steady state, although the growth rate of k̂ and ĉ become 0, the amount of capital and consumption level per capita are increasing with the exogenous technical progress x in the same manner as ex ante levels. Therefore, at least, we can say that the economy in the process of restoration grows faster than ever before.*

Discussion 1 seems to capture appropriately the situations that followed the two catastrophic earthquakes in Japan. As shown in Figures 3.1 and 3.2, the economies in the areas stricken by disaster grew for years immediately after the earthquakes occurred. However, the growth eventually ceased in the case of the Great Hanshin Earthquake in 1995.

One should note that our model does not consider any change in each region's population or population growth between *ex ante* and *ex post* levels. This is basically for convenience to simplify the issue. Endogenizing the migration process into the model necessarily makes calculations and conjectures too complicated and, thus, we omitted these components here. Approximately 20,000 people became victims of the Great East Japan Earthquake in 2011. However, at that time, the population of Iwate Prefecture was 1,330,530, Miyagi Prefecture 2,348,165, and Fukushima Prefecture 1,965,704. Therefore, the influence of the labor market seemed to be limited. However, the Census Return in 2015 (Ministry of Internal Affairs and Communications in Japan) shows that the population change in Iwate Prefecture was –4.3 percent, in Miyagi Prefecture –0.5 percent, and in Fukushima Prefecture –4.9 percent during the period 2010 to 2015. Such numbers are certainly not negligible, and one may be concerned about the effect on the regional economy (Nakajima and Sakamoto, 2015). Nevertheless, the GRPs of these regions during this period have been increasing, as shown in Figures 3.1 and 3.2. The real situation seems to be consistent with the restoration process that Discussion 1 indicates.

Now, we try to demonstrate verification of the damage cost. Let us remember that SS_0 is the steady state equilibrium of the economy. Hence, it satisfies equation (3.10), and is captured as below.

$$f(\hat{k}_0) - (n + x + \delta_0)\hat{k}_0 = \hat{c}_0 \qquad (3.12)$$

Immediately after the disaster occurs, the economy jumps to the point **SA**; therefore, it also satisfies equation (3.8), as below.

$$\dot{k} = f(\hat{k}) - \hat{c} - (n + x + \delta_0)\hat{k} \qquad (3.13)$$

Let us combine these equations; we then obtain an expression of the trajectory.

$$\dot{k} = f(\hat{k}_1) - f(\hat{k}_0) + \hat{c}_0 - \hat{c}_1 + (n + x + \delta_0)(\hat{k}_0 - \hat{k}_1) \qquad (3.14)$$

Equation (3.14) clearly represents the concept of the so-called "dynamic effect" or "dynamic multiplier effect" as presented in Nakajima et al. (2017). It is supposed that the region will restore itself. Furthermore, equation (3.14) shows that the volume of capital accumulation (left-hand side of the equation) does not equal the victims of consumption ($\hat{c}_0 - \hat{c}_1$). The difference between these can be explained by two components. One is expressed as $(n + x + \delta_0)(\hat{k}_0 - \hat{k}_1)$ on the right-hand side of the equation. Because *ex post* capital stock level $\hat{k}_1$ is smaller than that of *ex ante* $\hat{k}_0$, the necessity of capital supplementation for population growth, technological change, and depreciation becomes relatively small. The other part is $f(\hat{k}_1) - f(\hat{k}_0)$, namely, the "income effect," where the productivity *ex post* is smaller than that *ex ante* due to the scarcity of capital stock.

Therefore, the problem is whether or not the sum of $f(\hat{k}_1) - f(\hat{k}_0)$ and $(n + x + \delta_0)(\hat{k}_0 - \hat{k}_1)$ is positive. To restore "the direct damage cost," which equals $(\hat{k}_0 - \hat{k}_1)$, it may not be sufficient to use the equivalent of the victims of consumption. To put it differently, "the damage cost of the incidence" (measured by the consumption base) may be larger than "the direct damage cost" (measured by the capital base) because of the "dynamic effect." In fact, we can show this as below.

Lemma 1:
*Let a point **F** in Figure 3.4 be depicted. **F** is located on the curve $\dot{k} = 0$; therefore, it satisfies the equation as follows:*

$$f(\hat{k}_1) - (n + x + \delta_0)\hat{k}_1 = \hat{c}^* \qquad (3.15)$$

Let equations (3.12) and (3.15) be combined; we then obtain the following equation.

$$f(\hat{k}_1) - f(\hat{k}_0) + (n + x + \delta_0)(\hat{k}_0 - \hat{k}_1) = \hat{c}^* - \hat{c}_0 \qquad (3.16)$$

Substituting equation (3.16) into (3.13) derives

$$\dot{k} = \hat{c}* - \hat{c}_1 \qquad\qquad (3.17)$$

As $\hat{c}* < \hat{c}_0$ from Figure 3.4, equation (3.17) can be rewritten as below, and is comparable with equation (3.14) and the arbitrary positive variable of A.

$$\dot{k} = -A + \hat{c}_0 - \hat{c}_1 \qquad\qquad (3.18)$$

Equation (3.18) reflects that the sum of $f(\hat{k}_1) - f(\hat{k}_0)$ and $(n + x + \delta_0)(\hat{k}_0 - \hat{k}_1)$ is negative.
[QED]

Lemma 1 proves clearly that "the damage cost of the incidence" is larger than "the direct damage cost." Because equation (3.18) is the capital accumulation of the first period after the disaster occurs, for the second period and later, the economy is also on the stable arm from *SA* to *SS$_0$*, therefore the discussion of Lemma 1 can be applied similarly to a case with larger numbers of $\hat{k}_1$, $\hat{c}_1$, and $\hat{c}*$.

Moreover, as an extension of the argument above, we can understand the role of the usual investment for recovery and reconstruction from outside regions. If it is done ideally, such investment from outside the disaster-struck region could restore the capital stock level to its original settings as $\hat{k}_0 = \hat{k}_1$ immediately. In such a case, there is no capital shortage problem in the production sector and also no "dynamic effect" as Lemma 1 suggests. Then, equation (3.14) is rewritten as follows:

$$\Delta\hat{k} = \hat{c}_0 - \hat{c}_1 \qquad\qquad (3.19)$$

This suggests that "the damage cost of the incidence" is equal to "the direct damage cost." The "dynamic effect" no longer appears here.

Let us bring the debate back to the original topic. Up to now, we have analysed why the ability to recover after a disaster varies for each incidence. In the context of this section, the amount of support and government funding might be effective explanatory factors. The smaller the amount of funding or the later the timing of such financial aid when implemented, the more the economy would suffer from damage above "the direct damage cost." However, in the cases of the Great Hanshin Earthquake and the Great East Japan Earthquake, the amount of assistance almost coincided with "the direct damage cost" (Ministry of Internal Affairs and Communications in Japan, n.d.). Therefore, at this time, we cannot provide sufficient conjecture to explain the difference in the ability to recover.

Meanwhile, there is also an alternative hypothesis. Let us consider the relative scale of "the direct damage cost" in relation to the amount of *ex ante* capital. We capture this in Discussion 2 below.

Discussion 2:

In Figure 3.4, $(\hat{k}_0 - \hat{k}_1)/\hat{k}_0$ is also equal to $(K_0 - K_1)/K_0$. The numerator is actually "the direct damage cost" for each disaster's incidence: 10 trillion yen for the Great Hanshin Earthquake and 16–25 trillion yen for the Great East Japan Earthquake. However, we cannot define the exact value of K_0, which is the amount of ex ante *private capital in the disaster-stricken region. The subject regions here are the Osaka and Hyogo Prefectures for the Great Hanshin Earthquake and the Iwate, Miyagi, and Fukushima Prefectures for the Great East Japan Earthquake. Instead of capital, GRP statistics are available to estimate the relative scale of these regional economies compared with the other 46 prefectures in Japan. In 2014, Osaka was the second largest economy at about 38 trillion yen; and Hyogo was seventh at about 20 trillion yen; at the same time, Miyagi was 14th at about 9 trillion yen, Fukushima 20th at about 7.4 trillion yen, and Iwate 28th at about 4.6 trillion yen. These measures are considered to be almost proportional to the regional amount of capital equipment. Therefore, $(\hat{k}_0 - \hat{k}_1)/\hat{k}_0$ of the Great East Japan Earthquake was much larger than that of the Great Hanshin Earthquake. In Figure 3.4, this means that there was more distance from **SA** to **SS_0** in the case of the Great East Japan Earthquake and the residents might have seen longer economic growth.*

3.4 STEADY STATE SHIFTING MODEL

3.4.1 Corollary

Until now, we have discussed the regional restoration process from the representative earthquakes in the past. With the restoration model developed in Section 3.3 and Discussion 1, we can explain why a disaster-stricken region grows faster than ever before in a period. In addition, because of the "dynamic effect," Lemma 1 proves that "the damage cost of the incidence" is larger than "the direct damage cost," in general. Therefore, financial assistance from other regions is an effective policy to reduce the gap, making it as small as possible.

As an extension of these issues, we submitted a proposal to explain the difference between restoration length and strength for the Great Hanshin Earthquake and the Great East Japan Earthquake. Discussion 2 asserts that the difference is based on only the relative scale of economic damage. In our analytical framework of the Ramsey model, the larger the region is that suffers damage from the disaster, the faster and longer its economy will grow.

The reliability of this hypothesis depends heavily on special characteristics of our country. Japan is well known as a highly seismic country. Moreover, all of the regions seem to have the "resilience" to restore themselves even from the greatest disasters we have known. Therefore, many past incidences appear highly consistent with the neoclassical growth model. We cannot unconditionally deny the argument of Discussion 2. It must be one of the reasons that the economies of Iwate and Miyagi Prefectures continue growing still.

However, Discussion 2 cannot fully explain the situation of the Great Hanshin Earthquake. Let us revisit Figure 3.2. The GRP of both Osaka and Hyogo Prefectures reflects earthquake shock in 1994. Subsequently, the prefectures experienced economic growth or restoration for a few years. Following that period, these economies entered an era of decline for about ten years regardless of the fact that the overall GDP of Japan showed no weakness during the period. It is clear that our restoration process model has no precise explanation for this. The model just suggests that economic growth will cease when the amount of capital returns sufficiently to the original level.

To understand this situation, we need to introduce an alternative component to our theoretical model. This might be more of a long-term concern, affecting and displacing the steady state directly.

3.4.2 History

Table 3.1 reveals the twentieth and twenty-first century historical perspective of the large earthquakes in Japan and captures examples of incidences with over 1,000 victims or maximum seismic intensity (SS) of 7 as the new criterion. The Japan Meteorological Agency Seismic Intensity Scale has ten classes according to shaking degree. Among them, seismic intensity (SS) 7 is the largest, introduced after the outbreak of the Fukui Earthquake in 1948, and the scale was applied for the first time to the Great Hanshin Earthquake. Of note, during several decades, from 1948 to 1995, there was no prominent, large and rare earthquake in Japan. The Fukui Earthquake is positioned to be the last incidence of sequential large earthquakes during the 1920s to the 1940s. This period was considered as an intensive time for relatively large-scale earthquakes.

Currently, we may be in such an intensive period. The SS7 has been observed five times during the past 30 years: the Great Hanshin Earthquake in 1995, the Niigata Chuetsu Earthquake in 2004 (total damage cost estimated around 3 trillion yen), the Great East Japan Earthquake in 2011,

Table 3.1   History of the large earthquakes in Japan

Year	Incidence	Victims	Old	New
1923	The Great Kanto Earthquake	105385	SS6	SS7-eq
1927	Kitatango Earthquake	2925	SS6	SS7-eq
1933	Showa Sanriku Earthquake	3064	SS6	–
1943	Tottori Earthquake	1083	SS6	–
1944	Tonankai Earthquake	1223	SS6	–
1945	Mikawa Earthquake	2306	SS6	SS7-eq
1946	Nankai Earthquake	1223	SS6	–
1948	Fukui Earthquake	3769	SS6	SS7-eq
	New criteria of seismic intensity (Max 7) has been introduced.			
1995	The Great Hanshin Earthquake	6437	–	SS7
2004	Niigata Chuetsu Earthquake	68	–	SS7
2011	The Great East Japan Earthquake	18446	–	SS7
2016	Foreshock of Kumamoto Earthquake	9	–	SS7
2016	Kumamoto Earthquake	204	–	SS7

Note: "eq" means equivalent.

and a two-time occurrence of the Kumamoto Earthquake in 2016 (total damage cost estimated around 4.6 trillion yen). Thus, there is academic opinion that we live in a period of brisk seismic activity not only in Japan but also all over the world.

Consequently, we suggest a new hypothesis as a subsidiary proposition to Discussion 2. Suppose that the people living in a disaster-stricken region hereafter change their foresight about the frequency of large earthquakes. Namely, they predict that the frequency will be higher in the future than before. In accordance with the assumption of their rationality and perfect foresight in our model setting, their foresight becomes reality. This means that the depreciation rate of capital δ increases in particular.

3.4.3   Depreciation Rate Increasing and Shift of Steady State

The model introduced here has the same structure as the ones in our prior research (Morisugi and Morisugi, 2012; Nakajima et al., 2014, 2015). In earlier studies, we assume that the annual flood damage cost will increase due to climate change. We use the analytical framework here as well. Let us suppose that people can estimate the expected value of the annual damage cost to their assets from several disasters. Here, immediately after the rare disaster, the impact for the residents is assumed to be the increase in the annual physical damage of capital stock loss, namely, δ_0 to $\delta_1 (> \delta_0)$. This happens due to the change in the residents' foresight regarding the frequency of large earthquakes.

Incidentally, as in the restoration model process, there are also "the direct damage cost" and "the dynamic damage cost" concepts for this case; these each have different values. To understand the reason for this, we present comparative statics in Lemma 2 below.

Lemma 2:
Differentiating equations (3.10) and (3.11) with respect to $\hat{k}$, $\hat{c}$, and δ derives

$$f''(\hat{k})d\hat{k} = d\delta \quad \Rightarrow \quad \frac{d\hat{k}}{d\delta} = \frac{1}{f''(\hat{k})} < 0 \qquad (3.20)$$

$$\{f(\hat{k}) - (n + x + \delta)\}\, d\hat{k} - \hat{k}d\delta = d\hat{c}$$

$$\Rightarrow \quad \frac{d\hat{c}}{d\delta} = \frac{\{\rho + (\theta - 1)x - n\}}{f''(\hat{k})} - \hat{k}$$

$$\Rightarrow \quad \frac{d\hat{c}}{d\delta} = -\left[\frac{\{\rho + (\theta - 1)x - n\}}{-f''(\hat{k})\hat{k}} + 1\right]\hat{k}. \qquad (3.21)$$

The change of δ causes the annual damage to private capital to increase. "The direct damage cost" here is $d\delta\hat{k}$ in equation (3.21) or $(\delta_1 - \delta_0)\hat{k}$. From the results of the comparative statics on the steady state equilibrium, we can obtain a form of "the dynamic damage cost (comparative statics)" as equation (3.21) shows. The large bracket [] in this equation is the so-called "dynamic multiplier." The bracket {} in the equation is the same value of bracket [] in equation (3.4) of the transversality condition, so it has a positive value with the assumption of $f'' < 0$. Therefore, "the dynamic multiplier" certainly exceeds 1.
[QED]

Such a measurement of "the direct damage cost" can be derived easily from the general and official statistics related to details on the disaster's damage to assets. However, here again, we should suggest that such an evaluation method is neither adequate nor a correct evaluation. This is because the damage cost should be evaluated with and without comparison to consumption (or expenditure) as the incident form. "The dynamic damage cost (comparative statics)" is larger than "the direct damage cost" in general.

To understand the relationship between these types of damage cost, a phase diagram as shown in Figure 3.5 is useful. The *ex ante* steady state equilibrium for depreciation rate δ_0 is the point SS_0. The two fine arrows

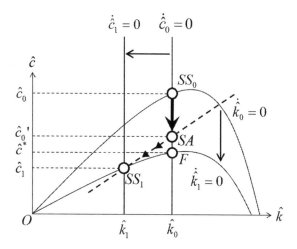

Figure 3.5 Phase diagram: notion of the dynamic damage cost (comparative statics)

represent the impact of the rare disaster. The increase of the depreciation rate as δ_0 to δ_1 shifts the vertical line of $\hat{c} = 0$ to the left-hand side, the curve of $\hat{k} = 0$ downwards, and the steady state equilibrium from SS_0 to SS_1. Both the capital stock per effective labor $\hat{k}$ and the consumption per effective labor $\hat{c}$ decrease due to the steady state relocation.

Let us define the point F as the cross point of $\hat{k}_1 = 0$ and $\hat{c}_0 = 0$, and $\hat{c}^*$ as the corresponding consumption level. At this point, it satisfies the condition as below as an extension of equation (3.12).

$$f(\hat{k}_0) - (n + x + \delta_1)\hat{k}_0 = \hat{c}^* \tag{3.22}$$

Hence, the distance from point F to point SS_0 is $(\delta_1 - \delta_0)\hat{k}_0$, namely, just "the direct damage cost." Similarly, $\hat{c}_0 - \hat{c}_1$ is "the dynamic damage cost (comparative statics)"; therefore, we can see easily this measurement is larger than the "the direct damage cost."

The disparity between "the direct damage cost" and "the dynamic damage cost (comparative statics)" relates strongly to capital accumulation in the dynamic process of the economy. If we set $d\hat{k} = 0$ in the process of combining equations (3.20) and (3.21), then the result would show $\hat{k}d\delta = d\hat{c}$. In another situation, if we suppose that the discount rate ρ, technological progress x, and population growth n are 0 (namely, remove the dynamic components from the model), we can obtain the same conclusion as well. In the new steady state equilibrium, the representative principal rationally selects a smaller value of capital stock than before. This moves the productivity downwards as well as the level of annual consumption. Then, the economy should pay more victims of consumption to compensate for the annual increase in damage cost to capital stock.

For more information, see the studies of Nakajima et al. (2015), who measured "the dynamic damage cost" of floods under climate change using a multi-regional, multi-sectoral, and forward-looking dynamic computable general equilibrium model (this consisted of 8 sectors and 20 sectors, respectively) and the theoretical framework based on Morisugi and Morisugi (2012). The degree of the "dynamic multiplier" may be around 1.2 to 1.5.

In terms of political concerns, there may be none worthy of special mention in this case. That differs from the theoretical consequence of the previous section; Lemma 2 only suggests that "the direct damage cost" is not an adequate way to evaluate the annual increase in damage costs due to disasters in the future and may rather underestimate this generally. In this neoclassical growth model setting, there is no political method to diminish the value of the damage cost without any loss of resource allocation efficiency.

3.4.4   Transitional Dynamics

Here, we extend the discussion above to the transitional dynamics of the economy. The model introduced in this section is inspired by Acemoglu (2009, see chapter 8). In the study by Acemoglu, the effects of a change in capital tax rate are considered, which are assumed to be unanticipated and to occur at some date. According to political action, the economy will ultimately tend to a new steady state equilibrium. The author references the method of analysis as "comparative dynamics." Contrary to the previous section and as seen in the restoration process model of Section 3.3, the disaster-struck region cannot shift its position to the new steady state equilibrium instantaneously in general (see Figure 3.5).

Considering the discussion about the phase diagram in Section 3.3, under the assumption of the principal's rationality and perfect foresight, the economy jumps to SA in Figure 3.5 by adjusting its level of consumption immediately after the disaster occurs. The point SA is on the stable arm, which is the lower left direction curve that moves to the new steady state equilibrium SS_1. From the point of SA, the economy begins to decline, gradually reducing both the amount of capital per effective labor and the consumption level per effective labor. However, the annual rate of decrease falls gradually as well (Figure 3.6).

The left graph is almost the same phase diagram as Figure 3.5; however,

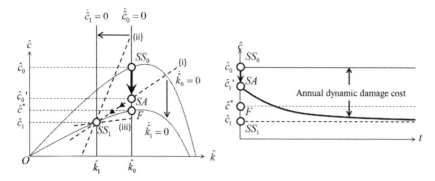

Figure 3.6 Phase diagram: notion of the dynamic damage cost (transitional dynamics)

three candidates for the stable arm are newly considered. The right panel displays the exact dynamic path of the consumption per effective labor as a typical case of stable arm (i) in which SA is located between SS_0 and F.

As explained above, "the dynamic damage cost (comparative statics)" is $\hat{c}_0 - \hat{c}_1$. Furthermore, we introduce here another concept, namely, "the dynamic damage cost" of transitional dynamics. It is measured by the average distance between $\hat{c}_0$ and $\hat{c}(t)$ on the path of the stable arm to SS_1. Unlike the case in equation (3.21), this type of measurement of the dynamic damage cost cannot be expressed in a normative analytical way. Alternatively, in Nakajima et al. (2014, 2015), there are numerical simulations in the original dynamic computable general equilibrium model. These empirical results are also consistent with these discussions.

"The dynamic damage cost of comparative statics" is generally larger than "the dynamic damage cost of transitional dynamics." In the case of (i) in Figure 3.6, we can see easily that the law is satisfied. In the case of (iii), SA locates under the point F, and $\hat{k}$ has begun to increase from the origin; therefore, it is not a sustainable trajectory. In the case of (ii), we cannot deny that such a trajectory might exist. However, it seems also to follow the law, while "the dynamic damage cost (transitional dynamics)" is negative around the beginning of convergence to SS_1. Therefore, we have no difficulty in treating "the dynamic damage cost (comparative statics)" as the maximum value of "the dynamic damage cost."

3.4.5 Integrated Model

In summarizing the discussions above, we can derive an integrated model (Figure 3.7). This model incorporates not only the restoration process

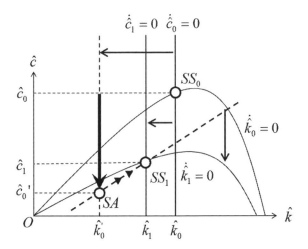

Figure 3.7   Phase diagram: restoration process and increase of the depreciation rate

model but also the steady state shifting model developed in this section. The *ex ante* steady state equilibrium for the depreciation rate δ_0 is at the point SS_0. The impact of the disaster is expressed as the drastic and instantaneous reduction in capital stock $\hat{k}_0$ to $\hat{k}_1 (<\hat{k}_0)$ as in Figure 3.4. In addition, the two finer arrows represent the impact of the rare disaster. The increase in the depreciation rate as δ_0 to δ_1 shifts the vertical line of $\hat{c} = 0$ to the left-hand side, the curve of $\hat{k} = 0$ downwards, and the steady state equilibrium from SS_0 to SS_1.

The economy jumps to SA immediately by adjusting the level of consumption. The point SA is on the stable arm, which is the upward-sloping curve that goes to the new steady state SS_1. From the point of SA, the economy begins to restore itself by accumulating the amount of capital per effective labor and increasing the consumption level per effective labor. This is just as Discussion 1 suggests and it explains appropriately the actual economic situation after the Great East Japan Earthquake or the Great Hanshin Earthquake. However, in this case, the economy would grow or restore up to SS_1 at the most. The scale of the economy at SS_1 falls short of the one at SS_0. Therefore, the period of growth or restoration might feel much shorter than expected. Furthermore, if the depreciation rate increases repeatedly due to a change in people's predictions about the frequency of large earthquakes in the future, the model would clearly describe the situation of the Great Hanshin Earthquake.

3.5 CONCLUSION

To summarize the content of this chapter, under our theoretical and historical examinations, the difference in the economic situations following two extreme earthquake incidences does not depend on any difference in physical "resilience" in these regions nor on the size of assistance from other regions but rather on the future expectations of the residents. Such a factor is mostly accidental and inherent; thus, it is hard to obtain through an intentional policy-making process.

Throughout this chapter, we suggest that evaluating the damage costs of the disaster in terms of the value of assets is more likely to underestimate the damage. This is because of the existence of a "dynamic effect." It should be noted that calculating the damage cost with and without a comparison of consumption (or expenditure) per incident form is a better method. As an extension of these discussions, we also suggest the economic significance of investment or financial assistance for recovery and reconstruction from outside the disaster-struck region. These would be effective in eliminating the "dynamic effect" in the process of restoration.

In recent years in Japan, extensive preliminary investments against future disasters have been implemented to literally acquire "resilience." The establishment of this as a policy might make some people feel better as well as safer. Therefore, these people might consume more than ever before based on the decreasing necessity to save as a precautionary move against future disasters. If the majority of people behave in such a way, the disaster-stricken region would enjoy a higher and longer economic growth following its restoration process. However, does the general Japanese citizen actually respond to a policy that way? From the current available statistics, the prospect of such a policy effect is doubtful. The effectiveness of such "resilience" obtained through the implementation of public capital for disaster prevention depends heavily on the accuracy of the prediction of earthquakes in terms of both timing and location. Needless to say, that is too difficult to accomplish. Moreover, will a drastic budget expansion for disaster prevention measures create anxiety among residents that a large-scale disaster is coming again? The situation is very similar to the one of the Great Hanshin Earthquake. In fact, the earthquake may fade in the minds of consumers and make the economic restoration process short and very small.

Contrary to such pessimistic views, in recent years, the disaster-stricken regions of the Great East Japan Earthquake have been restored and seen steady economic growth. Today, post-earthquake statistics for the related prefectures are available for only three to four years at most; therefore, we avoid making an estimate of these regions here. However, the case of the

Great Hanshin Earthquake serves as a cautionary tale, with the key being the residents' anxiety about their future. Years from now, we will discover whether several current policies and plans have or have not been effective in a real sense.

REFERENCES

Acemoglu, D. (2009). *Introduction to Modern Economic Growth*, Princeton, NJ: Princeton University Press.

Arrow, K.J. (1951). "Alternative Approaches to the Theory of Choice in Risk-taking Situations," *Econometrica*, **19** (4), 404–37.

Barro, R.J. and Sala-i-Martin, X. (2004). *Economic Growth*, 2nd edn, Cambridge, MA: MIT Press.

Cass, D. (1965). "Optimum Growth in an Aggregate Model of Capital Accumulation," *Review of Economic Studies*, **32**, 233–40.

Economic and Social Research Institute, Cabinet Office, Government of Japan website, http://www.esri.cao.go.jp/jp/sna/sonota/kenmin/kenmin_top.html (accessed 12 August 2018).

Harrod, R.F. (1942). *Toward a Dynamic Economics: Some Recent Developments of Economic Theory and their Application to Policy*, London: Macmillan.

Koopmans, T.C. (1965). "On the Concept of Optimal Economic Growth," in J. Johansen (ed), *The Econometric Approach to Development Planning*, Amsterdam: North Holland, pp. 410–48.

Loayza, N.V., Olaberria, E., Rigolini, J., and Christiaensen, L. (2012). "Natural Disasters and Growth: Going Beyond the Averages," *World Development*, **40** (7), 1317–36.

Ministry of Internal Affairs and Communications in Japan (n.d.), Population Census, Statistics Bureau of Japan, http://www.stat.go.jp/english/data/kokusei/index.html (accessed 12 August 2018).

Morisugi, H. and Morisugi, M. (2012). "Definition and Measurement of Natural Disaster Damage Cost by Ramsey Growth Model," in *Proceedings of the 52nd European Congress of the Regional Science Association International*, Ordinary Session 52, http://www-sre.wu.ac.at/ersa/ersaconfs/ersa12/e120821aFinal00591.pdf (accessed 12 August 2018).

Nakajima, K. and Sakamoto, N. (2015). "General Equilibrium Analysis of Regional Redistributive Effects of Investment for Reconstruction from the Great East Japan Earthquake," in *Proceedings of the 55th European Congress of Regional Science Association International*, Paper 00320, pp. 1–36, http://hdl.handle.net/10419/124628 (accessed 12 August 2018).

Nakajima, K., Morisugi, H. Morisugi, M., and Sakamoto N. (2014). "Measurement of Flood Damage due to Climate Change by Dynamic Spatial Computable General Equilibrium Model," in *Proceedings of the 54th European Congress of the Regional Science Association International*, Paper 00673, pp. 1–27, http://hdl.handle.net/10419/124347 (accessed 12 August 2018).

Nakajima, K., Morisugi, H. Morisugi, M., and Sakamoto, N. (2015). "Measurement of Long-term Flood Damage in Japan using Spatial Computable General Equilibrium Model," in *Proceedings of the European Association of*

Environmental and Resource Economists 21st Annual Conference, pp. 1–31, http://www.u-hyogo.ac.jp/shse/nakajima/English/work/EAERE2015.pdf (accessed 12 August 2018).

Nakajima, K., Morisugi, H., Sakamoto, N., and Morisugi, M. (2017). "Measurement of Dynamic Damage Cost of the Great East Japan Earthquake with Reconstruction Process," *Journal of JSCE*, **5**, 45–57.

Okuyama, Y. (2003). "Economics of Natural Disasters: A Critical Review," Regional Research Institute Research Paper, 2003–12, West Virginia University, Morgantown.

Pratt, J.W. (1964). "Risk Aversion in the Small and in the Large," *Econometrica*, **32** (1/2), 122–36.

Ramsey, F.P. (1928). "A Mathematical Theory of Saving," *Economic Journal*, **38**, 543–59.

Solow, R. (1956). "A Contribution to the Theory of Economic Growth," *Quarterly Journal of Economics*, **70**, 65–94.

4. Population change and economic impacts on the affected region: the case of massive earthquakes in Japan

Yoshifumi Ishikawa

4.1 INTRODUCTION

Japan has suffered numerous earthquakes, and, as of 2017, had experienced 51 massive earthquakes[1] over a quarter of a century. Among these earthquakes, four have affected people's lives: the 1995 Great Hanshin-Awaji Earthquake, the 2004 Chuetsu Earthquake, the 2011 Great East Japan Earthquake and the 2016 Kumamoto Earthquake. In particular, the Great Hanshin-Awaji Earthquake and the Great East Japan Earthquake caused severe human and material damage, and the number of deaths, including earthquake-related deaths and individuals reported missing, exceeded 6000 and 20,000, respectively.

The Great Hanshin-Awaji Earthquake occurred in 1995 in the southern part of Hyogo Prefecture. It measured 7.3 on the moment magnitude scale and 7 on the intensity scale. The hypocenter of the earthquake was located on the northern end of Awaji Island, 20 kilometers (km) away from the city of Kobe (Figure 4.1). Kobe was closest to the epicenter and was hit by the strongest tremors; 6437 people lost their lives, including those missing, and about 4564 of them were from Kobe City. This was Japan's worst earthquake in the twentieth century after the Great Kanto Earthquake in 1923.[2] On the other hand, the Great East Japan Earthquake of 2011 was the most powerful earthquake ever recorded in Japan. The earthquake had a magnitude of 9.0 with the epicenter approximately 70 km east of the Oshika Peninsula of Tohoku, and the hypocenter at an underwater depth of approximately 29 km (Figure 4.1). It affected many people's lives

---

[1] Earthquakes with a seismic intensity of 6 or greater on the seven-point Japanese scale.
[2] The earthquake had a magnitude of 7.9 on the moment magnitude scale.

Figure 4.1   The location of the Great Hanshin-Awaji Earthquake and the Great East Japan Earthquake

in the three prefectures of Iwate, Miyagi and Fukushima, and the number of deaths exceeded 20,000, including earthquake-related deaths and individuals reported missing. The number of deaths in Miyagi was largest. The earthquake triggered powerful tsunami waves, causing massive damage to coastal areas in the Tohoku region. The human damage in Miyagi is attributable to the tsunami waves. While the number of deaths in Fukushima was relatively small, many people in Fukushima were forced to evacuate due to the nuclear plant accident; 55,608 people were relocated from Fukushima to other regions just after the earthquake. Thus, the population of the affected area has decreased owing to deaths, those declared missing, and the evacuation of people from their hometowns. Furthermore, it is believed that the population decline has resulted in a fall in consumer demand, which, in turn, has negatively affected the regional economy. From this perspective, Ishikawa (2017) analyzed the economic impact of the population decline after the Great East Japan Earthquake. The study presented the impact of the population decline from the Great Earthquake on the regional economy at the prefectural level. As a result, it was observed that the impact was spread across the country, and while the amount of production in the Tohoku region decreased, that of the Kanto region, including Tokyo, increased because many evacuees moved from the three affected prefectures of Miyagi, Iwate and Fukushima, and then became consumers in their new region. The previous study focused on economic impacts at the prefectural level, while this study focuses on areas smaller than a prefecture. Among the three affected prefectures of the Tohoku region, Fukushima Prefecture is still suffering from the impacts of the nuclear power plant accident following the Great Earthquake. However, the population decline is not spread across Fukushima Prefecture. The population decline is considerably greater in the coastal area that was directly affected by the nuclear power plant because of evacuation from the area.

The purpose of this study is to analyze the population changes in affected regions due to the massive earthquakes, and the impact of those changes on regional economies at a small region level. Therefore, we first clarify the population recovery process from two massive earthquakes: the Great Hanshin-Awaji Earthquake and the Great East Japan Earthquake. The economic impact of population decline due to the Great East Japan Earthquake is then analyzed using an interregional input-output model for the small region where there was direct damage. However, the conventional model does not consider interregional commuting and consuming regions. Many people have been relocated from the affected region of Fukushima Prefecture to other regions, and commute and consume between the directly affected region and their relocation region. Therefore, we develop an interregional input-output model with interregional commuting and consumption regions, and analyze the economic impact of the population decline due to the Great East Japan Earthquake.

There are several studies on the economic impact of earthquakes that use various economic modeling frameworks. The input-output analysis has been widely employed in many studies to measure the economic impact of earthquakes, because it has the ability to reflect the structure of a regional economy (for example, Cochrane, 1974; Rose et al., 1997; Okuyama et al., 1999, 2004; Tsunerori Ashiya, 2005; Yonemoto, 2016; Ishikawa, 2017). Okuyama et al. (1999) analyzed the economic impact of the Great Hanshin Earthquake employing an analytical framework based on Miyazawa's multipliers. The study highlighted the impact on the two-region system of the Kinki region and the rest of Japan, and the 1985 interregional input-output table published by the Ministry of International Trade and Industry (MITI) was used. Further, Okuyama et al. (2004) modified the static framework of an input-output table into a dynamic formulation using a Sequential Interindustry Model (SIM) framework to measure the economic impact of the Great Hanshin-Awaji Earthquake considering the dynamic process of impact propagation. These studies measured the economic impact on the Kinki region and the rest of Japan. Kinki consists of several prefectures, and is larger than a prefecture. Moreover, these studies do not focus on the population decline due to the earthquake. Yonemoto (2016) investigated the input-output structures with the six regions of Fukushima Prefecture in the aftermath of the Great East Japan Earthquake and analyzed the changes in backward-linkage effects.[3] The study used a similar viewpoint as this study, although it also does not focus on the population decline, and does not consider the change of interregional commuting and consumption regions in regional input-output structures.

The next section describes the population recovery processes following the Great Hanshin Awaji Earthquake and the Great East Japan Earthquake. Section 4.3 presents the method used to measure the economic impact of population decline due to the earthquake. In Section 4.4, the economic impact of population decline due to the Great East Japan Earthquake in the affected region of Fukushima Prefecture is derived, taking into account interregional commuting and consuming regions. Finally, Section 4.5 summarizes and concludes the study, and presents future research needs.

4.2 POPULATION CHANGE IN THE AFFECTED REGIONS: CASES OF THE GREAT EAST JAPAN EARTHQUAKE AND THE GREAT HANSHIN–AWAJI EARTHQUAKE

Factors contributing to the population changes resulting from the earthquakes include natural decreases, such as deaths and persons declared missing, and social changes due to evacuations. The Great Hanshin-Awaji Earthquake of 1995 affected many people's lives, and resulted in natural decreases. The number of deaths was 6437, including earthquake-related deaths and individuals reported missing; most of the dead were people who lived in Hyogo Prefecture. In particular, numerous human lives were lost in Kobe City in Hyogo Prefecture. As the earthquake was an inland earthquake, Kobe City received the most serious damage (Table 4.1).

Social population changes included evacuations. The number of evacuees increased gradually due to destruction of homes and shutdown of lifelines, and reached 316,678 one week after the earthquake. The number decreased to 17,569 after six months (Figure 4.2), but many people were forced to

---

[3] The backward-linkage effects are the impacts created by one unit increase in final demand upon sectors that provide intermediate inputs.

Table 4.1   Human toll due to the Great Hanshin-Awaji Earthquake

Prefecture City	Deaths	(Ratio)	Earthquake-related Deaths	(Ratio)	Missing	(Ratio)	Injured	(Ratio)
Hyogo	5483	99.4%	919	100.0%	3	100.0%	40092	91.6%
Kobe City	4564	82.8%	–	–	2	66.7%	14678	33.5%
Rest of the Country	32	0.6%	0	0.0%	0	0.0%	3700	8.4%
Overall	5515	100.0%	919	100.0%	3	100.0%	43792	100.0%

Note: The number of deaths of Kobe City include earthquake-related deaths.

Source: Fire and Disaster Management Agency (2006).

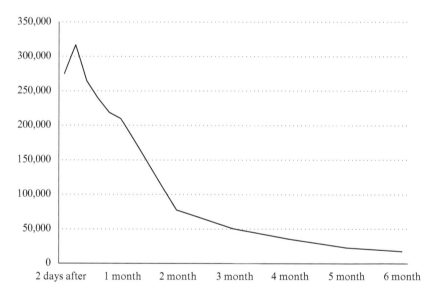

Source: The Great Hanshin-Awaji Earthquake: a record of Hyogo for a year (1996).

Figure 4.2   Change in the number of evacuees in places of refuge

evacuate to areas outside the area where they had lived. Figure 4.3 shows
the population change of Hyogo and its surrounding prefectures, such
Kyoto and Osaka. The population of Hyogo Prefecture had increased
before the earthquake, as had all of Japan. However, it declined just after
the earthquake, and then increased beginning the year after the earth-

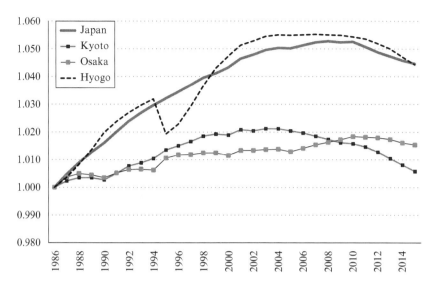

Source: Statistics Bureau.

*Figure 4.3   Changes in population of Hyogo and its surrounding
                prefectures*

quake; by 1997 it had recovered to almost the same level as in 1995. On the
other hand, the populations of the surrounding prefectures, such as Kyoto
and Osaka, were largely unaffected by the earthquake. The population in
Osaka had somewhat increased after the earthquake because of relocations
from Hyogo. At the prefectural level, the population recovery was rapid.
However, in the case of the Great Hanshin-Awaji Earthquake, the population of Kobe City dropped from 1.52 million to 1.42 million, decreasing by
about 100,000. As shown in Figure 4.4, it took ten years to recover to the
pre-earthquake level. When an earthquake's epicenter is right under a specific area of land, as in the case of the Great Hanshin-Awaji Earthquake,
the population number at the prefectural level quickly recovers to its pre-
earthquake level. However, the population of directly affected urban areas
such as Kobe City takes a long time to recover.

   The population change at the prefectural level due to the Great East
Japan Earthquake was investigated by Ishikawa (2017). Table 4.2 shows
the human toll due to the Great East Japan Earthquake. The number
of deaths including earthquake-related deaths was 19,300. In addition,
2565 were declared missing, and the population declined by 21,865 in
all. The earthquake significantly damaged the Tohoku region, including

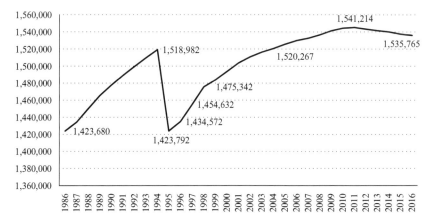

Source: City office of Kobe (2017).

Figure 4.4   Changes in population of Kobe City

Table 4.2   Human toll due to the Great East Japan Earthquake

Prefectures	Deaths		Earthquake-related Deaths		Missing		Injured	
		(Ratio)		(Ratio)		(Ratio)		(Ratio)
Iwate	4673	29.4%	455	13.4%	1125	43.9%	213	3.5%
Miyagi	9541	60.0%	918	26.9%	1237	48.2%	4145	67.4%
Fukushima	1612	10.1%	1979	58.1%	199	7.8%	183	3.0%
Rest of the Country	67	0.4%	55	1.6%	4	0.2%	1611	26.2%
Overall	15893	100.0%	3407	100.0%	2565	100.0%	6152	100.0%

Source: Ishikawa (2017).

prefectures such as Iwate, Miyagi and Fukushima, and most of the dead were people who lived in these three prefectures.

In terms of social population change, the number of evacuees reached 520,000 just after the earthquake; 174,000 people were still unable to return to their homes as of 2015. In particular, 43,497 people were relocated from Fukushima to other regions (Figure 4.5). Thus, the population of the affected areas decreased owing to deaths, those declared missing, and the evacuation of people from their hometowns.

As shown in Figure 4.6, the decline in the Japanese population began in 2009. The populations of the three prefectures had already begun to decline

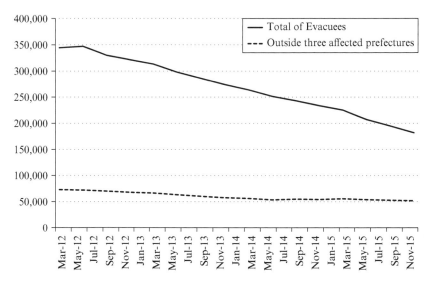

Source: Ishikawa (2017).

Figure 4.5 Change in the number of evacuees

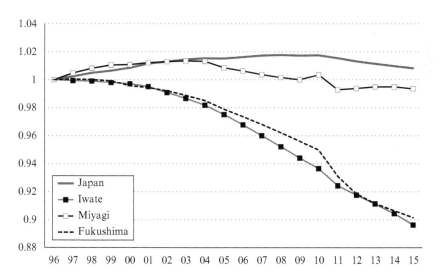

Source: Ishikawa (2017).

Figure 4.6 Changes in the populations of Fukushima, Iwate and Miyagi

before that. In 2010, prior to the earthquake, the population of Iwate was 1.33 million and those of Miyagi and Fukushima were 2.35 million and 2.03 million, respectively. The population of Miyagi and Fukushima dropped significantly just after the earthquake. However, Miyagi is the biggest prefecture in the Tohoku region, and recovered rapidly. In contrast, the population of Fukushima has continued to decrease, because many people are unable to return to their homes. However, the population decline is not spread across Fukushima Prefecture. The population decline is considerably greater in areas directly affected by the nuclear power accident. As shown in Figure 4.7, Fukushima can be divided into seven regions: Soso, Iwaki, Kenhoku, Kenchu, Kennan, Aizu and Minamiaizu. Among these, Soso is the area that suffered the most from the Great East Japan Earthquake, because the Fukushima Daiichi (No. 1) and Daini (No. 2) Nuclear Power Plants are in this area. As shown in Figure 4.8, the actual population of Soso declined from about 200,000 in 2010 to 110,000 in 2015. However, because the population of Soso was already declining prior to the earthquake, the population change due to the earthquake and the nuclear power plant accident was estimated by subtracting the actual population from the population for 2015 in the case without the disaster.[4] As a result, it was estimated that the population of Soso declined by 74,131 due to the earthquake and the nuclear power plant accident, primarily because many people relocated from this area to other regions.

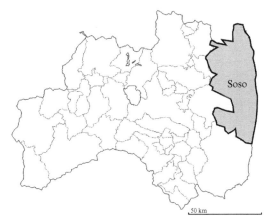

Figure 4.7   Regional division of Fukushima Prefecture

---

[4]   The population for 2015 in the case without the disaster was estimated by cohort analysis which uses population data by age group from the Statistics Bureau.

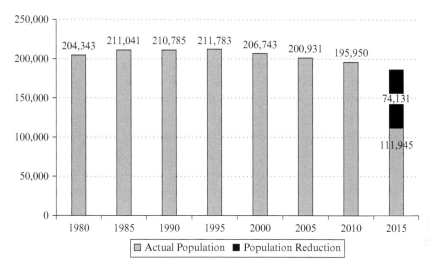

Figure 4.8   Changes in the population of Soso in Fukushima

4.3   METHOD FOR MEASURING ECONOMIC IMPACT

One of the purposes of this study is to analyze the economic impact of population decline on a region directly affected by earthquakes. In the case of the Great East Japan Earthquake, the Soso region in Fukushima Prefecture was directly affected by the earthquake and nuclear power plant accident. Most people who lived in Soso worked there before the earthquake, but moved out of Soso after the earthquake, while continuing to work in Soso. That is, many people commuted from outside Soso to Soso. Additionally, people who used to live in Soso made most of their purchases there before the earthquake. However, because they moved to other regions after the earthquake, it appears that consumption in Soso decreased (Figure 4.9). Thus, it appears that the population decline had a negative impact on the regional economy through a decline in consumer demand.

To analyze the economic impact on this region, we use the 2005 Input-Output Tables for Living Spheres of Fukushima Prefecture, which cover six regions including Soso. However, because the tables are intraregional input-output tables for a single region, they do not reflect interregional feedback effects and income distribution between the small region of Soso and other regions. When smaller regions such as Soso

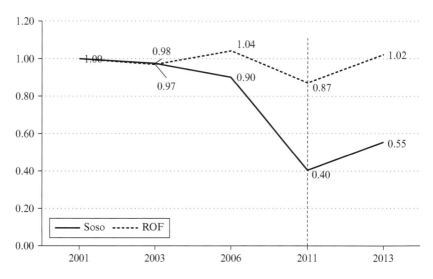

Source: Census of Commerce.

Figure 4.9   Index of changes in the sales of the retail industry

are examined, those factors are expected to be influential. Therefore, to
analyze the economic impact of the population decline considering these
factors, we developed an interregional input-output model that considers
interregional trade and income distribution between Soso and other
regions. The model endogenously determines consumption expenditure,
interregional income distribution and interregional trade. The theoretical
framework of the extended input-output framework considering these
points was given by Miyazawa (1976), and Hewings et al. (1999) described
the methodology in more detail. In addition, Hewings et al. (2001) analyzed the economic interdependence between inner-city communities and
suburbs within Chicago metropolitan area using Miyazawa's extended
input-output framework. However, the model shown in these studies is
based on the multiregional transaction matrix. Because we use the intraregional input-output tables for the affected region and the Input-Output
Table for Japan, we propose a two-region interregional model based on
an intraregional input-output table for a single region and the national
input-output table.

Dividing the whole country into a small region (Soso, region 1) and the
rest of the country (region 2), the regional economic circulation between
the small region and the rest of the country is shown in Figure 4.10. First,

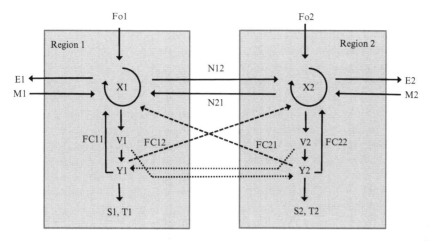

Figure 4.10   Regional economic circulation between the small region (region 1) and the rest of the country (region 2)

production activity in a small region (X1) is induced by final demand of the region (Fo1). At the same time, production of the rest of the country, region 2 (X2), is induced through the imports into region 1 (N21); that is, the export demand for region 2. Moreover, employees' income in region 1 increases with production inducement (X1). However, the income is distributed to each region (V1, V2) according to the region where workers live, with consumption in each region. As seen in Figure 4.10, the two regions have the same structure.

First, the structures of the supply-demand balance for a small region and the rest of the country are shown by equations (4.1) and (4.2), respectively. In these equations, household consumption, regional import and export, and international import and export are endogenously dealt with.

$$
\begin{aligned}
X_1 = {} & A_1 X_1 + F_{C1} + F_{O1} - \overline{N}_{21} A_1 X_1 - C_{21} F_{C1} - \overline{N}_{21} F_{o1} \\
& - \overline{M}_1 A_1 X_1 - C_{w1} F_{C1} - \overline{M}_1 F_{o1} \\
& + \overline{N}_{12} A_2 X_2 + C_{12} F_{C2} + \overline{N}_{12} F_{o2} \\
& + E_1
\end{aligned}
\tag{4.1}
$$

$$
\begin{aligned}
X_2 = {} & A_2 X_2 + F_{C2} + F_{O2} - \overline{N}_{12} A_2 X_2 - C_{12} F_{C1} - \overline{N}_{12} F_{o2} \\
& - \overline{M}_2 A_2 X_2 - C_{w2} F_{C2} - \overline{M}_2 F_{o2} \\
& + \overline{N}_{21} A_1 X_1 + C_{21} F_{C1} + \overline{N}_{21} F_{o1} \\
& + E_2
\end{aligned}
\tag{4.2}
$$

Also, regional distributed income is shown as the distributed compensation of employment, with payment according to the output of each region in terms of the region.

$$Y_1 = D_{11}V_1X_1 + D_{21}V_2X_2 + F_{DY1} \tag{4.3}$$

$$Y_2 = D_{12}V_1X_1 + D_{22}V_2X_2 + F_{DY2} \tag{4.4}$$

Where

$$
X_r = \begin{bmatrix} x_{1r} \\ \vdots \\ x_{ir} \\ \vdots \\ x_{nr} \end{bmatrix}
\quad
A_r = \begin{bmatrix} a_{11,r} & \cdots & a_{1j,r} & \cdots & a_{1n,r} \\ \vdots & \ddots & \vdots & \ddots & \vdots \\ a_{i1,r} & \cdots & a_{ij,r} & \cdots & a_{in,r} \\ \vdots & \ddots & \vdots & \ddots & \vdots \\ a_{n1,r} & \cdots & a_{nj,r} & \cdots & a_{nn,r} \end{bmatrix}
\quad
F_{Cr} = \begin{bmatrix} f_{C1,r} \\ \vdots \\ f_{Ci,r} \\ \vdots \\ f_{Cn,r} \end{bmatrix}
\quad
F_{or} = \begin{bmatrix} f_{o1,r} \\ \vdots \\ f_{oi,r} \\ \vdots \\ f_{on,r} \end{bmatrix}
$$

$$
\overline{N}_{rs} = \begin{bmatrix} n_{1,rs} & & 0 \\ & \ddots & \\ & n_{i,rs} & \\ & & \ddots \\ 0 & & n_{n,rs} \end{bmatrix}
\quad
\overline{M}_r = \begin{bmatrix} m_{1,r} & & 0 \\ & \ddots & \\ & m_{i,r} & \\ & & \ddots \\ 0 & & m_{n,r} \end{bmatrix}
$$

$$
E_{i,r} = \begin{bmatrix} e_{1,r} \\ \vdots \\ e_{i,r} \\ \vdots \\ e_{n,r} \end{bmatrix}
\quad
C_{rs} = \begin{bmatrix} c_{1,rs} & & 0 \\ & \ddots & \\ & c_{i,rs} & \\ & & \ddots \\ 0 & & c_{n,rs} \end{bmatrix}
\quad
Y_r = \begin{bmatrix} y_{1,r} \\ \vdots \\ y_{i,r} \\ \vdots \\ y_{n,r} \end{bmatrix}
$$

$$
D_{rs} = \begin{bmatrix} d_{1,rs} & & 0 \\ & \ddots & \\ & d_{i,rs} & \\ & & \ddots \\ 0 & & d_{n,rs} \end{bmatrix}
\quad
V_{ir} = \begin{bmatrix} v_{1,r} & & 0 \\ & \ddots & \\ & v_{i,r} & \\ & & \ddots \\ 0 & & v_{n,r} \end{bmatrix}
\quad
F_{DYr} = \begin{bmatrix} f_{dy1,r} \\ \vdots \\ f_{dyi,r} \\ \vdots \\ f_{dyn,r} \end{bmatrix}
$$

x_{ir} = output of commodity i in the region r
$a_{ij,r}$ = input coefficient of commodity j in the region r

$f_{oi,r}$ = final demand other than consumption demand of commodity i in the region r

$n_{i,rs}$ = regional import coefficient of commodity i in the region s

$m_{i,r}$ = international import coefficient of commodity i in the region r

$e_{i,r}$ = export coefficient of commodity i in the region r

$c_{i,rs}$ = consumption rate of commodity i from the region r to the region s

$y_{i,r}$ = reginal income of commodity i in the region r

$d_{i,rs}$ = distributed income rate of commodity i from region r to region s

$v_{i,r}$ = income rate of commodity i in the region r

$f_{dyi,r}$ = autonomous consumption of commodity i in the region r.

The consumption function for each region is shown as the product of the distribution of income and marginal propensity to consume for each region.

$$Fc_1 = c_1 Y_1 \qquad (4.5)$$

$$Fc_2 = c_2 Y_2 \qquad (4.6)$$

Where c_r = marginal propensity to consume for region r.

From these equations, the following equilibrium model with interregional commuting and consuming regions can be obtained.

$$
\begin{bmatrix} X_1 \\ Y_1 \\ X_2 \\ Y_2 \end{bmatrix} =
\begin{bmatrix}
[I-(I-\overline{N}_{21}-\overline{M}_1)A_1] & -(I-C_{21}-C_{w1})c_1 & -\overline{N}_{12}A_2 & -C_{12}c_2 \\
-D_{11}V_1 & I & -D_{21}V_2 & 0 \\
-\overline{N}_2 A_1 & -C_{21}c_1 & [I-(I-\overline{N}_{12}-\overline{M}_2)A_2] & -(I-C_{12}-C_{w2})c_2 \\
-D_{12}V_1 & 0 & -D_{22}V_2 & I
\end{bmatrix}^{-1}
$$

$$
\begin{bmatrix}
I-\overline{N}_{21}-\overline{M}_1 & 0 & \overline{N}_{12} & 0 \\
0 & I & 0 & 0 \\
\overline{N}_{21} & 0 & I-\overline{N}_{21}-\overline{M}_1 & 0 \\
0 & 0 & 0 & I
\end{bmatrix}
\begin{bmatrix} F_{o1} \\ F_{DY1} \\ F_{o2} \\ F_{DY2} \end{bmatrix}
+
\begin{bmatrix} E_1 \\ 0 \\ E_2 \\ 0 \end{bmatrix}
\qquad (4.7)
$$

In the above equations, economic effects can be estimated by providing exogenous demand to each region.

4.4   ECONOMIC IMPACTS OF POPULATION DECLINE IN THE AFFECTED REGION DUE TO THE GREAT EAST JAPAN EARTHQUAKE

In this section, the economic impact of population decline in the directly affected region (Soso in Fukushima) due to the Great East Japan Earthquake is estimated, and the economic effects of reconstruction are analyzed.

Soso region is in the coastal area of Fukushima Prefecture; it covers approximately 1737 km², the population pre-earthquake was approximately 200,000 in 2010. After the nuclear accident, more than half of the area of Soso region was either evacuated (primarily within 20 km) or had some restriction imposed on activities (mostly within 30 km).

Table 4.3 shows the percentage of people who commute to Soso. Before the earthquake (in 2010), 93 percent of the people who lived in the Soso region commuted from their home to a workplace in their own region. However, after the earthquake (2015), the percentage went down to 71 percent. For instance, the percentage of people who work for the electricity industry decreased by 30 percent due to the move from Soso to another region. That is, many people moved outside Soso, and commuted to Soso for work after the earthquake. It appears that people who work in Soso get paid in Soso, but they return to their home outside Soso and primarily spend their money there. Consumption also decreased after the earthquake, and the propensity to consume also went down from 0.713 (in 2010) to 0.600 (in 2015).[5]

To analyze the economic impact of the population decline in the Soso region due to the Great East Japan Earthquake using the model developed in Section 4.3, we need input coefficients, regional import coefficients, international import coefficients, propensity to consume, distributed consumption rate and distributed income rate for each region. As described in Section 4.3, the 2005 Input-Output Tables for Living Spheres of Fukushima Prefecture and the 2011 Input-Output Table for Japan are available. The former consists of six regions, including Soso, but a separate input-output table for Soso is also available. Therefore, we used this table. However, because it was the table for 2005, it was updated for 2011 using the RAS technique.[6] Data on consumption and income are available from the Statistics Bureau of the Japanese and Fukushima prefectural governments.

---

[5]   The family income and expenditure survey is conducted by the Statistics Bureau.

[6]   The RAS technique is widely used in the context of updating input-output tables, and known as a bipropotional matrix balancing technique.

Table 4.3   The percentage of people who commute to Soso

	2010 (%)	2015 (%)	difference (%)
Total	93	71	−22
Agriculture and forestry	100	100	0
Mining and quarrying of stone and gravel	86	60	−25
Construction	75	51	−24
Manufacturing	89	82	−7
Electricity, gas, heat supply and water	58	29	−30
Information and communications	74	79	5
Transport and postal activities	82	70	−11
Wholesale trade and retail trade	100	93	−7
Finance and insurance	83	84	1
Real estate and goods rental and leasing	87	69	−18
Scientific research, professional and technical services	81	58	−23
Accommodation, eating and drinking services	100	97	−3
Living-related and personal services and amusement services	99	100	1
Education, learning support	80	81	1
Medical, health care and welfare	93	94	1
Compound services	84	83	−2
Services, n.e.c.	72	41	−31
Government, except elsewhere classified	100	77	−23

Source: Statistics Bureau.

We estimated the consumer demand drop attributable to the population decrease by multiplying the population by per capita consumption.[7] As a result, it was estimated that the total consumer demand in Soso decreased by around 148 billion yen. Due to the decline in consumer demand, the amount of production in Soso and the rest of Japan declined by 187 billion yen and 157 billion yen, respectively. The Soso region accounts for 54 percent of the negative impact, while the production of the rest of Japan also decreased through interregional trade. With regard to employee salary, Soso and the rest of Japan decreased by around 43 billion yen and 47 billion yen, respectively (Table 4.4). The amount of production in

---

[7]   We estimated the decrease in consumer demand, as of 2015, by multiplying the population decrease estimated in Section 4.3 by per capita consumption from the family income and expenditure survey by the Statistics Bureau and population census.

Soso decreased by 7 percent compared to the pre-earthquake level, and employee salaries decreased by 9 percent.

As shown in the results of this analysis, the decrease in household consumption had a negative impact on the regional economy. On the other hand, the economy in Soso was supported by reconstruction-related demand. Therefore, we analyzed the economic effects of reconstruction demand. First, for a case study, we assumed that reconstruction demand increased to 100 billion yen in the Soso region; Tables 4.5, 4.6 and 4.7 show a summary of the results of the production inducement effect.

We estimated economic effects in the case of workers' residences and consumption regions of pre-earthquake (case 1) and of after-earthquake (case 2).

First, in the case of pre-earthquake (case 1), the demand increase in the Soso region brings about a production inducement effect, which is valued at approximately 145 billion yen; this affects not only the Soso region, but also the rest of Japan. Soso accounts for 47 percent of the impact, while

Table 4.4   Economic impacts of population decline (unit: million yen)

	Production	(ratio)	Salary of employees	(ratio)
Soso	−187 077	54.3	−43 059	47.6
Rest of Japan	−157 359	45.7	−47 467	52.4
Total (Japan)	−344 436	100.0	−90 526	100.0

Table 4.5   Economic effects of reconstruction demand (pre-earthquake: case 1) (unit: million yen)

	Production	(ratio)	Salary of employees	(ratio)
Soso	145 371	46.7%	35 503	38.9%
Rest of Japan	166 136	53.3%	55 877	61.1%
Total (Japan)	311 507	100.0%	91 380	100.0%

Table 4.6   Economic effects of reconstruction demand (after-earthquake: case 2) (unit: million yen)

	Production	(ratio)	Salary of employees	(ratio)
Soso	132 384	43.5%	22 977	25.7%
Rest of Japan	172 037	56.5%	66 364	74.3%
Total (Japan)	304 421	100.0%	89 341	100.0%

Table 4.7   Economic effects of reconstruction demand (the difference between case 1 and case 2) (unit: million yen)

	Production	(ratio)	Salary of employees	(ratio)
Soso	−12987	−3.2%	−12525	−13.1%
Rest of Japan	5901	3.2%	10487	13.1%
Total (Japan)	−7086	0.0%	−2039	0.0%

the production in the rest of Japan accounts for the remaining 53 percent. With regard to employee salaries, Soso and the rest of Japan increased by around 36 billion yen and 56 billion yen, respectively. The current propensity to consume is small, and many people go to areas outside Soso for consumption. Therefore, as shown in Table 4.6, the effect on the Soso region is small compared to pre-earthquake. Table 4.7 shows the difference between case 1 and case 2. It can be seen that compensation of employees who live in Soso is small compared to the pre-earthquake level. Money has flowed outside the Soso region, because people who used to live in Soso moved to other regions. Therefore, as measures to help the affected region recover, the Japanese government needs to make an effort to enable people to live in the Soso region as well as carrying out reconstruction.

4.5   CONCLUSION

In this study, we first investigated the population decrease after two massive earthquakes. As a result, in the case of the Great Hanshin-Awaji Earthquake, the population of Kobe City, a major city, declined due to the evacuation. However, it began increasing gradually the year after the earthquake, and in the ten years after the earthquake, it had almost recovered to its former level. On the other hand, the area of Fukushima Prefecture with the nuclear power plants that was directly affected by the Great East Japan Earthquake had not recovered as of 2015. There is the possibility of a long-term population decline in the coastal area of Fukushima Prefecture: Soso region, because it appears that reconstruction and recovery is delayed.

Next, the economic impact of the population decrease after the Great East Japan Earthquake was analyzed using the interregional input-output model developed in this study. This model takes interregional commuting and consumption regions into account. Utilizing the model developed in this study, the economic impact was estimated considering the inter-regional feedback effects and workers' residences. As a result, it was observed that the amount of production in Soso, the affected region with the nuclear power plant, decreased due to the many evacuees. Money has flowed outside the Soso region, because people who used to live in Soso moved to other regions and consume there. It is believed that the population decline will continue in the affected areas in the long term. Therefore, there is concern that the regional economy in the affected region will also decline, if reconstruction and recovery from the earthquake damage is delayed. In particular, the government needs to make an effort to increase the population in the affected regions to provide economic recovery from the earthquake damage.

REFERENCES

City office of Kobe (2017), *The Kobe City Statistical Report* (in Japanese).

Cochrane, H.C. (1974), 'Predicting the Economic Impacts of Earthquakes', in H.C. Cochrane, J.E. Haas, M.J. Bowden and R.W. Kates (eds), *Social Science Perspectives on the Coming San Francisco Earthquake*, Natural Hazards Research Paper No. 25, NHRAIC, Boulder, CO: University of Colorado, pp. 1–41.

Fire and Disaster Management Agency (2006), *The Great Hanshin-Awaji Earthquake Final Report* (in Japanese).

Hewings, Geoffrey J.D., Michael Sonis, Moss Madden and Yoshio Kimura (eds) (1999), *Understanding and Interpreting Economic Structure*, New York: Springer-Verlag.

Hewings, Geoffrey J.D., Yasuhide Okuyama and Michael Sonis (2001), 'Economic Interdependence Within the Chicago Metropolitan Area: A Miyazawa Analysis', *Journal of Regional Science*, **41**(2), 195–217.

Ishikawa, Yoshifumi (2017), 'Economic Impacts of Population Decline Due to the Great East Japan Earthquake: An Inter-regional Input–Output Approach', in S. Tokunaga and Budy P. Resosudarmo (eds), *Spatial Economic Modelling of Megathrust Earthquake in Japan: Impacts, Reconstruction, and Regional Revitalization*, New York: Springer, pp. 237–57.

Miyazawa, Kenichi (1976), *Input-Output Analysis and the Structure on Income Distribution*, New York: Springer-Verlag.

Okuyama, Yasuhide, Michael Sonis and Geoffery J.D. Hewings (1999), 'Economic Impacts of an Unscheduled, Disruptive Event: A Miyazawa Multiplier Analys', in Geoffrey J.D. Hewings, Michael Sonis, Moss Madden and Yoshio Kimura (eds), *Understanding and Interpreting Economic Structure*, New York: Springer-Verlag, pp. 113–43.

Okuyama, Yasuhide, Geoffrey J.D. Hewings and Michael Sonis (2004), 'Measuring Economic Impacts of Disasters: Interregional Input-Output Analysis Using Sequential Interindustry Model', in Y. Okuyama and S. Chang (eds), *Modeling Spatial and Economic Impacts of Disasters*, New York: Springer, pp. 77–101.

Rose, A., J. Benavides, S.E. Chang, P. Szczesniak and D. Lim (1997), 'The Regional Economic Impact of an Earthquake: Direct and Indirect Effects of Electricity Lifeline Disruptions', *Journal of Regional Science*, **37**(3), 437–58.

Tsunenori Ashiya (2005), 'Economic Structural Change of Hyogo Prefecture

Given by the Hansin-Awaji Earthquake Disaster in 1995 – Use of Hyogo Prefecture Input-Output Table', *Input-Output Analysis*, **13**(1), 45–56 (in Japanese).

Yonemoto, Kiyoshi (2016), 'Changes in the Input-Output Structures of the Six Regions of Fukushima, Japan: 3 Years After the Disaster', *Journal of Economic Structures*, **5**(2), 1–20.

PART II

Case studies on resilience

5. An AHP-based methodology towards resilient tourism strategies: the Istanbul case

Ebru Seçkin

5.1 INTRODUCTION

The world is characterized by increasingly fast and deep transformations, boundless interconnectedness and pervasive interdependencies. Therefore, an economic or political crisis that takes place in one place in the world can affect a different place in a profound way. In the tourism industry there is a direct relationship between the place where tourism takes place and its surroundings. Tourists' perceptions are affected by the social, political and economic conditions of tourist destinations, making them vulnerable to crisis. Developing resilience planning or crisis management planning to reduce the disaster risks, strengthen the adaptive capacity, prepare for potential crisis events in the tourism industry and protect the image of touristic cities has therefore become very important.

Resilience and adaptive capacity are closely linked with vulnerability. Vulnerability, in the tourism context, relates to the extent to which the industry may be affected or disrupted by a crisis event. Tourism disaster is a situation when the tourist destination is confronted with sudden, unpredictable changes over which it has little control. However, the revival process is complex because it is based on many complex and uncertain conditions such as travel motivations, political stability and security. These conditions shape the image of the tourist destination and affect tourists' behaviour. The complexity of the tourism revival process necessitates a systematic approach with a detailed analysis of a variety of internal and external environmental factors (Wickramasinghe and Takano, 2010). In this context, tourism resilience planning has emerged to provide adjustments to a rapidly changing world (Lew, 2014).

In the early years of the twenty-first century, the global tourism industry was affected by terrorist attacks. In the literature, scholars have examined the relationship between terrorism and tourism (Enders and Sandler, 1991;

Richter, 1999; Bhattarai et al., 2005; Yaya, 2009; Feridun, 2011; Raza and Jawaid, 2013; Romagnoli, 2016) and discuss steps in tourism recovery, tourism's vulnerability and resilience to terrorism (Richter, 1999; Calgaro et al., 2014; Liu and Pratt, 2017), the implications for tourism marketing and the effects on tourist behaviour (Sönmez and Graefe, 1998). Sackett and Botterill (2006) mentioned that the flow of international tourists is more sensitive to terrorist attacks or other risks, since the perception of risk varies according to the spatial, emotional and cultural proximity, and nationality of the tourists.

The aim of this chapter is to enhance understanding of how the resilience of the tourism industry can be improved in Istanbul. A review of the literature on the vulnerability and resilience of tourist destinations is first provided. This is followed by a case study on the current vulnerability and resilience of Istanbul as a tourist destination. The situation was analysed by using SWOT analysis. SWOT analysis facilitates decision-making by determining the internal capabilities and limits (strengths and weaknesses) and external conditions (opportunities and threats) in a given context. SWOT factors were weighted using the analytical hierarchy process (AHP) method. As a result, six strategies for Istanbul were determined using the TOWS method. The TOWS matrix is used to discuss the strategies and policies that Istanbul should adopt as a tourist destination to cope with and recover from shocks and stresses. The final section concludes the study.

5.2   THE VULNERABILITY AND RESILIENCE OF TOURIST DESTINATIONS

In order to effectively manage risk, it is essential to understand how vulnerability is generated, and how it increases. Vulnerability is usually portrayed in negative terms as the susceptibility to be harmed. It is the state of being exposed to the possibility of being attacked or harmed, either physically or emotionally. It also means the ability of an exposed unit to cope, recover or fundamentally adapt (become a new system or become extinct). There are three dimensions of vulnerability: exposure, sensitivity and adaptive capacity. Exposure is the degree to which a system could be affected by stressors or shocks. It includes shocks and stresses (magnitude, intensity, frequency, duration), and the character of threatened elements (the built or natural environment, population). Sensitivity is the degree to which a system is modified or affected by disasters. Adaptive capacity is the ability of a system to evolve in order to accommodate environmental hazards or policy change and to expand the range of variability with which it can cope. It reflects the pre-existing economic, social, political and environmental conditions that shape anticipatory and immediate response capabilities. Adaptive capacity refers to a process of change against shocks and stresses, and anticipatory actions for preparedness, immediate and short-term actions and long-term adjustments (Adger, 2006; Nelson et al., 2007; Polsky et al., 2007; Calgaro and Lloyd, 2008; Cardona et al., 2012).

System adaptation refers to the preconditions that are necessary to enable adaptation and includes economic, human, social, physical capital and governance mechanisms (Nelson et al., 2007). Economic capital includes livelihood portfolios, the accumulation of liquid and fixed assets, credit histories and insurance, employment opportunities, business stability and access to welfare safety. Human capital includes knowledge of risk (including traditional/ historical responses to past shocks and stressors that aid preparedness), skills that enable greater employment flexibility if employment opportunities are interrupted, and labour capacity. Social capital embodies networks and connectedness, group membership, relationships and levels of trust and reciprocity (Calgaro et al., 2014). Physical capital includes access to natural resources, the biophysical carrying capacity of a destination and access to infrastructure and communication systems (Nelson et al., 2007). Formal and informal governance structures and processes play an important role in influencing destination vulnerability and resilience level. They also dictate how resources are used (e.g., the types of buildings that are permitted, and the amount of financial capital that is available for development). Interventions are made to address pre-existing weaknesess in the systems and increase preparedness. Tourist flows are influenced by national visa rules, aircraft regulations and airport taxes. These rules and regulations may affect costs, destination attractiveness and tourist choices (Calgaro et al., 2014).

Resilience is the ability of an exposure unit or system to absorb recurrent stresses and shocks without losing its fundamental structure and function (Tompkins and Adger, 2004). Carpenter et al. (2001) suggest answering the question, 'Resilience of what to what?' – that is, over what time period and at what scale – to avoid confusion. Resilience is a direct expression of the strength of the coupled human–environment system reflecting its immediate response, self-organization, learning and adaptive capabilities (Carpenter et al., 2001).

In the tourism literature, many studies have focused on why some destinations are more vulnerable than others. Some factors that constitute sensitivity to shocks and adaptive capacity have been underlined in these studies: (a) tourism as a dominant sector especially for regions with scarce resources; (b) high levels of perceived risk and negative perceptions of a destination's image (Ritchie, 2004; Calgaro and Lloyd, 2008; Liu and Pratt, 2017). Rittichainuwat and Chakraborty (2009) note that the risk perceptions of tourists, rather than actual risk circumstances, impact their decision-making and behaviour. The authors found that in the case of Thailand, tourists familiar with the destination affirm they would continue to travel as the threat of terrorism is part of life nowadays. Tourists' socio-demographic profiles, nationality and level of previous experience influence their perception (Calgaro et al., 2014). In spite of that, Sönmez and Graefe (1998) emphasized that perceived risks regarding terrorism deter tourists from travel in the short run but do not have a long-term effect on internal tourists' travel motivation (Sönmez and Graefe, 1998). In addition, Fuchs and Reichel (2004) found significant differences in the overall risk perception of a given tourist destination and a variety of risk perception dimensions among tourists of various nationalities. They also captured religious affiliation as associated with varying degrees of destination risk perceptions (Fuchs and Reichel, 2004). Risk perceptions are not only affected by nationality or cultural background, but also by familiarity with a destination (Karl et al., 2015).

5.3   CASE STUDY: ISTANBUL

The aim of the chapter is to determine the current vulnerability and resilience of Istanbul as a tourist destination and to discuss the strategies and policies for becoming more resilient. Its research question is: How should the tourism industry in Istanbul prepare for risks and increase its resilience? This requires the identification of factors that increase its vulnerability. A three-step method has been used for the purpose. In the first step, the current situation and the relevant factors in the external and internal environment were analysed using SWOT analysis. In the second step, pair-wise comparisons of factors within each SWOT group were carried out using the AHP method (see Figure 5.7). Using these pair-wise comparisons, the relative priority value of each factor in each SWOT group was calculated using the eigenvalue method. By utilizing the AHP in SWOT analysis, individual SWOT factors are analysed to determine the intensity or priority order of each factor. Finally, the TOWS matrix was used to discuss the strategies for becoming more resilient. Four sub-strategic groups for alternative strategies are defined in the TOWS matrix: strengths-opportunities (SO), strengths-threats (ST), weaknesses-opportunities (WO) and weaknesses-threats (WT).

5.3.1 Tourism Characteristics of Istanbul

Istanbul is the most important tourist destination in Turkey with historical and cultural heritage, and natural beauty. With 15 million inhabitants (2017 data), Istanbul is Turkey's largest city. There are palaces, pavilions, mosques, churches and fountains belonging to different periods. For example, the Hagia Sophia Museum and Topkapi Palace Museum are the most attractive places for tourists. In 2015, the Hagia Sophia Museum and the Topkapi Palace Museum, with 3,425,000 and 3,252,000 visitors, respectively, became the most visited places in Turkey. Unfortunately, their visitor numbers decreased after the terror attacks. The number of visitors to these two museums decreased by 56 per cent between 2015 and 2016. Visitor numbers started to increase again in 2017, but have not yet reached the 2015 level (Figure 5.1). The number of foreign visitors to Istanbul in 2017 was 10.8 million. Although the terrorist attacks in 2016 caused a decrease in the number of foreign visitors, there has been an increase from 2017. But it is still behind the visitor numbers in 2014 (11.8 million).

Tourism activities in Istanbul are concentrated in the historical centre of the city. Tourists are mostly attracted to the Historical Peninsula, Beyoğlu, Beşiktaş, Şişli on the European side and Kadıköy on the Anatolian side of Istanbul. In other words, tourists are mostly in the region known as

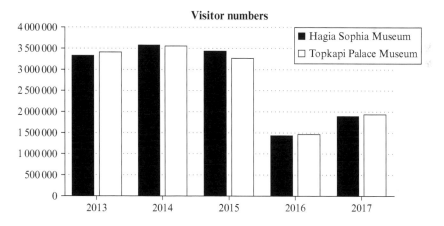

Source: Hagia Sophia Museum Statistics, Visitor Number (2013–17), http://ayasofyamuzesi. gov.tr/tr/content/istatistikler (accessed 17 December 2017); Provincial Directorate of Culture and Tourism, Museum Visitor Number (2009–17), http://www.istanbulkulturturizm.gov.tr/ TR,168166/muze-ziyaretci-sayilari.html (accessed 17 December 2017).

Figure 5.1   Visitor numbers to Hagia Sophia Museum and Topkapi Palace Museum

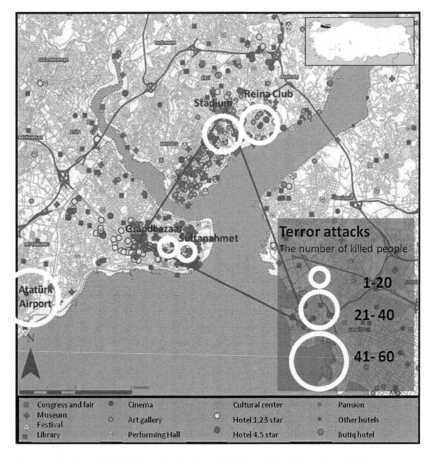

Source: Enlil et al. (2010). See also Mortiner (2016) and New York Times (2017).

Figure 5.2 The areas where the terror attacks took place and tourism attractions

the cultural triangle (Enlil et al., 2010). In 2016, suicide bomb attacks took place in this area where tourists are most intense. This situation has increased the sensitivity of the tourism sector (Figure 5.2).

5.3.2 The Influence of Terror Attacks

Terror attacks have reached record levels since 2016 in many countries. The attacks by ISIS in Paris, Brussels and Ankara were amongst the most devastating in the history of these nations and a worrying return of transnational group-based terrorism after September 11 (Institute for Economics & Peace, 2016). Tourism is one of the sectors of the economy that suffers the most from terrorism. Tourism's contribution to gross domestic product (GDP) is twice as large in countries with no terrorist attacks targeting tourists. The adverse economic effects of terrorism on the tourism sector are felt by all countries that suffer terrorist attacks, regardless of whether or not they target tourists (Institute for Economics & Peace, 2017).

Turkey ranked 14th on the Global Terrorism Index 2016[1] with a score of 6.7 points. Turkey has never been ranked in the ten countries most impacted by terrorism, but it rose from 27th place in 2015 to 14th place in the 2016 Global Terrorism Index ranking. After Turkey, France (5.6 points) was the Organisation for Economic Co-operation and Development (OECD) nation with the second highest number of deaths in 2016 (Institute for Economics & Peace, 2016).

Terrorism reduces economic activity due to increases in actual and perceived risks. Investors come to expect reduced returns on capital. This results in decreased foreign direct investment. For instance, in Turkey, an increase in terrorism caused significant decreases in foreign direct investment after 2015 (Figure 5.3). Advanced and diversified economies are economically more resilient and have shorter recovery periods from incidents of terrorism. This is mainly due to their ability to reallocate resources such as labour and capital from the sector affected by terrorism. The Turkish economy has also experienced two important financial crises since 2000. The first crisis was the 2000–01 banking crisis. The second crisis happened in 2008 when Turkey was affected by the global economic crises. These crises caused declines in foreign capital inflows (World Bank Open Data, 2017) and GDP per capita (Turkey GDP, 2001–16) (Figure 5.4).

In 2016, Istanbul was struck by terrorist attacks, and they occurred in places where tourist attractions are located. This is why the number of visitors who arrived in Istanbul decreased after 2015. The number of visitors to Istanbul decreased from 12.5 million in 2015 to 9 million in 2016. In 2017, the number of visitors started to increase. The number of foreign visitors in the first three-quarters of 2017 was equal to the previous year's total figure. While in 2015 about 35 million foreign visitors came to Turkey, this number was 25 million in 2016. This number became 32.4 million in 2017 (Figure 5.5).

---

[1] Measuring 163 countries and covering 99 per cent of the world's population, one of the principle aims of the Global Terrorism Index is to help us to understand the global, regional and local impacts of terrorism. With this understanding, we can inform a positive practical debate about the future of terrorism and, importantly, how we respond.

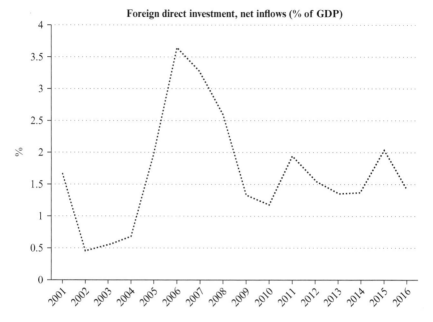

Source: World Bank Open Data (2017).

Figure 5.3   Foreign direct investment in Turkey

The change in tourist profile of Istanbul is also striking. The interest of tourists from the Middle East countries is an important factor in ensuring that the number of foreign visitors reaches the figures of previous years. While the number of tourists from Middle East countries who visit Istanbul has been increasing, the number of European tourists has fallen since 2016 (Figure 5.6).

5.4   RESULTS

The results of the study are explained in three steps outlined below.

5.4.1   Step 1: Identification of the Relevant Factors (SWOT Analysis)

In the first step, a SWOT hierarchy was structured for the goal. Internal capability or limits (strengths and weaknesses) and external conditions (opportunities and threats) are determined by SWOT analysis for decision-making (Kajanus et al., 2004; Hai, 2011). On its own, SWOT analysis has

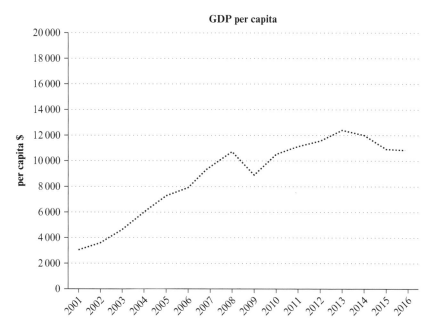

Source: Turkey GDP (2001–16).

Figure 5.4   GDP per capita in Turkey

no way of determining the significance of each SWOT factor (Shinno et al., 2006), and it is difficult to identify the most determinant factors in the decision-making process. That is why this study integrated the analytic hierarchy process (AHP) with SWOT analysis. AHP is a multi-criteria decision-making method that utilizes a hierarchical formation to define a problem and then develop priorities for alternatives.

In this context, the SWOT analysis was carried out in order to determine factors which affect the vulnerability/resilience of the tourism sector in Istanbul. This study attempts to discuss the strategies and policies for making Istanbul's tourism sector more resilient. The overall goal is to determine such strategies and policies. There are four SWOT criteria. They are classified into 24 sub-criteria under SWOT. Finally, six alternative competitive strategies are evaluated in terms of 24 sub-criteria (Figure 5.7).

Relevant factors of the SWOT comprise the results of the Search Conference and focus group discussions held during the preparation phase of the Istanbul Tourism Master Plan (Enlil et al., 2013). After preparing

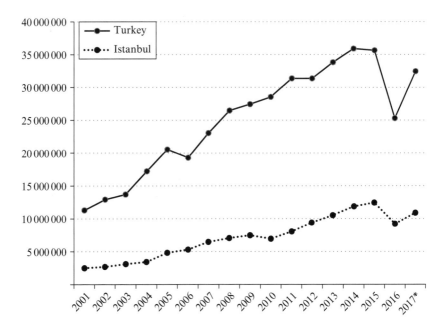

Figure 5.5   Number of foreign visitors

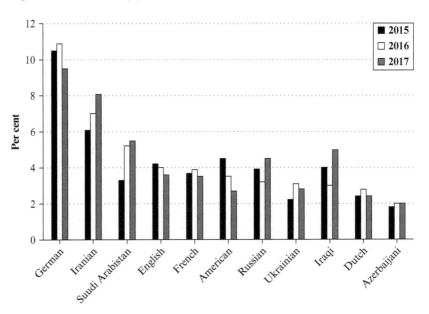

Figure 5.6   Number of foreign visitors according to nationality

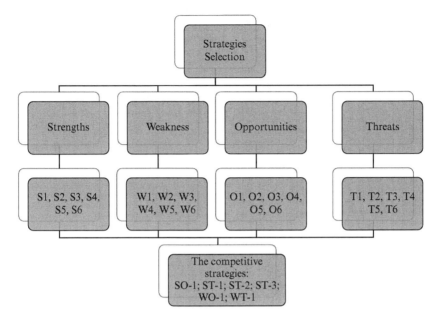

Figure 5.7   SWOT hierarchy for selecting the competitive strategies

the preliminary list of decision factors, these were categorized into 24 major factors, six of which were placed in each SWOT group (Table 5.1).

5.4.2   Step 2: Pair-wise Comparison of Factors

The second step consists of the results of a pair-wise comparison of SWOT factors. A matrix of pair-wise comparisons indicates how strongly or important one factor is than another with respect to the criterion by which they are being compared (Saaty, 2008). The analytical hierarchy process (AHP) and its eigenvalue calculation are integrated with the SWOT analysis (Kurttila et al., 2000).

The SWOT factors were used to develop a questionnaire for pair-wise comparison using SWOT-AHP methods. The questionnaire included a rating scale to weigh each factor relative to the others. The respondents were asked to evaluate if both factors were equally important or if one was more important than the other. The data from pair-wise comparisons were used to evaluate a priority value for each factor. Throughout this analysis, consistency ratios were maintained at < 0.1 as suggested by Saaty (2008).

The results of the AHP-SWOT analysis show that experts placed more emphasis on avoiding the disadvantage of threats, but also emphasized

Table 5.1   Factors placed in each SWOT group

STRENGTHS [S] Factors that increase the adaptive capacity	WEAKNESSES [W] Factors that increase vulnerability
(S1) *Historical buildings and places*: The architecture of the city, cultural heritage (S2) *Geographical advantages*: Sea, Bosporus, climate, natural beauty, scenery (S3) *Istanbul is a financial, congress and exhibition centre*: The attraction of Istanbul for congresses and fairs (S4) *Cultural richness*: There have been many different cultures which have immigrated to Istanbul. They bring the richness of their cultures (Turkish gastronomy etc.) (S5) *Thematic tourism attractions and experiences* (health tourism, cultural tourism) (S6) *Culture and art events*: Film, music festivals, concerts etc.	(W1) *Foreign tourists cannot fully experience the whole city* because the Historical Peninsula is highlighted as a main tourism centre in Istanbul (W2) *Insufficient promotional activities*: The lack of promotional and marketing strategies for Istanbul (W3) *Inadequate preservation* of historical works in the city (W4) *Inadequate security* in the city (W5) *Unsatisfactory accommodations* in terms of price and quality (W6) *Absence of a holistic management plan for tourism*

OPPORTUNITIES [O] Factors that increase the adaptive capacity	THREATS [T] Factors that increase vulnerability
(O1) *Increasing private and public investments*: Museums established by private sector in various regions (O2) *In the Middle East countries, positive perception of Turkey and Istanbul*: Arabians have started to become interested in Istanbul as a tourism location more than Europeans (O3) *Expansion of flight capacity and routes in air transport*: Opportunity to reach wider geographic area (O4) *Multiculturality of Istanbul*: Foreign tourists can experience the feeling of belonging because of the multiculturality of Istanbul (O5) *Culture and art* plays an important role in promotional and marketing activities: Turkish film industry, Turkish TV series (O6) *Colours of Istanbul*: traditions, festivals, mentality and lifestyle: Residents of Istanbul have several distinct national characteristics	(T1) *Terrorist attacks* in Istanbul (T2) *Negative perceptions* of Turkey, after terror attacks (T3) *Natural disaster*: Earthquake risk (T4) *Degeneration* for cultural treasures (T5) *The worst quality of life*: Inadequate urban transportation infrastructure, unplanned urbanization, inadequate green space, pollution etc. (T6) *Economic crisis*

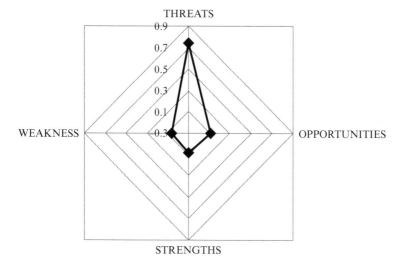

Figure 5.8   The results of the AHP-SWOT analysis

the significance of strengths for developing strategies to make Istanbul tourism more resilient (Figure 5.8).

Scale parameters that were used to calculate the overall priority score of each factor within each of the SWOT groups are obtained by using the rating process. Each strength, weakness, opportunity and threat was rated based on nine intensity ratings (see Appendix). Relative local priorities of the factors were computed using the eigenvalue calculation method. Finally, the global priority of each SWOT factor was calculated as the product of local priority and the scale of each SWOT group as shown in Table 5.2.

5.4.3   Step 3: Identifying Strategies Using the TOWS Matrix

The third level identifies alternative competitive strategies using the TOWS matrix. The TOWS matrix, developed by Weihrich (1982), creates four different strategy types (or logical combinations):

1.   SO strategies: using internal strengths to realize external opportunities.
2.   WO strategies: reducing internal weaknesses or developing strengths to realize external opportunities.
3.   ST strategies: using strengths to minimize external threats.
4.   WT strategies: reducing internal weaknesses to avoid external threats (only defensive strategy, worst case scenario) (Weihrich, 1982; Table 5.3).

Table 5.2 Pair-wise comparison matrices for SWOT factors

SWOT group Scaling factor		SWOT Factors	Local priority	Global priority
STRENGTHS 0.0815	1	(S1) Historical buildings and places	**0.3662**	**0.0299**
	2	(S4) Cultural richness	**0.2796**	**0.0228**
	3	(S3) Istanbul is a financial, congress and exhibition centre	**0.1233**	**0.0101**
	4	(S2) Geographical advantages	0.0981	0.0080
	5	(S5) Thematic tourism attractions and experiences	0.0796	0.0065
	6	(S6) Culture and art events	0.0532	0.0043
WEAKNESSES 0.0668	1	(W4) Inadequate security in the city	**0.5157**	**0.0345**
	2	(W3) Inadequate preservation of historical works in the city	**0.2189**	**0.0146**
	3	(W6) Absence of a holistic management plan for tourism	**0.1030**	**0.0069**
	4	(W2) Insufficient promotional activities	0.0695	0.0046
	5	(W1) Foreign tourists cannot fully experience the whole city	0.0530	0.0035
	6	(W5) Unsatisfactory accommodations in terms of price and quality	0.0398	0.0024
OPPORTUNITIES 0.1172	1	(O3) Expansion of flight capacity and routes in air transport	**0.2864**	**0.0344**
	2	(O5) Turkish film industry, Turkish TV series	**0.2209**	**0.0265**
	3	(O2) Positive perception of Turkey and Istanbul in the Middle East countries	**0.2154**	**0.0259**
	4	(O4) Multiculturality of Istanbul	0.1667	0.0200
	5	(O6) Colours of Istanbul	0.0594	0.0071
	6	(O1) Increasing private and public investments	0.0512	0.0061
THREATS 0.7342	1	(T2) Negative perceptions of Turkey	**0.3456**	**0.2537**
	2	(T1) Terrorist attacks in Istanbul	**0.3302**	**0.2425**
	3	(T3) The worst quality of life	0.1232	0.0905
	4	(T6) Economic crisis	0.0681	0.0500
	5	(T5) Natural disaster	0.0667	0.0490
	6	(T4) Degeneration for cultural treasures	0.0662	0.0486

Table 5.3   TOWS strategic alternatives matrix

	STRENGTHS (T)	*WEAKNESSES (W)*
OPPORTUNITIES (O)	*The SO Strategy (maxi-maxi):* The aim of this strategy is to *maximize both strengths and opportunities.* This strategy is used to cope with threats and overcome weaknesses.	*The WO Strategy (mini-maxi):* The aim of this strategy is to *minimize the weaknesses and to maximize the opportunities.*
THREATS (T)	*The ST Strategy (maxi-mini):* This strategy is based on the strengths and threats. *Strengths are used to deal with threats* in the external environment.	*The WT Strategy (mini-mini):* The aim of the WT strategy is to *minimize both weaknesses and threats.*

Source: Weihrich (1982).

The competitive strategies were developed according to this matching between components of the SWOT analysis (e.g., strength S1, S2, S4, S6 and opportunity O1, O4, O5, O6 were considered for the SO 1 Strategy) (Table 5.4).

5.5   CONCLUSION

The aim of resilience planning is to define priorities and create a system that is adaptive to stressors and shocks. The adaptive capacity aims explicitly at equipping systems to deal effectively with slow and radical changes. The enhancement of adaptive capacity is a necessary condition for reducing vulnerability. In this context, some alternative strategies for use by policy makers are suggested in this study as a result of the SWOT-TOWS analysis for the tourism sector in Istanbul. It may serve as a guide for developing resilience tourism planning for politicians and tourism enterprises.

Tourism is one of the sectors that is the most sensitive to stresses and shocks such as economic crises, political turmoil, natural disasters and terrorist attacks. Terrorist attacks shook the global tourism industry in the early part of the twenty-first century. Turkey is among the countries which recorded particularly sharp drops in foreign tourist arrivals after terrorist attacks. Therefore, developing resilience planning or crisis management

Table 5.4   The TOWS matrix

	STRENGTHS	WEAKNESSES
	(S1) Historical buildings and places (S4) Cultural richness (S3) Istanbul is a financial, congress and exhibition centre (S2) Geographical advantages (S5) Thematic tourism attractions and experiences (S6) Culture and art events, festivals	(W4) Inadequate security in the city (W3) Inadequate preservation of historical works in the city (W6) Absence of a holistic management plan for tourism (W2) Insufficient promotional activities (W1) Foreign tourists cannot fully experience the whole city (W5) Unsatisfactory accommodations in terms of price and quality
OPPORTUNITIES (O3) Expansion of flight capacity and routes in air transport (O5) Turkish film industry, Turkish TV series (O2) Positive perception in the Middle East countries (O4) Multiculturality (O6) Colours of Istanbul (O1) Increasing investments	SO-1: To develop cultural tourism, to provide experience with abstract and concrete inheritance (O3, S1, S4)	WO-1: To develop multi-segment marketing strategy and promoting activities reinforcing positive perception (W2, O5, O2, O4, O6)
THREATS (T2) Negative perceptions (T1) Terrorist attacks (T3) The worst quality of life (T6) Economic crisis (T5) Natural disaster (T4) Degeneration	ST-1: To ensure integration of various types of tourism, to attract different tourist profiles to the city and extend the duration of stay (S1, S4, S3, T2, T1) ST-2: To diversify attractions and spread tourist flows over the entire city (S3, S5, S6, T2, T1) ST-3: To prepare resilience tourism planning (S1, S2, S3, S4, S5, S6, T1, T2, T3, T4, T5, T6)	WT-1: To satisfy the tourists by increasing the quality of service (W4, W3, T3, T4)

planning to reduce the disaster risks, prepare for potential crisis events in the tourism industry and protect the image of touristic cities has become very important. Tourists' perceptions, their attitude towards travel and their image of the destinations are very vulnerable to the shocks or stressors (Baker, 2014). The safety and security of a destination is the most important factor influencing foreign tourists' decision-making on choosing a destination (Tasci and Boylu, 2010). The change in the number and profiles of international visitors to Turkey after the terrorist attacks in 2016 could also support this view. The number of foreign visitors to Turkey fell by approximately 28 per cent in 2016, with 10 million fewer visitors than in 2015. In this period, while the visitor arrivals in Istanbul from the Middle East countries such as Saudi Arabia, Afghanistan, Jordan, Algeria and Kuwait increased by approximately 17 per cent, the number of European tourists dropped by approximately 26 per cent. The experts in the sector have also highlighted the positive perception of Turkey and Istanbul in the Middle East countries as a powerful feature that affects the resilience of tourism. This result may depend on both geographical and ethnic-religious proximity. Religious similarity with tourists from the Middle East countries is the main factor in the increasing tourism demand in spite of risks. It is possible to say that culture and political relations are the main factors affecting the perception of tourists. Therefore, to develop a multi-segment marketing strategy and promote activities to change the negative image affected by terror attacks was defined as a strategy for building resilience. Ensuring the integration of various types of tourism, attracting different tourist profiles to the city and extending the duration of stay (ST-1 Strategy) and providing experience with abstract and concrete inheritance (SO-1 Strategy) are strategies which will make Istanbul become more resilient. Despite the fact that there are a lot of different tourist attractions (historical buildings and places, cultural richness), culture and arts events, foreign tourists cannot fully experience the whole city. The main problem is that many potential tourists are not aware of Istanbul's tourist attractions because of lack of marketing. More promotional activities are required to promote tourism in Istanbul. Therefore, WO-1 Strategies become very important for the resilience of Istanbul. In this way, it is possible to diversify attractions and spread tourist flows over the entire city (ST-2 Strategy). As a result, resilience tourism planning contributes to improve the competitiveness of a tourist destination and prepare for potential risks (ST-3 Strategy).

REFERENCES

Adger, N.W. (2006), 'Vulnerability', *Global Environmental Change*, **16**, 268–81.
Baker, David Mc. A. (2014), 'The effects of terrorism on the travel and tourism industry', *International Journal of Religious Tourism and Pilgrimage*, **2** (1), 58–67.
Bhattarai, K., D. Conway, and N. Shrestha (2005), 'Tourism, terrorism and turmoil in Nepal', *Annals of Tourism Research*, **32** (3), 669–88.
Calgaro, E. and K. Lloyd (2008), 'Sun, sea, sand and tsunami: examining disaster vulnerability in the tourism community of Khao Lak, Thailand, Singapore', *Journal of Tropical Geography*, **29**, 288–306.
Calgaro, E., K. Lloyd, and D. Dominey-Howes (2014), 'From vulnerability to transformation: a framework for assessing the vulnerability and resilience of tourism destinations', *Journal of Sustainable Tourism*, **22** (3), 341–60.
Cardona, Omar-Dario, Maarten K. van Aalst, Jörn Birkmann et al. (2012), 'Determinants of risk: exposure and vulnerability', in C.B. Field, V. Barros, T.F. Stocker, D. Qin, D.J. Dokken, K.L. Ebi et al. (eds), *Managing the Risks of Extreme Events and Disasters to Advance Climate Change Adaptation*, Cambridge and New York: Cambridge University Press, pp. 65–108.
Carpenter, S., B. Walker, M. Anderies, and N. Abel (2001), 'From metaphor to measurement: resilience of what to what?', *Ecosystems*, **4**, 765–81.
Country Economy (2017), 'Turkey GDP – gross domestic product', http://www.countryeconomy.com/gdp/turkey (accessed 21 December 2017).
Enders, W. and T. Sandler (1991), 'Causality between transnational terrorism and tourism –the case of Spain', *Terrorism*, **14** (1), 49–58.
Enlil, Zeynep, İclal Dinçer, Yiğit Evren, and Ebru Seçkin (2010), *İstanbul'da Kültür Turizmi için Yenilikçi Stratejiler*, İstanbul: İstanbul Bilgi Üniversitesi Yayınları.
Enlil, Zeynep, Iclal Dinçer, Ebru Seçkin et al. (2013), 'İstanbul Turizm Master Planına Yönelik Veri Toplama İşi', Unpublished research report, financed by Istanbul Metropolitan Municipality, İstanbul.
Feridun, M. (2011), 'Impact of terrorism on tourism in Turkey: empirical evidence from Turkey', *Applied Economics*, **43** (24), 3349–54.
Fuchs, G. and A. Reichel (2004), 'Cultural differences in tourist destination risk perception: an exploratory study', *Tourism*, **52** (1), 21–37.
Hai, Hui-Lin (2011), *Assessing the SMEs' Competitive Strategies on the Impact of Environmental Factors: A Quantitative SWOT Analysis Application, Environmental Management in Practice Elzbieta Broniewicz*, Intech Open, https://www.intechopen.com/books/environmental-management-in-practice/assessing-the-smes-competitive-strategies-on-the-impact-of-environmental-factors-a-quantitative-swot (accessed 21 December 2017).
Institute for Economics & Peace (2016), Global Terrorism Index 2016, Measuring and Understanding the Impact of Terrorism, accessed 21 December 2017, available from: https://reliefweb.int/report/world/global-terrorism-index-2017.
Institute for Economics & Peace (2017), Global Terrorism Index 2017, Measuring and Understanding the Impact of Terrorism, https://reliefweb.int/report/world/global-terrorism-index-2016 (accessed 21 December 2017).
Kajanus, M., J. Kangas, and M. Kurtilla (2004), 'The use of value focused thinking and the A'WOT hybrid method in tourism management', *Tourism Management*, **25** (4), 499–506.

Karl, M., C. Reintinger, and J. Schmude (2015), 'Reject or select: mapping destination choice', *Annals of Tourism Research*, **54** (C), 48–64.

Kurtilla, M., M. Pesonen, J. Kangas, and M. Kajanus (2000), 'Utilizing the analytic hierarchy process (AHP) in SWOT analysis – a hybrid method and its application to a forest-certification case', *Forest Policy and Economics*, **1** (1), 41–52.

Lew, A.A. (2014), 'Scale, change and resilience in community tourism planning', *Tourism Geographies*, **16** (1), 14–22.

Liu, A. and S. Pratt (2017), 'Tourism's vulnerability and resilience to terrorism', *Tourism Management*, **60**, 404–17.

Mortiner, C. (2016), 'Istanbul bombing: terror attack death toll rises to 38 including 30 police as PKK offshoot claims attacks', *Independent*, 11 December 2016, http://www.independent.co.uk/news/world/europe/istanbul-bomb-turkey-car-terror-death-toll-dead-police-pkk-isis-killed-latest-a7468001.html (accessed 30 December 2017).

Nelson, R.D., W.N. Adger, and K. Brown (2007), 'Adaptation to environmental change: contributions of a resilience Framework', *Annual Review of Environment and Resources*, **32**, 395–419.

New York Times (2017), 'Wave of terror attacks in Turkey continue at a steady pace', http://www.nytimes.com/interactive/2016/06/28/world/middleeast/turkey-terror-attacks-bombings.html (accessed 21 December 2017).

Polsky, C., R. Neff, and B. Yarnal (2007), 'Building comparable global change vulnerability assessments: the vulnerability scoping diagram', *Global Environment Change*, **17** (3–4), 472–85.

Raza, S.A. and S.T. Jawaid (2013), 'Terrorism and tourism: a conjunction and ramification in Pakistan', *Economic Modelling*, **33**, 65–70.

Richter, L.K. (1999), 'After political turmoil: the lessons of rebuilding tourism in three Asian Countries', *Journal of Travel Research*, **38**, 41–5.

Ritchie, W.B. (2004), 'Chaos, crises and disasters: a strategic approach to crisis management in the tourism industry', *Tourism Management*, **25** (6), 669–83.

Rittichainuwat, N.B. and G. Chakraborty (2009), 'Perceived travel risks regarding terrorism and disease: the case of Thailand', *Tourism Management*, **30** (3), 410–18.

Romagnoli, M. (2016), 'The effects of terrorism on tourism: (inter)relations, motives & risks', *AlmaTourism Journal of Tourism Culture and Territorial Development*, **7** (5), Special Issue: SI, 125–33.

Saaty, T. (2008), 'Decision making with the analytic hierarchy process', *International Journal of Services Sciences*, **1** (1), 83–98.

Sackett, H. and D. Botterill (2006), 'Perceptions of international travel risk: an exploratory study of the influence of proximity to terrorist attack', *e-Review of Tourism Research* (eRTR), **4** (2), 44–9.

Shinno, H., H.Yoshioka, S. Marpaung, and S. Hachiga(2006), 'Quantitative SWOT analysis on global competitiveness of machine tool industry', *Journal of Engineering Design*, **17** (3), 251–8.

Sönmez, S.F. and A.F. Graefe (1998), 'Influence of terrorism risk on foreign tourism decisions', *Annals of Tourism Research*, **25** (1), 112–44.

Tasci, A.D.A. and Y. Boylu (2010), 'Cultural comparison of tourists' safety perception in relation to trip satisfaction', *International Journal of Tourism Research*, **12** (2), 179–92.

Tompkins, E.L. and W.N. Adger (2004), 'Does adaptive management of natural resources enhance resilience to climate change?', *Ecology and Society*, **9** (2), 1–14.

Turkey GDP (2001–16), 'Gross Domestic Product, Evolution: Annual GDP Turkey (2001–2016)', http://www.countryeconomy.com/gdp/turkey (accessed 21 December 2017).

Weihrich, H. (1982), 'The TOWS matrix – a tool for situational analysis', *Long Range Planning*, **15** (2), 54–66.

Wickramasinghe, V. and S. Takano (2010), 'Application of combined SWOT and analytic hierarchy process (AHP) for tourism revival strategic marketing planning: a case of Sri Lanka tourism', *Journal of the Eastern Asia Society for Transportation Studies*, **8**, 954–69.

World Bank (2017), World Bank Open Data, http://www.data.worldbank.org/indi cator/BX.KLT.DINV.WD.GD.ZS?locations=TR (accessed 24 December 2017).

Yaya, M.E. (2009), 'Terrorism and tourism: the case of Turkey', *Defence and Peace Economics*, **20** (6), 477–97.

Table 5A.1   Pair-wise comparisons between SWOT factors

	STRENGTHS 1	STRENGTHS 2	STRENGTHS 3	STRENGTHS 4	STRENGTHS 5	STRENGTHS 6
STRENGTHS 1	1	5	7	3	5	5
STRENGTHS 2	1/5	1	3	1/5	1	3
STRENGTHS 3	1/7	1/3	1	5	1/5	1
STRENGTHS 4	1/3	5	5	1	5	7
STRENGTHS 5	1/5	1	3	1/5	1	1
STRENGTHS 6	1/5	1/3	1	1/7	1	1
	CI: 0.1020			CR: 0.0822		

	WEAKNESS 1	WEAKNESS 2	WEAKNESS 3	WEAKNESS 4	WEAKNESS 5	WEAKNESS 6
WEAKNESS 1	1	3	1/7	1/9	1	1/9
WEAKNESS 2	1/3	1	1/7	1/9	1	5
WEAKNESS 3	7	7	1	1/9	5	7
WEAKNESS 4	9	9	9	1	9	9
WEAKNESS 5	1	1	1/5	1/9	1	1/3
WEAKNESS 6	9	1/5	1/7	1/9	3	1
	CI: 0.0303			CR: 0.024		

Table 5A.1 (continued)

	OPPORTUNITIES 1	OPPORTUNITIES 2	OPPORTUNITIES 3	OPPORTUNITIES 4	OPPORTUNITIES 5	OPPORTUNITIES 6
OPPORTUNITIES 1	1	1/3	1/7	1/3	1	1/3
OPPORTUNITIES 2	3	1	1/3	5	1	7
OPPORTUNITIES 3	7	3	1	5	1/5	3
OPPORTUNITIES 4	1/3	1/5	1/5	1	5	5
OPPORTUNITIES 5	1	1	5	1/5	1	5
OPPORTUNITIES 6	3	1/7	1/3	1/5	1/5	1
	CI: 0.008				CR: 0.007	

	THREATS 1	THREATS 2	THREATS 3	THREATS 4	THREATS 5	THREATS 6
THREATS 1	1	1	9	9	9	1
THREATS 2	1	1	9	5	9	9
THREATS 3	1/9	1/9	1	5	3	7
THREATS 4	1/9	1/5	1/5	1	3	3
THREATS 5	1/9	1/9	1/3	1/3	1	7
THREATS 6	1	1/9	1/7	1/3	1/7	1
	CI: 0.057				CR: 0.0465	

6. Resilience of urban systems in the context of urban transformation: lessons from Beykoz-Istanbul

Tuba İnal-Çekiç and Mehmet Doruk Özügül

6.1 INTRODUCTION

Resilience has been an important discourse in urban studies and urban policy, prioritized by researchers as well as policy makers (Wilkinson, 2011). However, the fact remains that what resilience means for planning is not clear and yet to be explored. Efforts to understand urban systems are still in an exploratory stage and there is a great opportunity for creative approaches and perspectives. At this point, understanding resilience to be more than a metaphor, it is argued that transformation (by regeneration and renewal) and the displacement agenda of a given urban system could be read, discussed and measured over such a resilience conceptualization. From this point of view, cities, such as Istanbul, that are subject to dynamic spatial changes are especially worth working on.

Departing from the gap in the literature and a focus on community and urban system resilience, we discuss the concept of "resilient neighborhoods" through a district located on the northern shores of the Bosphorus (Istanbul) where a mega investment – the third bridge – has been constructed and has commenced to transform its vicinity. In respect thereof, planning here is supposed to be a tool to shift vulnerable features of an urban system, which has to be sustained, to a resilient one. Therefore, we aim to present the resilience of an urban system (neighborhood) and resilience against a displacement problem and social change. We attempt to make our assessment through 17 individual neighborhoods in the Beykoz District within the context of resilience in a transformation environment and represent planning tools through a resilience perspective. We focus on the role of planning activities and define a framework that planners can use or enhance during the planning process of a sub-urban system. Planning, in addition to all its objectives, has to serve to enhance the vulnerable features of an urban system and provide planning decisions given the system's resilience or vulnerability. Consequently, we propose to define systems as resilient which are not vulnerable according to the features and indicators we put forth.

Seeking a resilient urban system and social structure, the next section provides a brief summary of the literature and a conceptual background relating to the resilience concept in urban studies. The methodological framework and the features of the research field are then given. Drawing from the empirical research, the fourth section presents the findings of the analysis. Finally, a discussion is aimed particularly at planning authorities that may provide some takeaway lessons for neighborhoods that are subject to physical and social change through investments or planning activities.

6.2 FROM AN ABSTRACT TO A MORE MEASURABLE CONCEPT: RESILIENCE

The concept of resilience has a longer history in physics, psychology and ecology compared to its reflections in urban studies. As a milestone in this specific literature field, Holling (1973) described resilience as a measure of the ability of systems to absorb change and disturbance without losing the pre-disturbance relationships between their constituent elements. After this very well-known description, several types of conceptualizations were developed given the field/discipline, the problematic or the context.

Within the context of global environmental change, resilience was first discussed at the 2002 World Summit on Sustainable Development in Johannesburg. The statement that was put forth in the summit was that sustainability and resilience both follow the precautionary principle regarding resource use and emerging risks, avoiding vulnerability and promoting ecological integrity into the future (Adger, 2003). While economists measure resilience with regard to the ability of a place or region to recover from an economic crisis, for example loss of industry, ecologists tend to use the term for measuring the ability of an ecosystem to return to the state of equilibrium after a temporary disturbance (Holling, 1973; Vale, 2014).

Some can easily observe that descriptions of resilience are similar in some ways and paradigmatically differ in others. Pickett et al. (2004) define resilience as "the ability of a system to adjust in the face of changing conditions" (p. 373), while according to Ahern (2011), resilience means "the capacity of systems to reorganize and recover from change and disturbance without changing to other states . . . systems that are 'safe to fail'", and Romero-Lankao and Gnatz (2013, p. 359) describe the concept as "a capacity of urban populations and systems to endure a wide array of hazards and stresses". Within the socio-ecological systems (SES) framework, resilience is often defined as "the capacity of a system to absorb disturbance and reorganize while undergoing change so as to still retain essentially the same function, structure, identity, and feedbacks" (Walker et al., 2004, p. 1).

Just as Meerow et al. (2016, p. 43) argue, it is worth mentioning that the logic behind any of these descriptions depends on a kind of equilibrium assumption. While Holling (1996) emphasizes the engineering conceptualization of resilience as an equilibrium state and the ecological resilience as an evolving system approach, Meerow et al. (2016), divides resilience literature into three categories: "single-state equilibrium", "multiple-state equilibrium", and "dynamic non-equilibrium". "Single-state equilibrium" is a concept generally referred to as "engineering resilience" where resilience is defined as "the capacity of a system to revert to a previous equilibrium post-disturbance" or "the ability of an object to return to its original position after receiving a hit and the ability to successfully survive a shock or trauma". Within such a conceptualization any healthy system has an ideal equilibrium state. In a "multiple-state equilibrium" perception, systems have multiple stable states and under the effects of disturbance move from one stable state to another. This assumption is also known as "ecological resilience". Regarding the third category, due to a "dynamic non-equilibrium" paradigm change in systems, it is not exceptional but a permanent process where no stable state exists. Reading the definitions from this perspective, most often the "single-state equilibrium" paradigm replaces the others in recent urban studies.

More specifically, the context of resilience has been embraced within urban studies, especially given the complexity of urban systems. During the last decade, research on urban systems has evolved to integrate different disciplines in order to understand the unpredictable dynamics of cities. So, multidisciplinary approaches have brought new ways that may contribute to urban studies to explore urban systems in which resilience can be mentioned (Chelleri and Olazabal, 2012). As a result of these fruitful attempts, resilience has been used as a keyword in several planning topics such as climate change and adaptation (Fünfgled and McEvoy, 2012; Pelling and Manuel-Navarrete, 2011; Wardekker et al., 2010), urban design and planning principles (Allan and Bryant, 2011; Pickett et al., 2004) and disasters and related mitigation precautions (Allan and Bryant, 2011; Prashar et al., 2012; Vale and Campanella, 2005).

Moreover, the literature also offers some examples of indicators that help us evaluate the resilience of specific systems. Despite the below-mentioned indicator sets from different fields of interest, there is still the need for more empirical studies on the resilience of socio-ecological systems.

Using the same empirical perspective and searching for different indicators used to measure the resiliency of systems, it is found that ecological resilience studies focusing on "the ability to persist and the ability to adapt" provide some examples (Adger, 2003). Also, Walker et al. (2004) have a very unique position. They propose that the resilience of a given socio-ecological system is a function of "latitude" (the maximum amount the system can be changed before losing its ability to recover), "resistance" (the ease or difficulty of changing the system), "precariousness" (the current trajectory of the system, and how close it currently is to a limit or "threshold" which, if breached, makes recovery difficult or impossible) and "panarchy" (how the other three attributes are influenced by the dynamics of the (sub)systems at scales above and below the scale of interest).

Economic resilience studies are widely focused on regions and institutions. In some of the recent studies, the concept is related to spatial planning, and regional resilience principles are defined and indicators are mentioned as "flexibility", "modularity", "interdependency" and "sectoral diversity" (Albers and Deppisch, 2012).

However, in the urban context few studies concretely define features of resilience. For example, Ahern (2011) proposes "multifunctionality", "redundancy", "diversity", "multi-scale networks", "connectivity" and "adaptive planning" to assess the resilience of urban systems.

As a result of a considerable number of studies on community resilience, the concept has evolved from a one-dimensional concept into a hybrid and multi-dimensional one, namely, "socio-ecological" systems. Moreover, in the social sciences, this idea was operationalized into the ability of communities to withstand disturbances so as to maintain their social infrastructures (Adger, 2000). Departing mainly from studies on forest communities, dimensions of community resilience include: (1) community resources which are supposed to be natural, human, cultural, social, financial and political; (2) active agents so that community members can influence their community's well-being and take a leadership role in doing so; (3) collective action, which indeed needs collective effort to accomplish specific community objectives; (4) strategic action, which implies conscious deliberation, planning, implementation and learning activities; (5) equity for equal access to society's benefits and costs, and social justice for all economic and social groups; and (6) impact, which means a community's successful response to crisis-opportunity-change, its successful implementation of plans, its development of new trajectories and futures for itself, and its adaptation to changes within and outside the community (Colussi, 1999; Folke et al., 2003; Harris et al., 2000; Healy et al., 2003).

6.3 DATA, RESEARCH AND METHODOLOGY

This study is specifically focused on the last dimension of the above-mentioned categorization and the socio-ecological system resilience approach of Walker et al. (2004). The aim is to clarify, evaluate and compare the adaptation capacity of neighborhoods under the transformative effects of a panarchic driver using an indicator-based method. For this purpose, our theoretical framework is unfolded through a set of assumptions, followed by representation of the research field and the methodological approach.

6.3.1 Assumptions

Having defined the resilience framework, it is vital to mention that this study leans toward four major assumptions. In the first instance, resilience is a premature concept, and in particular its planning relevance is worth discussing. Within this context, concepts and explanations in the resilience literature might be enlightening for different planning problematics. This brings us to our second assumption.

In our case, the "Panarchic Transformative Driver" is accepted as the Third Bosphorus Bridge that would generate substantial spatial and social alteration in the case study area (Beykoz District) and its vicinity. This assumption has both a practical and a theoretical explanation. From the practical perspective, it is certain that the destiny of both the urban and rural settlements of the district would be changing due to this mega infrastructure investment. And from the theoretical point of view, despite the existence of widespread panarchic driver assumptions in the literature about local consequences of climate change such as sea level rise, drought, flooding or natural disasters such as earthquakes, a human-made/artificial driver conception seems to be quite rare.

Third, "disturbance" is the natural consequence of such a huge panarchic effect, and in this case "disturbance" is accepted as "displacement" through which the main characteristics of the neighborhoods should transform. Recalling Walker et al.'s (2004) "function of ecological resilience" explanation, the resiliency of urban systems against displacement is measured after a mega investment that changes the main characteristics of the neighborhood and eventually leads to a displacement. In addition, land value change is considered as an essential inducement of displacement considering the definition of "latitude" as the maximum amount the system can be changed before losing its ability to recover.

As the fourth assumption, since urban (sub)systems have to be conceptualized as dynamic systems, the "dynamic non-equilibrium" paradigm is basically accepted as an explanatory perspective for this study. Yet it is also thought that such an urban (sub)system reading still maintains some problems, such as reading the urban environment (and the mobility tendencies of local inhabitants) from only a market-oriented point of view and neglecting the precautionary or protective aims of planning.

6.3.2   Spatialization of the Research Problematic: Beykoz

Departing from these assumptions, it is worth mentioning the contextual relevance, unique position and properties of the selected case study. With a population of 15 million people, Istanbul is Turkey's largest city and its financial center. It generates capital accumulation and is witnessing a rapid transformation agenda. This transformation in Istanbul is realized through various planning and investment processes, such as: (1) capital investments (prestigious business centers, hotels, shopping malls, gated communities and so on); (2) mega infrastructure projects (the third bridge, the third airport and so on); (3) regeneration/revitalization/transformation projects in residential areas (Çalışkan et al., 2012; Kurtuluş and Türkün, 2005). This spatial transformation is accompanied by social change, given the increased land prices in the central city and urban fringes. Displacement seems to be the consequence of the transformation processes since existing users cannot afford new services provided by new physical structure in central places and cannot proceed to production in agricultural land on urban fringes (Gülöksüz, 2002; Kara and Karatepe, 2012; Karaburun et al., 2010; Musaoglu et al., 2005).

Our chapter mainly emphasizes this process in order to understand and discuss the resilience (and adaptive capacity) of neighborhoods as urban systems under such panarchic effects where displacement is accepted as the inevitable disturbing outcome. According to the above-mentioned framework, field research has been conducted in the Beykoz District hosting the mega infrastructure investment, the third bridge, as a state-driven planning decision.

Hearings about the third bridge in Istanbul date back to the construction of the second bridge in the late 1980s, but it could not generate much interest while the spatial consequences of the second bridge were still on the agenda. However, the fact remains that the city gained experiences on land use and land price changes due to the two bridges built previously over the Bosphorus. In particular, the second bridge triggered the development of new neighborhoods on the urban fringes, mostly inhabited by squatters, and unplanned settlements on both the Anatolian and European sides of the city. Beykoz was one of the districts where the second bridge caused a considerable amount of land use change. Kavacık – a neighborhood located near the bridge in Beykoz – almost totally transformed into a central business district zone, and gated communities were settled in the forest areas of Beykoz (Aksoylu, 2015; İnal-Cekic and Gezici, 2009; Kurtuluş, 2011).

The history and spatial changes triggered by the third bridge commenced at the beginning of the 2000s. Fluctuating locations were announced for the bridge; however, a strong and tightly organized opposition stopped the decision process for a few years. Opposition was held by the citizens from the neighborhoods located along the alternative routes. Afterwards, in 2010, debates on the third bridge accelerated again as a result of the declaration of a new route crossing the Bosphorus from north of the existing two bridges, between Beykoz and Sarıyer Districts. The planning authority revised the Istanbul Metropolitan Master Plan regarding the route of the third bridge. Revision of the master plan immediately resulted in a change in land prices and triggered the handover of the land, particularly around the route of the planned bridge. New residential and commercial projects directly used this location and its proximity advantage was used as a marketing strategy (Table 6.1, Figure 6.1).

The value of Beykoz undoubtedly comes from its natural environment with villages, groves and forest areas surrounding a central historical village located on the northern shores of the Bosphorus (Figure 6.2). Beykoz is also characterized by its historical state-led industrial investments from the time of the Ottoman Empire and the early Republican Period. The Paşabahçe Glass Industry, the Beykoz Leather and Shoe Factory and the Tekel Factory are examples of industrial businesses where the workers also settled on illegal land.

Beykoz has special legal conservation status because of its natural assets and its location on the Bosphorus. However, these qualities accelerate the demand and pressure on this district in terms of residential development (İnal-Cekic and Gezici, 2009). While increasing accessibility through the 2nd and the planned third bridges stimulates demand, the so-called "2b"

Table 6.1   Milestones of the process

Year	Event
1988	The 2nd bridge was in service; first ideas about the 3rd and 4th bridges
2003–04	Alternative routes about the 3rd bridge and opposition of NGOs
April 2010	Announcement of Garipçe-Poyrazköy Route (Beykoz)
June 2010	Revision to Istanbul Metropolitan Master Plan
September 2012	Construction of the 3rd bridge begins

Figure 6.1   Locations of the Bosphorus bridges and Beykoz

forest lands,[1] which are subject to privatization, provide justification for

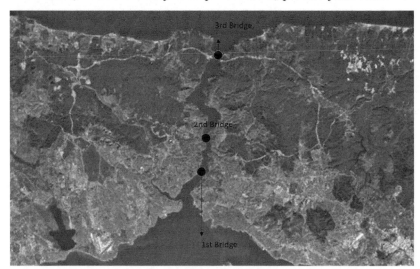

Figure 6.2   Beykoz

---

[1]   2b is an abbreviation for Forestry Law – Act 2, Article B. This abbreviation is used for the forest land that lost its natural character and cannot be used to create a forest anymore; in other words, the lands that were created under the cover of cadastral works by classifying them as poor lands not appropriate for forest development (Coşkun et al., 2015).

new developments (Musaoglu, 2005). Thus, land handovers in the fringe and rural areas of Beykoz and increasing land prices have been important in this area since the beginning of the 2000s.

From this viewpoint, it can be predicted that the third bridge and the connecting roads will increase the accessibility of Beykoz, and increasing accessibility will eventually be accompanied by physical and social alterations. Therefore, this chapter proposes a framework for accounting for the physical and social components of neighborhoods as an urban system in adaptation to a panarchic effect which has – in this case – transformative effects and socio-spatial consequences of the third bridge.

While ideas of place have been incorporated into research on social and community resilience, the current work aims to evaluate the adaptation capacity of different neighborhoods under given circumstances. Sense of place attachment and the features of the neighborhood which indicate the community's and the neighborhood's successful response to crisis and adaptation to changes within and outside the community are the main topics considered.

Regarding the usage of local urban services as the physical attachment to the space, Beykoz mainly stands in a self-sustaining context (Özügül and İnal-Çekiç, 2015). However, the aim is to reveal the distinction between the neighborhoods of Beykoz within a resilience context.

6.3.3   Data, Indicators and Methodology

To represent Beykoz as a whole, from its 25 neighborhoods and 20 villages, 17 neighborhoods and villages have been selected.[2] Throughout a stratified sampling methodology, their location, number of households, population and neighborhood status[3] were considered, and random selection was applied within the neighborhood clusters. Table 6.2 shows the distribution of a total of 392 questionnaires conducted according to the sample size, which is calculated on the basis of total households in these neighborhoods. A sample of households on a street basis within the selected neighborhoods represents Beykoz within a 95 percent confidence level and +/–0.05 confidence interval.

The applied survey generated data on personal information of the households, attachment to the neighborhood, inter-urban mobility, house-

[2]   According to a change in the urbanization law in 2014, the status of all villages within the borders of metropolitan areas shifted to neighborhoods.
[3]   Data are provided by the Veri Research Company and are calculated over Street Base-Land Prices per square meter (m²), Neighborhood Base-Education Level and Street Base-Development Index.

Table 6.2   Questionnaires conducted according to neighborhood status

	Estimated number of households 2010	%	Number of questionnaires	Total number of neighborhoods/ villages	Number of neighborhoods/ villages where questionnaire conducted
Mid status N.−4*	3691	5.7	22	2	1
Mid-low status N.−5	8913	13.8	54	5	3
Low status N.−6	35045	54.1	212	12	6
Lowest status N.−7	10713	16.5	65	6	3
Villages	6441	9.9	39	20	4
Total	64803	1000	392	45	17

Note: * Highest status N.-1, High status N.-2 and mid-high status N.-3 were not found within the sample.

hold income, status of the property and dwelling. Following the production of survey data, the necessary data were transformed into a neighborhood parameter. The available neighborhood-base institutional data were then inserted into the data set and analyzed using hierarchical cluster analysis. This explorative analysis tries to identify structures within the data. Regarding Cormack's (1971) and Gordon's (1999) work on cluster analysis, the term "cluster" emphasizes two main features so that a cluster is an integrity that has internal cohesion and external isolation. Regarding our methodology, cluster analysis is used to organize observed data into meaningful structures to develop groups of neighborhoods depending on the degree of similarities between them.

A total of 21 indicators were used in the hierarchical cluster analysis. Table 6.3 shows these indicators including the source and the year the data were obtained and Table 6.4 gives the meaning of the indicators within our contextual framework. Each indicator was described according to what it means for a more resilient neighborhood. In the follow-up phase of the study, neighborhoods within the clusters were ranked from I to IV regarding these indicators and their meanings describing the resiliency against an outside factor as the disturbance.

Table 6.3 Indicators used in cluster analysis

Indicator	Indicator code	Level of indicator	Data source	Year of data
Change in land price per year	Land_Prc_Chn	Neighborhood	gib.gov.tr	2000–14
Percentage of population over 65	Age65_Pop	Neighborhood	ADNKS	2008
Percentage of population increase	Pop_Increase	Neighborhood	TUIK	2000
Percentage of university graduates	Unv_Grd	Household	Questionnaire	2013
Percentage of detached houses	Dtch_House	Household	Questionnaire	2013
Rooms per household member	Room_Prs	Household	Questionnaire	2013
Percentage of building with occupancy permit	Ocpncy_Prm	Household	Questionnaire	2013
Monthly average income of household (TL)	Avrg_Incm	Household	Questionnaire	2013
Percentage of rent within income	Rent_Expndt	Household	Questionnaire	2013
Percentage of transportation expenditure within income	Trnsp_Expndt	Household	Questionnaire	2013
Percentage of private car owner households	Car_Owner	Household	Questionnaire	2013
Percentage of head of households born in this neighborhood	Nghbrh_Born	Household	Questionnaire	2013
Percentage of households using Beykoz for health services	Health_Usg	Household	Questionnaire	2013
Percentage of households using Beykoz for education services	Edctn_Usg	Household	Questionnaire	2013
Average transportation duration to local retailers (minutes)	Shpng_Acs	Household	Questionnaire	2013
Percentage of households with workplace on the Anatolian side	Antln_Wrk	Household	Questionnaire	2013
Percentage of households with workplace within walking distance	Wrkplc_Walk	Household	Questionnaire	2013
Average transportation duration to workplace (minutes)	AvTime_WrkIpc	Household	Questionnaire	2013
Percentage of households willing to move from this neighborhood	Will_Move	Household	Questionnaire	2013
Percentage of workplaces within the whole land use types of urban fabric	Wrkplc_Lnduse	Neighborhood	TUIK-ADNKS	2008
Percentage of homeowners	Hmown	Household	Questionnaire	2013

Table 6.4   Meanings of indicators

Code	Meanings and assumptions
Land_Prc_Chn	Increase in land prices increases vulnerability
Age65_Pop	Low capacity of mobilization increases neighborhood dependency
Pop_Increase	Change in population decreases place identity
Unv_Grd	Given the indirect relation with income, defines consciousness in neighborhood preference and increases place attachment
Dtch_House	When the proportion of detached houses decreases (fewer homeowners), persistence/resistance against displacement decreases
Room_Prs	Increase in number of people per room increases the tendency to change the living environment depending on discomfort
Ocpncy_Prm	Legality decreases the vulnerability
Avrg_Incm	Mobilization capacity increases with income
Rent_Expndt	Increase in expenditures in rent increases the tendency to change living environment
Trnsp_Expndt	Increase in expenditures in transportation increases the tendency to change living environment
Car_Owner	Car ownership indicates economic power
Nghbrh_Born	Being born in the neighborhood increases neighbourhood attachment
Health_Usg	The more people using public services from the neighborhood means more neighborhood dependence
Edctn_Usg	The more people using public services from the neighborhood means more neighborhood dependence
Shpng_Acs	The more people using retailers from the neighborhood means more neighborhood dependence
Antln _Wrk	Spatial proximity to job increases neighborhood dependence
Wrkplc_Walk	Spatial proximity to job increases neighborhood dependence
AvTime_Wrklpc	Spatial proximity to job increases neighborhood dependence
Will_Move	Direct relation with place attachment and increases resilience capacity
Wrkplc_Lnduse	Increase in businesses in the neighborhood increases the tendency of residents to move out
Hmown	More homeowners increases neighborhood attachment

6.4   RESILIENCE VERSUS VULNERABILITY IN BEYKOZ NEIGHBORHOODS

To categorize neighborhoods with homogeneous patterns according to a resilience context, hierarchical cluster analysis was used in which an observation (in our study a neighborhood) is joined to a cluster if it has a

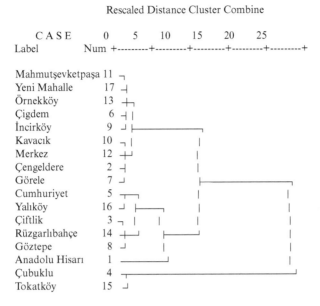

Dendrogram using Average Linkage (Between Groups)

Rescaled Distance Cluster Combine

```
        C A S E       0      5     10     15     20     25
     Label          Num  +---------+---------+---------+---------+---------+

Mahmutşevketpaşa  11  ┐
Yeni Mahalle      17  ┘
Örnekköy          13  ┐
Çigdem             6  ┐│
İncirköy           9  ┘├────────────────┐
Kavacık           10  ┐│                │
Merkez            12  ┤┘                │
Çengeldere         2  ┐                 │
Görele             7  ┘          ┌──────────────────────┐
Cumhuriyet         5  ┬─┐        │                      │
Yalıköy           16  ┘ ├────┐   │                      │
Çiftlik            3  ┐ │    │   │                      │
Rüzgarlıbahçe     14  ┤─┘    ├──────┘                   │
Göztepe            8  ┘      │                          │
Anadolu Hisarı     1  ────────┘                          │
Çubuklu            4  ┬────────────────────────────────────┘
Tokatköy          15  ┘
```

Figure 6.3   Findings of hierarchical cluster analysis

certain average level of similarity with all current members of the clusters. The average linkage within groups combines clusters so that the average distance between all cases in the result is as small as possible (Rousseeuw, 1987). Thus, the distance between two clusters is the average of the distances between all possible pairs of cases in the resulting cluster.

According to the findings of the analysis, clustered neighborhoods independent from the geographical context can be seen in Figure 6.3. Cluster-I includes five neighborhoods: Cumhuriyet, Yalıköy, Çiftlik, Rüzgarlıbahçe and Göztepe. Çiftlik, Rüzgarlıbahçe and Göztepe demonstrate homogeneity given their proximity and their location in the water catchment area with the illegal structure that joins them together in the first stage of the analysis. Even though Yalıköy and Cumhuriyet stand in a different locational context, accessibility is the main factor being combined. Yalıköy has the advantage of being on the shore of the Bosphorus and Cumhuriyet has strong connections with the bridges compared with other rural units (Mahmutşevketpaşa, Örnekköy, Görele).

Cluster-II consists of one neighborhood, Anadolu Hisarı, which does not combine with any cluster given the outstanding features of the others. Location in the vicinity of the second bridge gives leverage to Anadolu

Hisarı, which has a very steady property structure with a high level of income as its distinguishing character.

Cluster-III consisting of nine neighborhoods reveals a homogeneity dependent on rapid change due to the status of much of the land in a 2b forest area and consequent turnovers in the land property. Cluster-IV includes Çubuklu and Tokatköy which are located close to the central area of Beykoz. Both have had a rapid change in land values accompanied by turnovers. Çubuklu has been exposed to rapid land use change due to a transformed industrial area which still remains as a brownfield site and is planned as a tourism area (Figure 6.4).

Results of the cluster analysis assert homogeneous neighborhood struc-

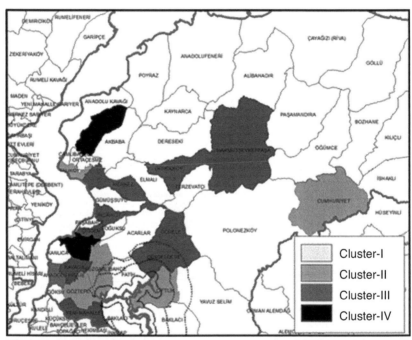

	Neighborhoods
1st Cluster	Cumhuriyet, Yalıköy, Çiftlik, Rüzgarlıbahçe, Göztepe
2nd Cluster	Anadolu Hisarı
3rd Cluster	Çigdem, İncirköy, Mahmutşevketpaşa, Yeni Mahalle Örnekköy, Kavacık, Merkez, Çengeldere, Görele
4th Cluster	Çubuklu, Tokatköy

Figure 6.4　Mapping the findings of hierarchical cluster analysis

tures and features in the mean of the indicator which combines them in a cluster. Once the clusters are decided upon, they are ranked due to the indicators' definition which directly points out the resilient structure of the neighborhood through a disturbance of transformation caused by the third bridge. Findings of this ranking analysis are given in Figure 6.5.

Figure 6.5 shows the rankings of all indicators within the clusters. With reference to the indicator rankings, enlargement in the total area of the radial graphic indicates more resiliency for the cluster. At this point, the second graphic demonstrates that Anadolu Hisarı alone is the most resilient neighborhood under risk of possible displacement, in which the homeownership rate is high and a low level of population increase is observed. Cluster-III follows Anadolu Hisarı in a sequence. Both clusters have different indicators which show resilience in the overall evaluation. Therefore, they will be less affected by a possible displacement problem.

As a result of such indicator-based research, it is possible to highlight which neighborhoods are vulnerable against displacement due to what indicators. In order to reach a more "displacement resilient neighborhood" in our case, plans should pay special attention to land use decisions such as locating urban facilities and workplaces and improving the quality and legality of housing stock for the less resilient clusters (Cluster-1 and Cluster-IV).

Remembering "zero-displacement" would be neither a realistic nor a healthy goal. Some sort of clarity would help planners to shape relevant strategies against these disturbing effects and build more successful resiliency plans. Within the same context, a planning system should also be supported with legal precautions (like rent control or local employee priority mechanisms), on the one hand, and should be improved with the help of new toolkits (like resiliency indexes), on the other.

6.4 DISCUSSION

Planning cannot be located in just a reflexive position, but should also orient the direction and extent of change (and determine at least some end-states) for urban environment(s). In other words, transforming any given value cannot be the only perspective of planning. Each planning practice should make several kinds of decisions according to the features of the planning area and the problematic, such as what and how to protect (persistence), rehabilitate (adaptability) or renew (transform). In doing so, and for better resilience planning, the vulnerabilities of subsystems should be well analyzed. This study particularly aims to contribute to the current literature from this point of view.

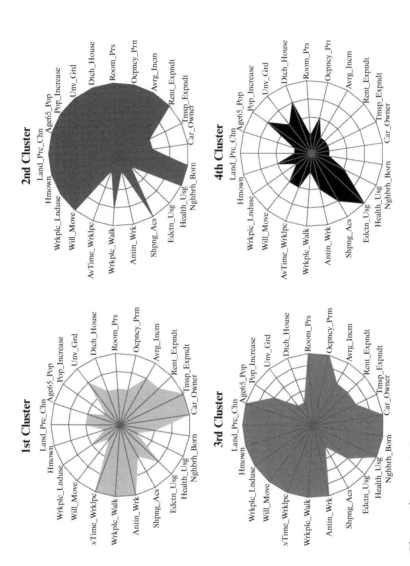

Figure 6.5   Cluster characteristics

Even though this field research which has been conducted in Beykoz does not give generalizable results for all cities and neighborhoods, it still emphasizes the role of planning to expose the vulnerable features of communities while sustaining the resilient ones. Regarding the planning exercises which aim to change the physical environment without entailing a displacement, this chapter presents some clues and takeaways for planning studies. Particularly when a mega infrastructure project or an investment is on the agenda, it seems to be crucial to evaluate the inevitable consequences and social impact of the planned investment in the area.

Moreover, our research reveals that tackling the "urban environment" as a monolith would be a negligent approach. Instead, planners should seek for some new tools to consider the vulnerable and resilient features of a neighborhood through a planning decision process. Within this context, land value change, population change, legal status, place attachment and property rights were used as the assets of a neighborhood given the unique features of Beykoz. It is also possible and essential to develop new indicators for further studies and the site-specific conditions of different localities. The findings of the study clearly suggest that resilience seeking practices will always entail a more continuous process for planners rather than achieving some sort of endpoint.

REFERENCES

Adger, W.N. (2000). Social and ecological resilience: are they related? *Progress in Human Geography*, **24**(3), 347–64.
Adger, W.N. (2003). Building resilience to promote sustainability, *IHDP Update*, **2**, 1–3.
Ahern, J. (2011). From fail-safe to safe-to-fail: sustainability and resilience in the new urban world, *Landscape and Urban Planning*, **100**(4), 341–3.
Aksoylu, S. (2015). Development of the urban periphery and issues related to urban landscape due to gated communities, *Journalism*, **5**(8), 415–27.
Albers, M. and Deppisch, S. (2012). Resilience in the light of climate change: useful approach or empty phrase for spatial planning? *European Planning Studies*, **21**(10), 1598–610.
Allan, P. and Bryant, M. (2011). Resilience as a framework for urbanism and recovery, *Journal of Landscape Architecture*, **6**(2), 34–45.
Çalışkan, Ç., Çılgın K., Dündar, U., and Yalçıntan, M.C. (2012), İstanbul Dönüşüm Coğrafyası (Transformation geography of Istanbul), 3. Kentsel ve Bölgesel Araştırmalar, Symposium presentation, Ankara.
Colussi, M. (1999). The community resilience manual: a new resource will link rural revitalization to CED best practice, *Making Waves*, **10**(4), 10–14.
Cormack, R.M. (1971). A review of classification, *Journal of the Royal Statistical Society A*, **134**, 321–67.
Coşkun, A.K., Türker, M.F., and Öztürk, A. (2015). Türkiye'de tek başına iktidar

olan partilerin seçim beyannameleri ve hükümet programlarında ormancılık (Election statements of political parties of Turkey and forestry in government programs), *Artvin Çoruh Üniversitesi Orman Fakültesi Dergisi*, **16**(1), 72–88.

Chelleri, L. and Olazabal, M. (eds) (2012). *Multidisciplinary Perspectives on Urban Resilience: A Workshop Report*, BC3, Basque Centre for Climate Change.

Folke, C., Colding, J., and Berkes, F. (2003). Synthesis: building resilience and adaptive capacity in social-ecological systems, *Navigating Social-Ecological Systems: Building Resilience for Complexity and Change*, **9**(1), 352–87.

Fünfgled, H. and McEvoy, D. (2012). Resilience as a useful concept for climate change adaptation? *Planning Theory & Practice*, **13**(2), 324–8.

Gordon, A.D. (1999), *Classification* (2nd edn), Boca Raton, FL: Chapman and Hall/CRC.

Gülöksüz, E. (2002). Negotiation of property rights in urban land in Istanbul, *International Journal of Urban and Regional Research*, **26**(3), 462–76.

Harris, C., McLaughlin, W., Brown, G., and Becker, D.R. (2000). *Rural Communities in the Inland Northwest: An Assessment of Small Rural Communities in the Interior and Upper Columbia River Basins*, United States Department of Agriculture Forest Service General Technical Report.

Healy, K., Hampshire, A., and Ayres, L. (2003). Engaging communities for sustainable change: promoting resilience. Available at http://www.bensoc.org.au/research/engaging_communities.html (accessed 6 May 2005).

Holling, C.S. (1973). Resilience and stability of ecological systems, *Annual Review of Ecology and Systematics*, **4**, 1–23.

Holling, C.S. (1996). Engineering resilience versus ecological resilience. In P. Schulze (ed.), *Engineering Within Ecological Constraints*, Washington, DC: National Academies Press, pp. 31–44.

İnal-Çekiç, T. and Gezici, F. (2009). Gated communities leading the development on the periphery of Istanbul Metropolitan Area, *ITU A-Z*, **6**(2), 73–95.

Kara, F. and Karatepe, A. (2012). Uzaktan algılama teknolojileri ile Beykoz ilçesi (1986–2011) arazi kullanımı değişim analizi (Land use change analysis of Beykoz through remote sensing systems), *Marmara Coğrafya Dergisi* **25**, 378–89.

Karaburun, A., Demirci, A., and Suen, I.S. (2010). Impacts of urban growth on forest cover in Istanbul (1987–2007), *Environmental Monitoring and Assessment*, **166**(1), 267–77.

Kurtuluş, H. (2011). Gated communities as a representation of new upper and middle classes in Istanbul, *İstanbul Üniversitesi Siyasal Bilgiler Fakültesi Dergisi*, **44**, 49–65.

Kurtuluş, H. and Türkün, A. (2005). Introduction. In H. Kurtuluş (ed.), *İstanbul'da Kentsel Ayrışma* (Urban disintegration in Istanbul), Istanbul: Bağlam Yayınları, pp. 9–25.

Meerow, S., Newell, J.P., and Stults, M. (2016). Defining urban resilience: a review, *Landscape and Urban Planning*, **147**, 38–49.

Musaoglu, N., Coşkun, M., and Kocabas, V. (2005). Land use change analysis of Beykoz-Istanbul by means of satellite images and GIS, *Water Science and Technology*, **51**(11), 245–51.

Özügül, D. and İnal-Çekiç, T. (2015). Kentsel Saçaklanmayı Yerel Kentsel Hizmetlere Erişim Perspektifinden Okumak; Beykoz Üzerine bir Çözümleme (Reading urban sprawl in terms of local urban services; case of Beykoz), *Mimarist*, **54**, Autumn, 65–70.

Pelling, M. and Manuel-Navarrete, D. (2011). From resilience to transformation:

the adaptive cycle in two Mexican urban centers, *Ecology and Society*, **16**(2), Art. 11. Available at http://www.ecologyandsociety.org/vol16/iss2/art11/ (accessed August 2018).

Pickett, S.T.A., Cadenasso, M.L., and Grove, J.M. (2004). Resilient cities: meaning, models, and metaphor for integrating the ecological, socio-economic, and planning realm, *Landscape and Urban Planning*, **69**(4), 369–84.

Prashar, S., Shaw, R., and Takeuchi, Y. (2012). Assessing the resilience of Delhi to climate-related disasters: a comprehensive approach, *Natural Hazards*, **64**, 1609–24.

Romero-Lankao, P. and Gnatz, D.M. (2013). Exploring urban transformations in Latin America, *Current Opinion in Environmental Sustainability*, **5**(3–4), 358–67.

Rousseeuw, P.J. (1987). Silhouettes: a graphical aid to the interpretation and validation of cluster analysis, *Journal of Computational and Applied Mathematics*, **20**, 53–65, doi:10.1016/0377-0427(87)90125-7

Vale, L.J. (2014). The politics of resilient cities: whose resilience and whose city? *Building Research & Information*, **42**(2), 191–201.

Vale, L.J. and Campanella, T.J. (2005). *The Resilient City: How Modern Cities Recover from Disaster*, New York: Oxford University Press.

Wardekker, J.A., de Jong, A., Knoop, J.M., and van der Sluijs, J.P. (2009). Operationalising a resilience approach to adapting an urban delta to uncertain climate changes, *Technological Forecasting and Social Change*, **77**(6), 987–98.

Walker, B., Holling, C.S., Carpenter, S.R., and Kinzig, A. (2004). Resilience, adaptability and transformability in social–ecological systems, *Ecology and Society*, **9**(2), Art. 5. Available at http://www.ecologyandsociety.org/vol9/iss2/art5 (accessed August 2018).

Wilkinson, C. (2011). Social-ecological resilience: insights and issues for planning theory, *Planning Theory*, **11**(2), 148–69.

7. Arctic urbanization: resilience in a condition of permanent instability – the case of Russian Arctic cities

Nadezhda Zamyatina and Ruslan Goncharov

Both the natural and socio-economic environment of the Arctic are characterized by strong spatio-temporal variability and high sensitivity to external influences, which has brought questions of urban sustainability to the forefront in the study of the Arctic. It is not surprising that the Arctic is an area of constant changes and constant instability. The Arctic Council on Arctic Resilience supports this notion, including this statement in a recent report: "Change – even rapid change – is the norm in the Arctic" (Arctic Council, 2016, p. ix).

Absolutely all features in the Arctic – not only natural but also socio-economic – change very rapidly: climate, marine ice conditions and permafrost regime on land, social and gender structure, economic conditions and so on. Thus, the fundamental problem of resilience studies focused on the Arctic can be formulated as a contradiction between the exceptional variability of the Arctic environment and the approach to the definition of resilience. Here it is necessary to work out new principles for studying the Arctic resilience of dynamic, internally variable natural and socio-economic systems, which in turn are integrated into dynamic networks of Arctic settlements and economic development.

7.1 RESEARCHING THE RESILIENCE OF RUSSIAN ARCTIC CITIES – THE MOTIVATION

The Arctic is increasingly faced with the phenomenon of urbanization. In a key work on social development in the Arctic, Larsen and Fondahl state that "Of Arctic countries, all but the Faroe Islands have three-quarters or more of their populations residing in urban areas. Iceland, with much of the population residing in the capital of Reykjavik and a few other urban centers, has the highest percentage of urban population of Arctic countries at 94 percent, followed by Greenland and Sweden at 86 percent" (Larsen and Fondahl, 2015, p. 6). In the Arctic zone of Russia, 89 percent of the population lives in cities, which intriguingly makes the Arctic zone the most urbanized region in the country (National Statistical Service, 2018). This puzzling statistic raises our first research question: Are the levels of urbanization of various Arctic countries and regions true and comparable between each other?

In trying to compare the level of urbanization in all Arctic countries, the researcher is faced with a major challenge – the different national criteria for defining urban settlement. To overcome these inconsistencies, it is necessary to reevaluate urbanization levels using a common set of criteria. Due to myriad differences in the statistical systems of Arctic countries and the lack of necessary data, the only universal indicator available is the population of all settlements. For the purposes of our research, we collected data about all settlements in the Arctic region and analyzed those with populations greater than 5000 inhabitants (see Section 7.3).

It should be noted that our reassessment of urbanization levels according to common criteria (referring only to a city population with more than 5000 inhabitants) gives significantly lower rates of urbanization of some Arctic territories, especially for the European Arctic, where very soft official criteria for urbanized areas are used (Table 7.1). However, this does not reduce the importance of the problem of urbanization in the Arctic; it just reflects the complexity of research on this issue and the numerous methods for estimating urbanization.

The theme of the Russian Arctic cities deserves special attention, as the region has faced the most dramatic changes in the preceding decades and continues to face them in the present (Figure 7.1).

These changes are caused by a variety of reasons: from climate change to fluctuations in state policy regarding the development of the Arctic since the 1990s. The fact that the development of natural resource deposits was accompanied by the construction of new cities during the Soviet period was, of course, supported by political motivations (the non-Russian reader can gain exposure to the topic with McCannon, 1998). After the collapse of the Soviet Union, the Russian Arctic development model was reformulated to resemble the model for the development of the American and Canadian Arctic, and shift in the methods of development occurred.

The contrast between Soviet and Russian Arctic development policies can be seen in the comparison of the Nenets and Yamal-Nenets Autonomous Districts, which are quite similar in their specialization but have different development trajectories. The development of oil fields in the Nenets Autonomous District began in the 1990s without being

Table 7.1   Reevaluation of the level of Arctic urbanization based on common criteria

Country or territory	Arctic population,* thousands of inhabitants	Reevaluation of the Arctic urban population, thousands of inhabitants	Assessment of the level of urbanization, %
Russia	2669	2086	78.2
Alaska (USA)	742	371	50.0
Norway	468	208	44.5
Iceland	333	257	77.3
Sweden	191	135	70.8
Finland	170	101	59.4
Canada	114	47	41.4
Greenland	57	22	38.9
Faroe Islands	49	13	26.4
Total	4271	3240	67.6

Note: * The boundary of the Arctic zone was set at the most southern boundary of the Arctic within different variants of its determination (see below).

Source: Authors, based on national statistics data.

accompanied by the emergence of new cities, as was the case in the Yamalo-Nenets Autonomous District some decades earlier (Table 7.2).

The rapid decline in the population of Russia's Arctic cities in the post-Soviet period casts doubt on the possibility of the existence in the Arctic of large cities with populations greater than 100,000. Examples of large cities of the non-Russian Arctic – such as Anchorage, Reykjavik or even Tromsø – are deceptive, as they are located in the most climatically favorable regions of the Arctic, where ocean currents contribute to warmer atmospheric conditions. These largest cities of the American and European Arctic are therefore categorically incompatible with the conditions of development of such cities as Norilsk and Novy Urengoy. The only Russian city climatically comparable with Anchorage and other cities of Alaska and Nordic countries is Murmansk. This makes the Arctic cities of Russia a unique phenomenon that deserves independent consideration from the viewpoint of revealing regularities of the viability of these cities.

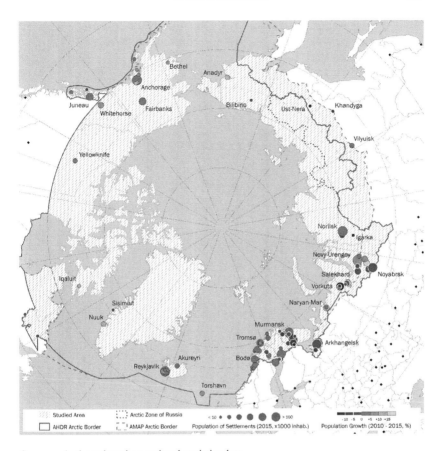

Source: Authors, based on national statistics data.

Figure 7.1 The different variants of boundaries of the Arctic, Arctic cities and the dynamics of their population, 2010–15

7.2 LITERATURE REVIEW

The theme of resilience in urban development is being explored through two main and currently unrelated directions.

On the one hand, the specific phenomenon of urban development in the Arctic is being actively studied by Russian, European and American scientists (inter alia Hansen et al., 2013; Heleniak, 2008; Jull, 2017; Laruelle, 2017; Nordregio, 2015; Orttung, 2016; Pilyasov, 2011). The study of the specifics of Arctic urban development lies, apparently, in the general trend of increasing attention to the study of regionally specific features of cities.

Table 7.2   *Soviet and post-Soviet types of settlement in resource extraction*
              regions: relative "overurbanization" of the Arctic in the Soviet
              model

Region	Post-Soviet model of development (example)	Soviet model of development (example)	Non-Russian analogues of the post-Soviet model of development of resource regions	
	Nenets autonomous *okrug* (2017)	Yamal-Nenets autonomous *okrug* (2017)	Yukon (Canada) (2016)	Northwest Territories (Canada) (2016)
The population of the administrative center, inhabitants	24 654	48 500	28 225	19 569
The population of the largest city, inhabitants	24 654	113 300	28 225	19 569
The population of the whole region, inhabitants	43 937	536 000	35 874	41 786
Area, thousands of square kilometers	177	769	475	1144

Source: Russian and Canadian National Statistical Services.

There is a natural stage in the development of interdisciplinary studies of urbanism when the limitations of "universal" approaches to city research become apparent. Analogously, in recent years, studies of tropical cities as a special phenomenon have become increasingly popular (Collier and Venables, 2017).

On the other hand, the study of resilience has experienced a research boom in recent years. Some important works that explore the principles of sustainability and viability of cities in general include Collier et al., 2014; Meerow et al., 2016; Pikea et al. 2010; Weichselgartner and Kelman, 2014, amongst others. Many researchers of regional development (geographers and economists) have contributed to the development of the theme of resilience regardless of the priorities of their own research. This was demonstrated in 2017 during the Congress of the European Association for Regional Studies which was held under the slogan "Social progress for resilience regions".

We can note here a curious trend: according to publication statistics in

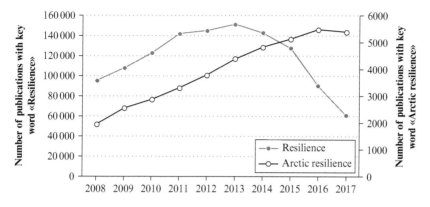

Source: Authors.

Figure 7.2   The rising popularity of Arctic resilience studies

Google Scholar (Figure 7.2), the number of publications on the topic of actual viability has declined since 2014; concurrently, the issue of viability in the Arctic (the query "Arctic resilience"), on the contrary, rose during that period and is currently at its peak of popularity (about 5000 publications annually in 2015–17).

Paradoxically, there is almost no intersection between studies on Arctic cities and studies on the stability of Arctic socio-economic systems. The theme of sustainability of the Arctic territories is mainly based on analyses of natural areas or small settlements (see, e.g., the Arctic Council's *Arctic Resilience Report*, 2016); moreover, the lacunae in Arctic urban development literature are explicitly noted in recent works (Petrov et al., 2016).

One of the few exceptions is the work of an international research group based at the University of George Washington (UGW); its first results were published in the collection by Orttung (2016). This group is currently developing a universal international sustainability index of cities in the Arctic (Suter et al., 2017). However, the UGW group focuses on international comparisons, and the Russian Arctic cities – which are currently subject to the most dramatic changes – are only tangentially addressed. Although the UGW project has produced many useful developments, there is still the need to develop fundamental principles for studying the resilience of the Russian Arctic settlements.

In particular, the issue of resilience of Arctic cities in terms of migration has not been practically developed. In the case of Arctic cities, it is clear that migration should be considered as a critical node in the study of socio-economic (non-natural) sustainability factors.

Migratory mobility of indigenous peoples is considered to be a form of their adaptation and a condition of their viability in the North (Arctic Council, 2016, p. 97). Meanwhile, in most studies on resilience, the issue of migration is not specifically considered (the exception being the mention of the risk of population growth), and in the study of the Arctic urban sustainability index mentioned above, a stable migration balance is even considered as one of the factors (and measures) of sustainability (Suter et al., 2017). Therefore, with regard to the stability of Arctic cities, the migration theme deserves more attention. Below, we consider the peculiarities of migration in Arctic cities with regard to their viability.

Due to the paradoxical nature of these Arctic settlements, we use a very simplified definition of resilience. In the first approximation, the mere existence of a city in Arctic conditions already indicates its resilience. A lack of resilience in such a severe region leads to the city's death, and there are many examples of the loss of urban resistance in the Arctic and Northern regions in general. There are numerous contemporary examples of Northern ghost towns that dramatically lost their resilience in the last two or three decades. Among them are the city of Gagnon in Canada, many towns in the Komi Republic such as Promyshlenniy (population of 15,000 people in 1979), Oktyabrsky (more than 5000 people in 1979) and others totally abandoned as well as Kadykchan (more than 5000 in 1989) and other towns in the Magadan Region. This chapter is conceived as one of the first approaches to studying the resilience of the Arctic cities and therefore considers just one of the possible aspects of resilience, namely, the study of ways of obtaining and assimilating new knowledge by Arctic urban communities.

7.3   DATA AND METHODS

The assessment of levels of urbanization in the different Arctic regions of the world presents a number of challenges.

The first problem is the border of the Arctic. The literature and legislation of different countries differentially and inconsistently define the boundaries of the Arctic. The most widely adopted are the borders defined by the Arctic Monitoring and Assessment Programme (AMAP) working committee of the Arctic Council, based primarily on natural criteria, and the boundaries of the Arctic used by the editors of the *Arctic Human Development Report* (AHDR) (Larsen and Fondahl, 2015). In Russia (where the Arctic zone makes up about a half of the Arctic territories of the world), the border of the Arctic zone (Arctic Zone of the Russian Federation – AZRF) is officially defined by decree of the President. All three boundaries are not the same and repeatedly intersect each other. Comparison and selection criteria of the Arctic border is a separate issue of interdisciplinary research, so for the purposes of the present work, the border criteria were simplified. The Arctic is defined here as an area lying to the north of the most southern (in each point) of these boundaries (AMAP, AHDR, AZRF) (see Figure 7.1).

The second problem is the absence of common assessments of urbanization levels of the Arctic territories. Different countries have different criteria for defining cities as mentioned above. For example, in Canada and Scandinavian countries, the threshold population for classifying settlements as cities is 2000. The Soviet threshold population for cities was 12,000 persons (with additional criteria regarding economic specialization), but the classification was more of a purely scientific endeavor; cities are sometimes settlements de facto with a significantly smaller population (e.g., Verkhoyansk) because of tradition. In Russia, there are no officially adopted criteria for defining cities as urban areas.

For the present study, we selected settlements with a population higher than 5000 people (similar to the methodology of the AHDR, but without regard to their functional specialization). In Russia, this initial sample included some settlements officially designated as "villages" (*poselki*) with populations greater than 5000 people (Ust-Nera, Khandyga, Purpe, Pangody and others).

The third major problem is that most of the statistics in all the countries are not attached to cities, but are fragmented statistical observations of municipal authorities, whose jurisdictional boundaries usually do not coincide with the city boundaries. We conventionally call such units "municipalities". In Russia, such municipalities are defined by the law on local self-government (Federal Law, 2003). Thus, there are three levels of administrative division: regional level; the level of municipal districts and urban municipalities (*okrugs*); and the level of urban and rural settlements. The adequate base for study are urban *okrugs* (second level) which in some cases, however, include rural settlements. The quality of statistics provided by the National Statistical Service Rosstat (as well as local statistical bodies) at the level of urban settlements (third level), as a rule, is poor.

There is also a problem with data availability – and unfortunately this forced us to reduce the final list of analyzed settlements. Official statistics in Russia correspond to the level of municipal government but not to cities as population centers. Large cities usually form their own urban municipality (so-called *gorodskoy okrug*), which have relevant statistical data. The municipal level of government includes urban municipalities and municipal districts containing mostly small settlements between cities. Our set of Arctic settlements with a population more than 5000 inhabitants contains only 19 cities that form their own urban municipality from the total number of 42 Arctic municipal bodies (except gated administrative units). Other settlements (although having the traditional status of a city such as as Nadym and Dudinka) are included in so-called municipal districts (*municipalnyie rayony*) and have authority at a sub-municipal level ("urban settlement administration"). The Russian context of fragmented sources of statistics primarily presents problems of statistical compatibility – we have comparable statistics only for the municipal units of the Russian administrative division ("urban municipalities" and "municipal districts"), but not for "urban settlements" within the boundaries of the municipal districts.

We decided to extend the basis of the study for some comparisons and to use data not only on urban municipalities but also on municipal districts in some cases. We decided to use statistics on those municipal districts that include Arctic settlements not designated as urban municipalities if the following conditions are met: (1) the population of such a settlement is more than 5000 residents and (2) it forms at least half of the population of the municipal district in which this settlement is included. Thus, we assumed that such settlements could be considered as local centers, providing services to surrounding populated places. Such conditions are quite common for towns forming urban municipalities.

Some of the Arctic settlements of the selected dataset resembling urban municipalities were excluded from the survey on the basis of criterion 2 – there are cities and towns that constitute less than half the population of the municipal districts within which they are located (e.g., the city of Viluysk, the settlements of Iskateley and Khandyga).

Our final list of Russian Arctic cities contained 29 entities (including 19 cities designated as "urban municipalities" and ten cities as "urban" municipal districts).

To reach our research goal to demonstrate the unique peculiarities of Arctic cities in terms of their knowledge adaptation capacity, we selected their counterparts within the main settlement area of Russia (most densely settled area) in order to compare and contrast these two modes of urban development. Our research idea is based on a hypothesized significant difference between the Arctic and "Southern" cities. The latter group is the collective name for "classical, typical cities".

The methodology for defining analogues was based on methods of comparative and similarity analysis of our pre-selected Arctic settlements and the whole dataset of Southern cities, for which we found comparable statistical data. To improve the objectivity of the results for each Arctic city, its city counterpart was, firstly, selected from the main settlement area of Russia and, secondly, met the following criteria of similarity to the particular Northern city: total population (via official data); the structure of employment by economic sector (via official data); and geographical location (in particular, proximity to the marine coastline) (via instruments of spatial analysis).

The main component of our methodology is a tool for similarity analysis, which performs a z-transformation for all incoming attributes and ranks the objects from the joined sample according to the degree of similarity with each object of the target sample. We used our set of Arctic cities (29 units) as the target dataset and the cities from the main settlement area as the joined dataset (more than 400 in total). Distance between cities was not considered in finding analogues to Arctic settlements. After automated completion analysis, an expert analysis of each received pair was conducted for the correction of results. The same methods were used for finding pairs for "urban municipalities" and "urban" municipal districts.

The main result of this research stage was 29 pairs of similar settlements in the Arctic and in the main settlement area, which formed the basis of further research.

7.4   RESULTS

Migration mobility is apparently one of the most important aspects of life of the Arctic urban settlements. We studied it from different points of view.

In the study of population, mobility refers to the magnitude of changes in the population of Arctic cities. In just five years (2011–15), the population of many of them changed in either direction by 5 to 10 percent (see Figure 7.1). Special studies confirm this observation. We assessed the overall mobility of the urban population M using the following formula:

$$M = (IN + OUT) / P,   \text{7.1}$$

where P is the city population at the end of the reporting year, IN is the in-migration flow for the same year, and OUT is out-going flow.

The analysis of our dataset showed that the average value of the mobility of the population for Northern cities was 9.8 percent in 2015 (in other words, migration processes involved almost every tenth resident of the "typical" Arctic city). For their Southern counterparts, the value of this indicator was only 5.8 percent. The average mobility rate over a five-year period (2011–15) showed similar results of 9.9 percent for the Arctic cities and 5.4 percent for the Southern analogues. Thus, the analysis of a broader range of data demonstrates an even more significant "separation" of Northern cities from their Southern analogues. It should be noted that we analyzed the statistical significance of all identified patterns using standard statistical methods, in particular, the Kolmogorov-Smirnov test, F-test and T-tests and all statistical differences of our data samples are representative (with p-value less than 0.0001).

One of the most interesting observations is that Arctic cities almost always have two-way flows of migration, regardless of whether they have a growing or decreasing population in the total calculation. We segregated the group of top Arctic cities losing their population. Eleven Arctic cities lost more than 1.0 percent of their population in 2015: these are the cities of Ust-Nera, Novy Urengoy, Nadym, Vorkuta, Dudinka, Muravlenko, Noyabrsk, Onega, Kovdor, Labytnangi and Murmansk. During the same year, each of these "shrinking" cities received an influx of migrants, which, on average for this group of cities, was 5.3 percent (from 2.4 percent in Onega to 9.0 percent in Novy Urengoy; Table 7.3). The example of Novy Urengoy is extraordinary: almost a tenth of its residents newly arrived in this "shrinking" city.

Similar data are also observed for other years: high inflows and high outflows characterize almost all Arctic cities.

Similarly, the fastest growing Arctic cities not only receive, but also lose population. For example, the city of Naryan-Mar, which grew by 1.4 percent in 2015, "acquired" 5.4 percent and simultaneously lost 4.0 percent of its population. "Stable" in the same year, the city of Arkhangelsk acquired and simultaneously lost about 2.7 percent of its population – that is, more than 9500 people.

Thus, an important feature of the Arctic cities is the constant "flowing" or "churning" mode of their migration. The rise or loss of population here is the result not of a radical "reversal" of trends, but only a shift in the unstable balance in one direction or another.

The picture observed in the Southern analogues is greatly flattened. For 2015, we chose the "top" declining cities, which lost at least 0.5 percent of their population. They also both acquired and lost population, but on average, this group of cities acquired 2.8 percent and lost 3.4 percent. These figures show that the population churn regime in Southern settlements was significantly weaker than in the Arctic. Most of these cities received no more than 3.0 percent of their population, except Southern Siberian cities like Slyudyanka and Tashtagol (it can be assumed that Arctic tendencies are also characteristic of Southern Siberia). The situation for other time periods is the same (at least during the last decade).

Another characteristic of the mobility of the population of Arctic cities

Table 7.3   Formally "shrinking" cities in the Arctic and the South, 2015

	Arctic cities				Southern cities		
Name	% of total loss of population	% of arrivals in relation to the general population	% of retirees in relation to the general population	Name	% of total loss of population	% of arrivals in relation to the general population	% of retirees in relation to the general population
Ust-Nera	-4.7	6.2	11	Berezniki	-0.9	1.2	2.1
Novy Urengoy	-4.7	9	13.7	Slyudyanka	-0.8	6.3	7.1
Nadym	-2.7	7.2	9.9	Desnogorsk	-0.8	2.4	3.2
Vorkuta	-2.2	4.9	7.1	Krasnoturinsk	-0.8	2.5	3.3
Dudinka	-1.7	4.9	6.5	Leninogorsk	-0.7	2	2.7
Muravlenko	-1.6	6.3	7.9	Michurinsk	-0.7	2.7	3.4
Noyabrsk	-1.5	4.6	6.2	Asbestos	-0.5	2.9	3.4
Onega	-1.5	2.4	3.9	Kamensk-Shakhtinsky	-0.5	1.6	2.1
Kovdor	-1.4	3.9	5.3	Tashtagol	-0.5	3.6	4.1
Labytnangi	-1.3	5.1	6.4	Astrakhan	-0.5	2.9	3.4
Murmansk	-1.3	3.8	5.1	Krasnobrodsky	-0.9	1.2	2.1
Average	-2.2	5.7	7.5	Average	-0.7	2.8	3.4

Source: Russian National Statistical Service.

Table 7.4   Percentage of long-distant migrations, 2016

Cities	In-migration from the external region, %	Out-migration to the external region, %
Arctic cities	67.9	71.3
Southern cities	44.4	45.2

Source: Russian National Statistical Service.

is the predominance of long-distant migration flows above other types of population flows (Table 7.4).

7.5   DISCUSSION

The Arctic cities share a significant common feature – high flows of both incoming and outgoing migration. This shows that the overall stability of the population is not a sign of resilience, it is a state of unstable equilibrium, and the fragile balance of thousands of migrants entering and leaving the city every year can easily move in any direction.

Moreover, significant fluctuations in the population are likely to be recognized as the natural state of Arctic cities. The increase in their stability should then depend on their ability to adapt to constant fluctuations in the population. There should be social, architectural, urban and other mechanisms that enable this adaptation. It is quite obvious, for example, that the construction of large concrete blocks of housing does not facilitate the rapid adaptation of a city to a decrease in population. Their construction and dismantling in arctic conditions are more expensive in comparison with lighter structures (Figures 7.3 and 7.4). For example, construction of the buildings in the photos started at a time when the city's population was projected to increase, but its growth suddenly stopped.

Significant changes in the population of a city create significant problems for its resilience. Thus, large flows of incoming migration create a load on infrastructure and a shortage of adequate housing and so on. But large flows of outgoing migration are also undesirable. In addition to the fall in the total volume of human and socio-economic capital, large volumes of outgoing migration create emptiness in the urban space that reduces the level of proximity, the possibilities for close interaction and increases the operating cost of urban communications that cross large "empty" areas. Finally, the unaesthetic appearance of such voids reduces the quality of the urban environment as a whole.

However, keeping the population at low volumes of both incoming

Source: Zamyatina (2013).

Figure 7.3   Unfinished residential buildings in Norilsk-Oganer District

and outgoing migration, and keeping the population at high volumes of incoming and outgoing migration should be viewed as fundamentally qualitatively different city conditions in comparison to stable population in both cases. The large volume of incoming migration, even if it is compensated by the outflow of migrants, inevitably creates problems of adaptation for those arriving in the urban community. The Arctic cities of Russia demonstrate this problem not less dramatically than do the large cities of Western Europe.

We should not forget about migration as a potential source of innovation – high migration turnover (while maintaining the total population) can be a positive factor for the development of the city. The innovations needed to ensure the resilience of the Arctic communities must be exactly in line with the specific Arctic requirements. However, migrants often carry their stereotypes and institutional factors formed in other regions of the Arctic, and often they do not contribute to the resilience in the Arctic. The situation is essentially the same as that described by Collier in relation to migrants from underdeveloped countries to developed countries. Migrants bring to the Arctic rigid behavioral attitudes that (albeit pertinent in extra-arctic

Source: Zamyatina (2013).

Figure 7.4   Unfinished residential buildings in Norilsk-Oganer District

conditions) inhibit resilience in the Arctic (Collier, 2013). The preference for high-rise housing "as in Moscow" is one of the most typical stereotypes (here the authors rely on many years of experience in the Arctic as consultants to city governments).

Migration by itself is not automatically a guarantee of "innovation". At one time, Soviet researchers identified two psychological types of migrants: some went to the North in the hope of "finding themselves" under severe conditions and were ready for internal changes. Others had already established behavioral attitudes that they brought with them (Razinskii, 1985). Therefore, it is necessary to study the behavioral attitudes of migrants, their identity and other institutional factors for further research on the connection between innovation and migration. It is the psychological mood of migrants (and not just quantitative indicators) that seems to be the key factor for stability in conditions of constantly fluctuating, large-scale migration flows.

7.6 CONCLUSIONS

The most prominent feature that distinguishes the Arctic cities from their Southern counterparts is high migration mobility. All Arctic cities (even those with a declining population) constantly experience both population outflow and inflow. The stability of the city population in the Arctic is the result of an unstable equilibrium.

Sustainability in the Arctic should, therefore, be ensured through the adaptation of local communities not only to harsh natural conditions but also to constant fluctuations in migration flows. In particular, we refer to the flexibility and adaptability of the urban environment and the housing stock of Northern cities.

The role of migrants in this aspect is twofold. On the one hand, large volumes of both incoming and outgoing migration create a special burden on the urban infrastructure. On the other hand, migrants can be described as potential carriers of innovation. However, migrants coming to the Arctic usually have more conservative behavioral attitudes than Arctic resilience requires. How much they promote resilience in many respects, apparently, will depend on behavioral attitudes and on the image of the Arctic city.

REFERENCES

Arctic Council (2016), *Arctic Resilience Report*, ed. M. Carson and G. Peterson. Stockholm: Stockholm Environment Institute and Stockholm Resilience Centre. Accessed 30 January 2018 at http://www.arctic-council.org/arr

Collier, F., Hambling, J., Kernaghan, S. et al. (2014), Tomorrow's cities: a framework to assess urban resilience, *Proceedings of the Institution of Civil Engineers: Urban Design and Planning*, **167** (2), 79–91.

Collier, Paul (2013), *Exodus: How Migration is Changing Our World*. Oxford and New York: Oxford University Press.

Collier, P. and Venables, A. (2017), Urbanization in developing economies: the assessment, *Oxford Review of Economic Policy*, **33** (3), 355–72.

Federal Law (2003), On General Principles of Organization of Local Self-government in the Russian Federation of October 6, 2003, No. 131-FZ. Accessed 30 January 2018 at http://www.consultant.ru/document/cons_doc_LAW_44571/6d3b1321c4f9966d07ca33533fc7ca347581c3a8/ (in Russian).

Hansen K., Rasmussen, R., and Weber, R. (eds) (2013), Nordregio Working Paper No. 6. In *Proceedings of the First International Conference on Urbanisation*, Arctic Conference, Ilimmarfik, Nuuk, Greenland, 28–30 August 2012.

Heleniak, Timothy (2008), Changing settlement patterns across the Russian north at the turn of the millennium. In M. Tykkylainen and V. Rautio (eds), *Russia's Northern Regions on the Edge: Communities, Industries and Populations from Murmansk to Magadan*. Helsinki: Kikimora Publications and University of Helsinki, pp. 25–52.

Jull, Matthew (2017), The improbable city: adaptations of an Arctic metropolis, *Polar Geography*, **40** (4), 291–305.

Larsen, J. and Fondahl, G. (eds) (2015), *Arctic Human Development Report: Regional Processes and Global Linkages*. Copenhagen: Nordisk Ministerråd.

Laruelle, Marlene (ed.) (2017), *New Mobilities and Social Changes in Russia's Arctic Regions*. London and New York: Routledge.

McCannon, John (1998), *Red Arctic: Polar Exploration and the Myth of the North in the Soviet Union, 1932–1939*. New York: Oxford University Press.

Meerow, S., Newell, J. and Stults, M. (2016), Defining urban resilience: a review. *Landscape and Urban Planning*, **147**, 38–49.

National Statistical Service (2018). Accessed 30 January 2018 at https://gks.ru

Nordregio (2015), City-region planning for everyday life. Experiences from four Nordic city-regions. NORDREGIO Policy brief No.7. Accessed 30 January 2018 at http://www.nordregio.se/en/Publications/Publications-2015/City-region-planning-for-everyday-life/.

Orttung, Robert (ed.) (2016), *Sustaining Russia's Arctic Cities: Resource Politics, Migration, and Climate Change*. New York: Berghahn Books.

Petrov, Andrey, BurnSilver, S., Chapin III, S. et al. (2016), *Arctic Sustainability Research: Past, Present and Future*. London: Routledge.

Pikea, A., Dawleya, S., and Tomaney, J. (2010), Resilience, adaptation and adaptability, *Cambridge Journal of Regions, Economy and Society*, **3** (1), 1–12.

Pilyasov, Alexander (2011), Towns of the Russian Arctic: comparison of the economic indicators, *Vestnik Moskovskogo Universiteta, Seriya 5: Geografiya*, **4**, 64–9 (in Russian).

Razinskii, G.V. (1985), Obraz zhizni naseleniia Noril'skogo promyshlennogo raion.

In V.V. Sartakov (ed.), *Problemy sovershenstvovaniia obraza zhizni v usloviiakh Severa* (Way of life of inhabitants of the Norilsk industrial area). Krasnoiarsk: Krasnoiarsk University Press, pp. 41–56 (in Russian).

Suter, Luis, Schaffner, C., Giddings, C., Orttung, R., Streletskiy, D. (2017), *Developing Metrics to Guide Sustainable Development of Arctic Cities: Progress & Challenges*. Arctic Yearbook. Akureyri, Iceland: Northern Research Forum.

Weichselgartner, J. and Kelman, I. (2014), Geographies of resilience: challenges and opportunities of a descriptive concept, *Progress in Human Geography*, **39** (3), 1–19.

Zamyatina, Nadezhda (2013), Kreativnyy klass, simvolicheskiy kapital i territoriya (Creative class, symbolic capital and territory), *Obshchestvennyye nauki i sovremennost*, **4**, 130–9 (in Russian).

PART III

Policy prevention and recovery analysis:
simulations and scenario building

8. Urban resilience and the politics of scale

Mojgan Taheri Tafti

Almost 35 years ago Rittel and Webber described urban planning problems as wicked, because of the inherent intractability of defining and
locating 'the problem' in cities. Urban planning policies and practices
aimed at building or enhancing resilience against specific disasters are
exemplars of such observations. Firstly, defining the problem, for example,
weak resilience, is difficult, as resilience is intrinsically linked to deeply
rooted socio-economic and political issues. In the social world of cities,
Davoudi et al. (2012) argue 'resilience has as much to do with shaping the
challenges we face as responding to them' (p. 306). Secondly, it is difficult
to locate 'the problem' and, therefore, the spatial boundaries and scales of
interventions for enhancing resilience are ill-defined. Interventions that
target one locality might have repercussions for other areas or across scales.
As Chelleri et al. (2015, p. 182) argue, 'trade-offs of enhancing resilience
at one scale or in one time for other scales, time periods or other systems
is poorly understood'. In the light of these two points, Rittel and Webber
(1973) suggest that urban problems rely upon elusive political judgement
for a 'resolution'. In the context of urban resilience policies and practices,
the entrenchment of political judgement for a resolution has been the
central concern of the politics of urban resilience (e.g., Coaffee, 2013;
White and O'Hare, 2014).

Seeking to contribute to the literature on the politics of urban resilience,
in this chapter I aim to explore how defining and locating the 'problem' of
enhancing urban resilience as a wicked problem in urban policies can carry
significant implications for other scales or areas. I focus on urban resilience
against earthquakes in Tehran, one of the most populous metropolitan
areas in the world, exposed to major earthquakes. Looking at a number
of policies and practices aimed at enhancing resilience in the city, I will
explain the re-articulation of meaning and scale in operationalizing and
translating resilience into urban policies and practices and the conflicts
and contradictions they entail. In particular, I will argue that determining
the scale and delineating the areas of policy intervention for enhancing

resilience are central to the politics of urban resilience. Locating and delineating the boundaries of such interventions are often based on vested interests, accompanied by techno-managerial policies and practices, which underpin existing priorities and programmes and accentuate pre-existing socio-spatial inequalities. Shi et al. (2016, p.132) suggest that examining how scalar and spatial dimensions of such policies and practices entrench or redress social inequality should be the first step towards identifying pathways to more transformative policies of urban resilience and adaptation.

In pursuing this argument, the rest of the chapter is organized as follows. In the first section, I draw on emerging debates on the politics of urban resilience and explain the analytical lens through which policies and practices of urban resilience against earthquakes in Tehran are examined. The next section describes the Tehran metropolitan region in terms of its exposure to, and vulnerability against, earthquakes. This sets the scene for the introduction of a major policy response for enhancing the resilience of the city against an anticipated earthquake. Locating and delineating boundaries in urban resilience policies in this case involve three levels: the first level involves 'the city' itself; the chapter explains how Tehran and its hazardscape is empirically, discursively and legally constructed by omitting its peripheral areas. The next level involves identifying 'deteriorated areas' within Tehran and the ramifications of the policies concerned with these areas for other areas and scales. The third level is the level of buildings. White and O'Hare (2014, p.934) argue that resilience within spatial planning leaves unaddressed 'wider sociocultural concerns and instead emerges as a narrow, regressive, techno-rational frame centred on reactive measures *at the building scale*' (emphasis added). This focus at the building scale is dominant in cases of urban earthquakes, reflecting one of the most familiar mantras in the field: 'earthquakes don't kill people, buildings do' (England and Jackson, 2011). Such understanding reduces the causes of earthquake-related fatalities and destruction to technical issues, sidelining the socio-economic factors behind the inaccessibility of safe construction technologies to the affected population. This inquiry about defining boundaries for promoting urban resilience raises serious concerns over justice and the right to live in a safe environment.

8.1   POLITICS OF URBAN RESILIENCE

The politics of urban resilience has been a major concern of academic writings on the social dimensions of resilience (Meerow and Newell, 2016). This body of work debates how the ill-defined and hence excessively malleable concept of urban resilience can be interpreted within a technical-reductionist framework in urban policies and practices (Vale, 2014; Weichselgartner and Kelman, 2015). The ambiguity of the term, these studies warn, can make it an 'empty signifier which can be filled to justify almost any ends' (Davoudi et al., 2012, p. 329) and in particular makes it liable to capture by vested interests (Fainstein, 2015; Vale, 2014).

Three interrelated concerns underpin the politics of urban resilience, all of which revolve around the issue of how framing urban resilience in policies and practices can lead to depoliticization of such interventions. The first concern relates to the question of 'resilience to what?' and the critical differences between the equilibrist and evolutionary interpretations of resilience in addressing this question (White and O'Hare, 2014). The equilibrist interpretation suggests a seemingly technical view of bouncing back to the status quo, while the evolutionary interpretation seeks to address the 'resilience to what?' question through aspiring to a deliberative transformation of the existing condition (Davoudi et al., 2012). Therefore, policies adopting these different normative interpretations have contrasting aims and outcomes (White and O'Hare, 2014). But even the evolutionary views of urban resilience are under increasing attacks (Fainstein, 2015; Kaika, 2017) because of the problems inherent in applying ecological concepts into the social world in this perspective. This problem can be conducive to constraining urban policies and practices within a technocratic mode and depoliticizing consequent urban transformations (Wilkinson, 2012).

The second concern relates to the question of 'how to frame resilience?'. Chelleri et al. (2015, p. 181) point out that resilience is often simplified as the opposite of vulnerability, undermining the social dimensions of the former, such as social learning, the willingness and capacity to self-organization and to transform organizational, material and policy frameworks (Zaidi and Pelling, 2015). Resilience from this perspective is framed as a specific product of a certain place and time period. But more importantly, current translations of the term resilience in urban policies and practices, according to Kaika (2017, p. 1), seem to prepare citizens and environments 'to take larger doses of inequality and degradation in the future', while doing little towards alleviating them. In these policies, urban resilience is increasingly conceptualized and measured through 'old methodological tools', which inevitably involves depoliticized, techno-managerial solutions, such as smart cities (Kaika, 2017).

The third concern relates to the question of 'resilience for whom?'. A number of studies have criticized the resilience literature, policies and practices for their insufficient attention to the issue of power (Cote and Nightingale, 2012; Davoudi et al., 2012; Wilkinson, 2012). Policies and practices of building and enhancing resilience often assume a universal benefit from enhancing urban resilience (Fainstein, 2015), which depoliticizes such interventions (Kaika, 2017). In the light of these concerns, a growing number of studies have highlighted the importance of unpacking normative questions such as 'resilience for whom?' in examining and scrutinizing resilience policies (Cote and Nightingale, 2012; Cretney, 2014; Meerow and Newell, 2016; Turner, 2014; Vale, 2014). While hazard literature has long paid attention to the root causes of risk, including inequality and poverty (e.g., Wisner et al., 2004), resilience thinking is still in a transitional phase from a descriptive concept to a normative agenda (Weichselgartner and Kelman, 2015).

These concerns notably are relevant when considering urban policies and practices for building or enhancing resilience in the context of cities. In their review of European policies and legislations, White and O'Hare (2014) argue that these policies have largely focused on the less challenging engineering and technical perspectives. These policies, they argue, are characterized by a 'simple return to normality that is more analogous with planning norms, engineered responses, dominant interests and techno-managerial trends', leaving unaddressed wider socio-cultural concerns (p. 934). Similarly, Walker and Salt (2012, p. 63) suggest 'when you hear managers and planners using the term resilience they may be thinking about engineering resilience in which the aim is to bounce back quickly to business as usual following a small disturbance'. In the context of cities of developing economies, adopting such views can arguably be irrelevant to the local realities and risks that urban residents face on a daily basis (Ziervogel et al., 2017).

In spite of the above-mentioned concerns over applying the concept of resilience to cities, most critical thinkers suggest that the concept still retains promise and significant potential to change mind-sets (Vale, 2014; Wilkinson, 2012). Rather than viewing the ambiguity of the term as problematic, Davoudi et al. (2012) see it as an opportunity, suggesting a reframing of the concept in ways that allow us to identify values and political pathways to pursue it. This reframing of urban resilience involves adopting a progressive view attentive to the questions of social justice and rights (Fainstein, 2015; Vale, 2014; Ziervogel et al., 2017), the root causes of risk (Weichselgartner and Kelman, 2015) and 'the practices that created the need to build resilience in the first place' (Kaika, 2017, p. 10).

This reframing of the concept implies embracing the politics of resilience. The politics of resilience, in this sense, 'is central to what the term has to offer' (Davoudi et al., 2012, p. 309). It involves questioning how dominant storylines on urban resilience are constructed (Vale, 2014), how they are applied to repackage the existing practices and reproduce power positions and how they assume that everyone will benefit if resilience is enhanced, disguising who is getting what (Fainstein, 2015). In reality, resilience building policies and practices might even further entrench vulnerabilities and socio-economic impoverishment (Shi et al., 2016).

8.2 SCALE, BOUNDARIES AND THE POLITICS OF URBAN RESILIENCE

One of the dimensions through which urban resilience politics is playing out relates to the ways policies and practices concerned with enhancing urban resilience define – and justify – the scale and boundaries of their interventions. Research concerning the scale of interventions for building or enhancing urban resilience is scant (Shi et al., 2016). In the context of resilience to climate change, most of the academic and grey literature as well as existing policies adopt a local framing of resilience and adaptation-related interventions (Nalau et al., 2015). To this, one can add institutional frameworks such as the budgetary, regulatory and governance structures that often prioritize a focus on local scale framing of 'problems' and 'solutions'. This is also the case in resilience policies and practices concerned with other types of risk (Chelleri et al., 2015).

The locally framed resilience interventions, however, might produce or transfer a negative spill-over impact at other scales or other areas (Chelleri et al., 2015; Corfee-Morlot et al., 2011). They can also carry implications in terms of justice, by producing and accentuating socio-economic inequalities or vulnerabilities (Shi et al., 2016). As Leichenko (2011) argues:

> Studies identify situations where promotion of resilience for some locations may come at the expense of others, or enhancement of resilience at one scale, such as the level of the community may reduce resilience at another scale, such as the household or individual. (p. 166)

Choices about the appropriate scale of interventions are essentially political choices (Shi et al., 2016). These choices and demarcating boundaries for urban resilience policies and programmes are politically and socially constructed and discursively justified by embedding 'scientific knowledge' into policy discourses. At the same time, these choices often reflect the same socio-political processes that shape the root causes of vulnerability and urban inequalities (Shi et al., 2016). As a result, local framing of resilience policies not only limits the potential to address justice, but also carries implications in terms of resilience at other scales or areas. This adds to the concern that the socio-spatial implications of these policies are not universal even within the identified boundaries.

In this chapter, I would like to contribute to this ongoing discussion by exploring in detail the politics of defining scale and demarcating boundaries for urban resilience policies and their implications at other scales or areas. The following sections explain the context, policies and politics of urban resilience against earthquakes in Tehran.

8.3   METHODS

The chapter draws on fieldwork data collection, conducted in 2016–17 in Tehran. Given that this research focuses on the issue of scale and demarcating boundaries for urban resilience policies, data collection concerned three scales; Tehran metropolitan region, Tehran municipality area and neighbourhoods. For the first two, the main sources of data consisted of policy documents, reports of the Iranian Urban Development and Revitalization Corporation, the Urban Renewal Organization of Tehran, census data from 1996 to 2011 and other secondary sources.

Regarding the scale of neighbourhood, data collection focused on one neighbourhood, namely, Farahzad. Data collection for this neighbourhood involved conducting semi-structured interviews, on-site mapping, archival review as well as examining planning documents including the latest version of the planning document of the neighbourhood (2015). Interviews were conducted with four municipality staff, 16 residents, two neighbourhood representatives and the manager of a non-governmental organization active in the Farahzad neighbourhood.

8.4   TEHRAN AND ITS HAZARDSCAPE

Between 1900 and 2013, the Iranian plateau experienced about 17 earthquakes with M7.0 or higher, which killed more than 164,000 people; that is, 1577 persons per year on average (Berberian, 2014, p. xlvi). Tehran metropolitan area, with a day-time population of around 12 million, is built on the active faults (Berberian, 2014, p. xlvi). Although other major issues, such as an alarming air pollution level and a prolonged drought, are posing significant risks to Tehranians, the frequent occurrence of massive earthquakes in the country has made them more self-conscious about their relationships with their shaky grounds.

In Tehran, the interrelated web of socio-ecological relations has brought about highly uneven urban environments: a dramatic height difference in the city has played a major role in shaping the physical and social characteristics of the city. In the context of the hot, arid climate of Tehran, the northern foothills with a more moderate climate and more rainfall have been colonized by the better off, while the poor have occupied the dry and hot areas close to the desert (Madanipour, 1999). Throughout the last two centuries political, economic and ecological processes have worked together to shape and reinforce sharp socio-spatial differences between the wealthy northern areas and majority poor areas of the south.

The uneven development has been even sharper when comparing areas inside and outside the municipality boundaries. Outside the municipality boundaries, immigrants from rural areas, war-torn areas and Afghanistan have shaped rapidly growing informal settlements around the city. Between 1976 and 1996, for instance, these settlements took up 40 per cent of the population growth in the Tehran metropolitan region (5 million people). In recent decades and in addition to this movement, out-migration from areas inside the municipality boundaries to these settlements has been taking place, due to increasing land and housing prices. Zebardast (2006) found that one-third of the population in these settlements were former residents of the city.

These settlements, however, provide better living conditions compared to most countries of the global south. Over 90 per cent of them are connected to the water and electricity networks, albeit mostly with the authorities turning a blind eye to illegal activities or sometimes with the agreement of the government for tapping into the existing network (Piran, 1987). Furthermore, these areas – except for rare cases – do not involve squatting on private land; rather, their practices of land transfer, subdivision and land use changes are located outside the legal/formal frameworks of the country (Zebardast, 2006).

In contrast to the marked spatial differences in terms of socio-ecological formation between the north and south of the city, the exposure to earthquakes is more evenly distributed. Major active faults of Tehran are located in both the north (North Tehran Fault) and south of the city (North and South Ray Fault). Nevertheless, the difference between the northern and southern areas as well as areas inside and outside the municipality boundaries in terms of the vulnerability of the social and built environment is significant. Figure 8.1, for instance, illustrates this contrast in terms of the percentage of housing with very low quality materials and construction techniques. It demonstrates the production of the uneven geography of vulnerability inside and outside the municipality boundaries. In line with Swyngedouw and Heynen (2003), in the Tehran metropolitan region urban resilience has been shaped and reshaped in the historical-geographical processes of production and reproduction of the urban environment.

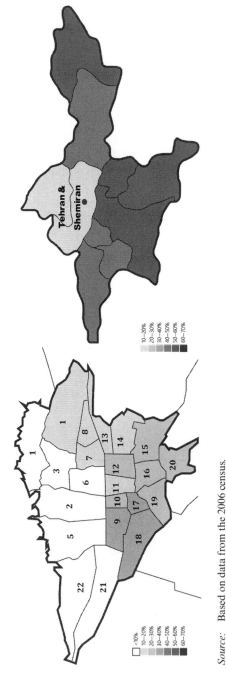

Source: Based on data from the 2006 census.

Figure 8.1 The percentage of housing with very low quality materials and construction techniques and its distribution among the 22 districts of Tehran – Tehran municipality area (right); areas between the municipality boundaries (left)

162

8.5   CONSTRUCTING THE BOUNDARIES OF TEHRAN'S HAZARDSCAPE

In this section I will explain the construction of the boundaries of Tehran's hazardscape in resilience-related policies and programmes. Arguably, the most important representation of hazardscape in the case of Tehran is a seismic risk assessment study conducted by the Japan International Cooperation Agency (JICA, 2000). The report was based on a detailed mapping of the urban landscape to make risk governable. This representation of Tehran's hazardscape manifests the abstract and conceptual depictions of 'Tehran' on the one hand and the logic, abstract understandings and forms of knowledge about seismic risk and hazards on the other.

The JICA report considered 'Tehran' as the area inside Tehran's municipality boundaries (comprising 22 districts), ignoring all settlements located on the urban periphery. As Hourcade (1997) highlights, these urban peripheries do not exist, neither in the image that Tehranians have of their city nor in the representations of the city as in its maps and plans. Tehran Disaster Mitigation and Management Organization also chiefly defines its territorial responsibility within Tehran's 22 districts. The sporadic, disjointed programmes of this organization for enhancing urban resilience in Tehran, such as the Davam plan (local volunteer groups for emergency response), are confined to the same area. Officials in their interviews after two weak earthquakes in 2017 were overwhelmingly concerned with Tehran's municipality boundaries, its exposure and vulnerability. While these events have made the relationships between people and their landscape self-conscious, general public imagination of an earthquake-devastated Tehran concerned the collapse of high-rise buildings of the north and middle-class housing, undermining the highly fragile settlements located outside the municipality boundaries.

Tehran's hazardscape, therefore, is empirically, discursively and legally constructed by omitting the peripheral areas. This does not mean that inside this imagined Tehran, the city and its residents are 'resilient'. Far from it, the knowledge produced by the JICA report was not used for developing a risk governance plan or a coherent programme for enhancing the city's resilience. Nevertheless, the defined boundaries signify a right to live in a safer environment for those inside Tehran's 22 districts compared to those living beyond this boundary. It also shows a scalar mismatch between a risk-related situation and existing regulations and programmes.

8.6 THE MARKET-LED ENHANCEMENT OF RESILIENCE

Within the municipal boundaries of Tehran new boundaries were demarcated for the implementation of policies and programmes aimed at – among other goals – enhancing urban resilience. The demarcated areas in cities are called 'deteriorated urban areas'. The renovation of these areas has been subject to a series of policies and programmes during the past 15 years. The latest of these policies is the 'National Strategy Document on Revitalizing, Upgrading, Renovating and Enabling Deteriorated and Underutilized Urban Fabrics' (2014). One of the main goals of the policy is mentioned as 'enhancing the safety, quality and durability of *buildings*' (emphasis added). The Ministry of Interior (2010) described the renovation and revitalization of these areas as the most effective way of enhancing resilience against earthquakes.

The Urban Renewal Organization of Tehran (UROT) highlights the Bam earthquake as a turning point in its policies concerned with the deteriorated urban areas. On 26 December 2003 a major earthquake registering 6.6 on the Richter scale devastated the city of Bam in south-east Iran. With a population of 104,469, the city's death toll was 23,503. The catastrophe destroyed 80 per cent of all buildings in the city and left 75,600 people in the city and surrounding villages homeless. Since the earthquake, resilience has entered the lexicon of the urban officials and urban renewal policies in the country. Ever since, the occurrence of every earthquake in cities – including one measuring 5.2 on the Richter scale in Tehran during the time of writing this chapter – has been an opportunity for authorities to highlight the importance of the renewal of 'deteriorated urban areas' as the most unsafe areas of cities. In fact, the Bam earthquake provided a much needed justification and impetus to the process of urban renewal of inner cities. Within a few months after the Bam earthquake, the City Council of Tehran introduced additional development incentives (e.g., higher Floor Area Ratio (FAR) level) for private sector developers in order to speed up the slow process of urban renewal in the city.

These urban renewal policies were dubbed as 'green earthquake' to discursively connect policies to the fear of an earthquake. Altheide (2006, p. 418) describes such discursive construction of fear as politics of fear, which means the promotion and use of the audience's belief and assumptions about danger, risk and fear to achieve certain goals. My argument is not about denying the existence of fear nor downplaying the necessity of raising awareness about a foreseeable earthquake among people. Instead, I am interested in fear being manipulated by those who seek to benefit from it for other purposes (Altheide, 2006, p. 418). This was the case in replacing the previous urban renewal policies that were unsuccessful with almost similar policies and programmes, repackaged through instigating fear. This fear, however, was soon replaced by people's fear of the consequences of these policies for their lifestyles.

According to these policies, locating and delineating 'deteriorated urban areas' have relied on three criteria: (1) the percentage of impervious road networks, measured based on roads narrower than 6 metres; (2) the percentage of fragile buildings, measured based on buildings aged 20 years and older; and (3) the percentage of fine-grained parcels of land, measured based on plots smaller than 200 square metres. Even inside these delineated boundaries, there is another set of boundaries, though invisible in the built environment. These new boundaries are delineated between parcels of land with and without formal ownership registration.

Relying on financial and development incentives to private developers and owners, the introduced policies intended to renovate these 'deteriorated areas' through widening roads and consolidating urban parcels of land. This means those currently living in one- or two-storey buildings with private courtyards in small parcels of land could not renovate their housing unless they consolidate their parcels of land with those of their neighbours to build apartment blocks. This often takes place through a joint venture with a private developer. Such movement would be indispensably associated with changes in habits and ways of living, particularly those concerning the use of space for livelihood purposes. As one of the residents says, 'They said this is a green earthquake. It is worse than a real earthquake . . . These people have never lived in apartments.' Furthermore, for those who moved to newly built apartments, such moves did not necessarily change their perception of risk. The reason is the general distrust of developers, who are often scornfully called *besaz-bendaz* (build and pass off), in adhering to and applying the country's seismic building code, accompanied by widespread corruption in the country's construction industry.

What is clearly related to the issue of boundaries, scale and politics of resilience is the displacement of low-income renters in the process of urban renewal in the demarcated areas. No provision was made for replacing the lost affordable rental housing in these areas. According to MRU (2014), however, more than half of the low-income renters in the country are living in the identified deteriorated urban areas. This comes as no surprise, as these urban areas provide an affordable rental housing solution for people. This is especially the case in Tehran, where the average rental price in district 18 with the lowest rental prices in Tehran was 100.6 per cent of the average income for the lowest income decile in 2010 (Shahr and Andisheh Pars, 2014). The displaced low-income renters, therefore, have little option but to move to the urban periphery.

While the property-led renewal of 'deteriorated urban areas' is creating a built environment that would perform better in the wake of an earthquake, it creates by nature a different socio-spatial setting through sweeping away the urban poor. These policies adopted an engineering understanding of risk and the rhetorical use of resiliency has been 'more a matter of name shift rather than introduction of new perspectives' (Hosseinioon, 2018, p. 77). Aligned with Weichselgartner and Kelman (2015), the rhetoric of resiliency has been used to repackage the same activities that have been unsuccessful under previous framings. These policies downplayed the social aspects of resilience and overlooked the root causes of vulnerability. Furthermore, the main instrument of implementing policies has been the reliance upon and encouragement of private sector involvement, without providing a housing option for those who were displaced as a result of the implementation of the policies. As a result, a combination of an engineering understanding of resilience and a reliance on the private sector to enhance it in particular localities has been conducive to transferring vulnerability to other areas and other scales, that is, Tehran metropolitan region.

8.7   ENHANCING RESILIENCE AS A GOVERNANCE TOOL

In this section, I focus on a neighbourhood, namely, Farahzad, in order to explain in more detail the implications of the aforementioned policies and programmes for enhancing resilience in Tehran. The neighbourhood presents an indicative case, as it is located on the edge of the municipal boundaries (Figure 8.2), is almost completely delineated as 'deteriorated urban area' and at the same time is mainly considered as an informal settlement.

Located in the foothills of the northern mountains of Tehran, Farahzad village has been engulfed by the expansion of the city. During the years following the 1979 revolution, migrants have settled in the areas adjacent to the village. A number of powerful state organizations (Setad Farman Imam, Bonyad Mostazafaan and Oghaf organization) have laid claim to most of the land in Farahzad and, hence, the neighbourhood comprises a rural core and an informal settlement that is continuing to grow. The neighbourhood receives a number of urban services, including access to water, electricity and surfaced roads. As Figure 8.3 shows, Farahzad is almost isolated from the more expensive, formal neighbouring areas by a highway on its south, mountains on its north and east and a valley on its west side.

Given that the expansion of the neighbourhood is constrained by these

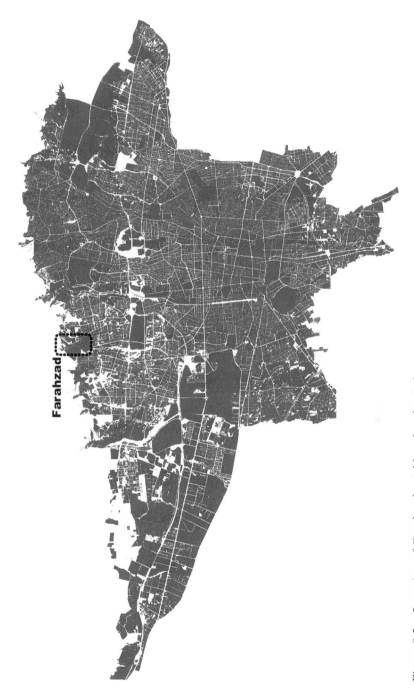

Farahzad

Figure 8.2   Location of Farahzad neighbourhood in Tehran

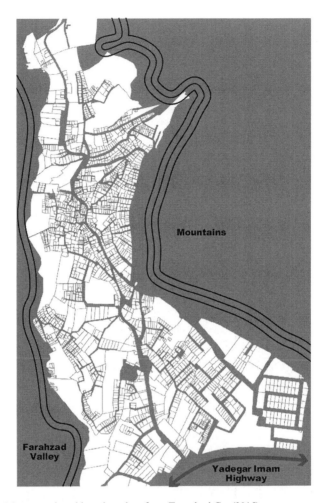

Source: Map reproduced based on data from Farnahad Co. (2015).

Figure 8.3   Farahzad neighbourhood is isolated and confined on four sides

obstacles and due to the heavy-handed reactions of the municipality staff in enforcing the no-construction zone (beyond the municipality boundaries), the neighbourhood is expanding vertically (Figure 8.4). The additional spaces provide affordable rental housing for the people on low incomes and the newcomers.

It is estimated that at least 40 per cent of residents in the neighbourhood are renters. Furthermore, around two-thirds of the residents of the neigh-

Source: Photograph by the author.

*Figure 8.4   The vertical and incremental expansion of Farahzad – each
             storey is built at different times and sometimes using different
             materials*

bourhood are migrants. In addition to those migrating from rural areas or
other cities and towns, Afghan migrants are estimated to comprise at least
a quarter of the population in this neighbourhood. Since state policies
have banned foreigners from buying properties and made it difficult for

those without a residency permit to rent a property, Afghan migrants have no choice other than the informal settlements, like Farahzad. Despite the fact that this neighbourhood is considered as an informal settlement, most of its residents are not from the lowest two income quintiles. As the city has reached and engulfed the neighbourhood, the land prices have become as high as those in the formal southern areas of the city.

As noted, most of the neighbourhood area is delineated as 'deteriorated urban area' and hence is subject to the latest policies and introduced incentives. According to the municipality staff, however, not a single unit has been renovated during the last 11 years in this area. The main issue has been the informality of land and housing ownership, which neither makes residents eligible for receiving subsidies to enhance the condition of their built environment nor allows them to rebuild, strengthen or renovate their properties using their own resources. A study conducted for the municipality of Tehran (Farnahad Co., 2015) shows that over 70 per cent of the buildings in this neighbourhood are unsafe in the face of an earthquake, due to the low quality of construction materials and building practices.

The case of Farahzad, therefore, illustrates the paradoxes embedded in urban renewal policies that are purportedly aimed at enhancing resilience: these policies make public subsidies inaccessible to those living in a precarious condition, while channelling resources towards the propertied and private sector developers. At the same time, those living in Farahzad are not allowed to make any changes to their housing to repair, strengthen or reconstruct. Any changes, especially adding new spaces, are being vehemently opposed by the municipality, which seeks to contain the neighbourhood expansion. As one of the municipality staff mentioned:

> If we wanted to follow the bureaucratic procedure to stop residents from construction activities in their housings, that would take at least two months. First, we should obtain a permit for entering the house, then we have to make a case against the residents and then the court would rule against them, so we can stop the construction activities. But it would be too late and by that time they would finish their construction. So we have to – sometimes – enter the property without obtaining a permit. Most of them [residents] are not properly literate and don't know about these procedures. So we can stop their construction activities.

In this case, the apparently extra-legal activities of residents are being constrained through illegal activities of the municipality. It can be argued that the real focus of policies concerned with deteriorated urban areas has been on the scale of individual buildings. The renewal of, or making alteration to, buildings is acceptable, so long as they occur within the 'formal' domain of urban governance and market. Zeiderman (2012) and Angell (2014) both explain how risk can be used as a governance tool. In the case of Farahzad, risk is used as a governance tool and at the same time is reinforced by the same tool.

8.8 CONCLUSION

Looking at the case of Tehran, I have explained how urban policies and practices purportedly aimed at enhancing resilience are characterized by a rhetorical use of urban resilience, a clear focus on disaster risk reduction strategies and 'fixing' the built environment as well as a reliance on the private market to enhance resilience. The spatial focus of these policies, in terms of the scale and spatial boundaries for interventions, were empirically, discursively and legally constructed at different levels. At the first level, the questions of resilience of what and whom were addressed by considering areas within Tehran's municipality boundaries. In the deeply unequal metropolitan region of Tehran, this dichotomy of within/outside Tehran's municipality boundaries for conceptualizing what is 'Tehran' left out millions of people living in highly vulnerable built environment outside the demarcated boundaries. They are excluded from the production of knowledge about, and the representation of, hazardscape as well as policy, material and discursive dimensions of enhancing resilience.

At the second level, demarcating boundaries for identifying 'deteriorated urban areas' and introducing area-based policies for enhancing resilience of these areas have concrete implications for their residents. Identifying, naming and subjecting these areas as 'deteriorated', as Rebotier (2012) discussed in the context of Latin American cities, became a critical driver of socio-spatial conditions and a lever for 'legitimate' actions on people and places. These areas and their residents have been subject to policies that have instrumentalized an engineering conception of resilience and have used property-led redevelopment strategies for enhancing it. In this sense, enhancing resilience has become a driver for social-spatial transformation of these areas, as low-income renters have to move to other localities sometimes outside Tehran's municipality boundaries.

At the third level, within the demarcated areas, and in fact in the city in general, the main focus of policies has been on the scale of individual buildings. Those without formal registration of ownership were marked out of the areas 'in need' of enhancing resilience. At the same time, resilience has become one of the concepts used as leverage for managing urban growth and governance. Therefore, using the rhetoric of resilience has affected the urban landscape, representations and perceptions of places, land and rent prices as well as spatial distribution and re-enforcement of vulnerability.

Along with exploring this particular case, the analysis made in this chapter aims to contribute to the debates on politics of urban resilience in several ways. First of all, and following the argument put forward by Fainstein (2015), the chapter calls into question the assumption of a universal benefit from enhancing urban resilience. It has showed that it is not enough to ask normative questions such as 'resilience for whom?', but it is also necessary to investigate who loses and what are the characteristics of the losers. The losers – in this case informal settlers and low-income renters – not only did none benefit from alleged enhancement of resilience, they have been locked in a precarious condition. In the second place, it is hoped that the chapter will contribute to current debates about market-based solutions for enhancing urban resilience (e.g., Kaika, 2017; Steele and Mittal, 2012). In particular, in the case of urban resilience against earthquakes, as shown, the predominant engineering 'solution' to the 'problem' – framed as fragile buildings – is associated with market-based transformation of the built environment, which can be conducive to gentrification and displacement of the poor. Finally, it is hoped that the chapter will contribute to the literature concerning the scale of interventions for building or enhancing urban resilience (Chelleri et al., 2015; Corfee-Morlot et al., 2011; Leichenko, 2011; Shi et al., 2016). The locally framed resilience interventions, shown in this case study, might produce or transfer the negative spill-over impact at other scales or other areas and accentuate socio-economic inequalities or vulnerabilities.

The case of Tehran and the Farahzad neighbourhood illustrates the importance of politicizing urban resilience. Politicizing urban resilience involves making the multiple root causes of vulnerability visible; revealing how and if policies purportedly aimed at enhancing resilience overlook people in an already unfavourable position and compound their vulnerability and marginalization; shedding light on who is getting what; explaining how seemingly neutral and rational policies for enhancing resilience mediate, reproduce and transfer vulnerability to other localities or at other scales; and, more importantly, potentially empower those affected by facilitating anticipatory learning.

REFERENCES

Altheide, D.L. (2006), 'Terrorism and the politics of fear', *Cultural Studies? Critical Methodologies*, **6**(4), 415–39.

Angell, E. (2014), 'Assembling disaster: earthquakes and urban politics in Istanbul', *City*, **18**(6), 667–78.

Berberian, M. (2014), *Earthquakes and Coseismic Surface Faulting on the Iranian Plateau*. Vol. 17, Amsterdam: Elsevier.

Chelleri, L., Waters, J.J., Olazabal, M., and Minucci, G. (2015), 'Resilience trade-offs: addressing multiple scales and temporal aspects of urban resilience', *Environment and Urbanization*, **27**(1), 181–98.

Coaffee, J. (2013), 'Rescaling and responsibilising the politics of urban resilience: from national security to local place-making', *Politics*, **33**(4), 240–52.

Corfee-Morlot, J., Cochran, I., Hallegatte, S., and Teasdale, P.-J. (2011), 'Multilevel risk governance and urban adaptation policy', *Climatic Change*, **104**(1), 169–97.

Cote, M. and Nightingale, A.J. (2012), 'Resilience thinking meets social theory: situating social change in socio-ecological systems (SES) research', *Progress in Human Geography*, **36**(4), 475–89.

Cretney, R. (2014), 'Resilience for whom? Emerging critical geographies of socio-ecological resilience', *Geography Compass*, **8**(9), 627–40.

Davoudi, S., Shaw, K., Haider, L.J. et al. (2012), 'Resilience: a bridging concept or a dead end? "Reframing" resilience: challenges for planning theory and practice interacting traps: resilience assessment of a pasture management system in Northern Afghanistan urban resilience: what does it mean in planning practice? Resilience as a useful concept for climate change adaptation? The politics of resilience for planning: a cautionary note', *Planning Theory & Practice*, **13**(2), 299–333.

England, P. and Jackson, J. (2011), 'Uncharted seismic risk', *Nature Geoscience*, **4**(6), 348–9.

Fainstein, S. (2015), 'Resilience and justice', *International Journal of Urban and Regional Research*, **39**(1), 157–67.

Farnahad Co. (2015), *Baznegareye sanade toseeye mahaleye Farahzad* (A revision study for Farahzad neighbourhood's development document). Tehran Municipality.

Hosseinioon, S. (2018), 'Measuring urban resilience to natural disasters for Iranian cities: challenges and key concepts'. In A. Fekete and F. Fiedrich (eds), *Urban Disaster Resilience and Security: Addressing Risks in Societies* (pp. 71–89). Cham: Springer International Publishing.

Hourcade, B. (1997), 'L'émergence des banlieues de Téhéran', *Cahiers d'études sur la Méditerranée orientale et le monde turco-iranien*. Available at http://journals.openedition.org/cemoti/1472 (accessed August 2018).

JICA (2000), *The Study on Seismic Microzoning of the Greater Tehran Area in the Islamic Republic of Iran*. Final Report. Japan International Cooperation Agency (JICA), Tehran Municipality. Available at http://open_jicareport.jica.go.jp/553/553/553_304_11611761.html (accessed August 2018).

Kaika, M. (2017), '"Don't call me resilient again!": the New Urban Agenda as immunology . . . or . . . what happens when communities refuse to be vaccinated with "smart cities" and indicators', *Environment and Urbanization*, **29**(1), 1–14.

Leichenko, R. (2011), 'Climate change and urban resilience', *Current Opinion in Environmental Sustainability*, **3**(3), 164–8.

Madanipour, A. (1999), 'City profile: Tehran', *Cities*, **16**(1), 57–65.

Meerow, S. and Newell, J.P. (2016), 'Urban resilience for whom, what, when, where, and why?', *Urban Geography*, 1–21. doi: 10.1080/02723638.2016.1206395.

Ministry of Interior (2010), *Renovation of Deteriorated Urban Fabric* (in Farsi). Available at https://www.moi.ir/portal/home/?73546/ Behsazi va nosazi bafte farsoodeh (accessed August 2018).

MRU (2014), *Motaleat baznegary tarhe jame maskan* (A revision study on the comprehensive plan for housing). Tehran Municipality (in Farsi). Available at http://

pnu.ac.ir/portal/File/ShowFile.aspx?ID=4ffc4ba2-da33-4f59-b4ee-5de53bb3c0a8 (accessed August 2018).

Nalau, J., Preston, B.L., and Maloney, M C. (2015), 'Is adaptation a local responsibility?', *Environmental Science & Policy*, **48**, 89–98.

Piran, P. (1987), 'Zaghehnishini dar Tehran' (Shanty dwelling in Tehran), *Ettelaat Siyassi Igtisadi*, **17**(23), 1–5.

Rebotier, J. (2012), 'Vulnerability conditions and risk representations in Latin-America: framing the territorializing urban risk', *Global Environmental Change*, **22**(2), 391–8.

Rittel, H.W.J. and Webber, M.M. (1973), 'Dilemmas in a general theory of planning', *Policy Sciences*, **4**(2), 155–69.

Shahr and Andisheh Pars (2014), *Tarhe Motaleati shenasaeeye rahkarhaye hemayat az maskan mahrooman* (Research project for identifying strategies for supporting housing for marginalized groups). Ministry of Roads and Urban Development, Tehran.

Shi, L., Chu, E., Anguelovski, I. et al. (2016), 'Roadmap towards justice in urban climate adaptation research', *Nature Climate Change*, **6**(2), 131–7.

Steele, W. and Mittal, N. (2012). *Building 'Equitable' Urban Resilience: The Challenge for Cities*. Dordrecht: Springer.

Swyngedouw, E. and Heynen, N.C. (2003), 'Urban political ecology, justice and the politics of scale', *Antipode*, **35**(5), 898–918.

Turner, M.D. (2014), 'Political ecology I: an alliance with resilience?', *Progress in Human Geography*, **38**(4), 616–23.

Vale, L.J. (2014), 'The politics of resilient cities: whose resilience and whose city?', *Building Research & Information*, **42**(2), 191–201.

Walker, B. and Salt, D. (2012), *Resilience Thinking: Sustaining Ecosystems and People in a Changing World*. Washington, DC: Island Press.

Weichselgartner, J. and Kelman, I. (2015), 'Geographies of resilience: challenges and opportunities of a descriptive concept', *Progress in Human Geography*, **39**(3), 249–67.

White, I. and O'Hare, P. (2014), 'From rhetoric to reality: which resilience, why resilience, and whose resilience in spatial planning?', *Environment and Planning C: Government and Policy*, **32**(5), 934–50.

Wilkinson, C. (2012), 'Social-ecological resilience: insights and issues for planning theory', *Planning Theory*, **11**(2), 148–69.

Wisner, B., Blaikie, P., Cannon, T., and Davis, I. (2004), *At Risk: Natural Hazards, People's Vulnerability and Disasters*. New York: Routledge.

Zaidi, R.Z. and Pelling, M. (2015), 'Institutionally configured risk: assessing urban resilience and disaster risk reduction to heat wave risk in London', *Urban Studies*, **52**(7), 1218–33.

Zebardast, E. (2006), 'Marginalization of the urban poor and the expansion of the spontaneous settlements on the Tehran metropolitan fringe', *Cities*, **23**(6), 439–54.

Zeiderman, A. (2012), 'On shaky ground: the making of risk in Bogotá', *Environment and Planning A*, **44**(7), 1570–88.

Ziervogel, G., Pelling, M., Cartwright, A. et al. (2017), 'Inserting rights and justice into urban resilience: a focus on everyday risk', *Environment and Urbanization*, **29**(1), 123–38.

9. Multi-hazard, exposure and vulnerability in Italian municipalities

Francesco Pagliacci and Margherita Russo

9.1 INTRODUCTION

Promoted and supported by the United Nations International Strategy for Disaster Risk Reduction (UNISDR), the Sendai Framework for Disaster Risk Reduction 2015–2030 has replaced the previous Hyogo Framework. This new framework aims to reduce disaster risk worldwide by 2030, mitigating the impact on the population of natural events (earthquakes, tsunamis, cyclones, volcanic eruptions, landslides and climate change). With respect to this objective, two key factors may be leveraged: before a disaster, preparing individuals, communities and economic and social organisations to face the danger; after the disaster, taking actions to better rebuild (reconstruction as an opportunity to mitigate the consequences of further future disasters) (UNISDR, 2015; Esposito et al. 2017). Accordingly, among the four priorities for action promoted by UNISDR (2015), understanding disaster risk can play a key role.[1] Indeed, the work of UNISDR promotes not only a systematic analysis of the factors that could make a natural event reach the proportions of a disaster, it also supports information and prevention activities. In the recommendations proposed by the Sendai Framework we find that communities must be at the core of systemic actions needed to reduce vulnerability and to activate processes of social innovation. Systemic actions are needed to ensure that natural disasters do not distort rhythms, established practices and social organisation (Sartori, 2017). Vulnerability is therefore the pivotal point of a reasoning that must consider the many material and immaterial characteristics of a territory and of the communities that live and work in that territory. To think about vulnerability requires us to think about the phase

---

[1] The other priorities are: Priority 2: Strengthening disaster risk governance to manage disaster risk; Priority 3: Investing in disaster risk reduction for resilience; Priority 4: Enhancing disaster preparedness for effective response and to "Build Back Better" in recovery, rehabilitation and reconstruction.

that precedes the occurrence of a destructive event: this is how we reveal the fragility on which to intervene, but also the ability to react and recover, on which we can leverage, and this is the core of the concept of resilience: a social process, not a black box. Vulnerability and resilience of territories, in their variety of socio-economic conditions, are essential to understand the magnitude of the effects of a disaster and for reconstruction. The concepts of vulnerability and fragility, together with that of resilience, refer, respectively, to responses and recovery and mitigation/preparedness, phases that are clearly outlined by the Sendai Framework. As stressed by Sartori (2017) and Pagliacci et al. (2017), reducing vulnerability and increasing resilience require collective resources to trigger processes of social innovation.

Within this analytical framework of resilience, a solid and shared knowledge-base on hazards is a preliminary condition to improve prevention and mitigation as well as the implementation of appropriate response measures. This is especially true for a country like Italy that shows the highest probability of a disaster and related economic losses in the European Union (EU) (Beck et al., 2012; Frigerio and De Amicis, 2016; Valensise et al., 2017). In addition, the theme of unpreparedness is particularly evident in Italy where, in ordinary language, the terms hazard and risk are generally used as synonyms.

In the Disaster Risk Reduction (DRR) framework, "natural" disasters are not expected to exist, only natural hazards actually occur. In fact, disasters are considered as external shocks, but disaster risk is the outcome of the interaction of natural and human elements (UNISDR, 2015). In particular, definitions of risk are probabilistic: the potential human and material losses, which may originate from a particular hazard to a specified element at risk, given a particular future timespan (Blaikie et al., 1994; Brooks et al., 2005; Carrão et al., 2016). This definition moves from the seminal work of the United Nations Disaster Relief Office (UNDRO). Following the UN definition (Cardona, 2005), the risk of suffering from material and immaterial losses can be defined as a function of three different components: natural hazard (a threat of a naturally occurring event will have a negative effect on humans); exposure (the elements at risk, such as the total population and its assets); and vulnerability (the conditions determined by physical, social, economic and environmental factors or processes which increase the susceptibility of an individual, a community, assets or systems to the impacts of hazards). Although the relation among the determinants of risk has been often schematised in mathematical terms (Risk = Hazard x Exposure x Vulnerability) (UNDRO, 1979; Dao and Peduzzi, 2003; Peduzzi et al., 2009; Cardona et al., 2012), this expression seems to represent more a teaching model – which can usefully show existing relationships among drivers – than a viable formula that can be adopted in assessing risk in a real environment. This is largely due to two factors: firstly, the unavailability of data at the appropriate spatial and temporal granularity, in order to implement relevant country/regions analyses over time; secondly, the meaning given to the operators that are supposed to combine the determinants of risks.

In general, according to that formulation, to reduce risks to zero, there are three alternative ways, namely, reducing to zero one of three multipliers. While the first two strategies are impossible – neither can hazards be eliminated nor can exposed persons and assets be removed – the only feasible way to implement DRR is increasing an exposed population's awareness of natural events (prevention) and reducing their burden of suffering from adverse effects when impacted by an event (mitigation), which means acting to reduce vulnerability. In a broader perspective, vulnerability has a lot to do with resilience of local communities, although the latter concept is not used here as it only emerges after the occurrence of a natural event.

A greater preparedness of a community (i.e., a deeper understanding of the existing hazards, also through a better recognition of warning signals) could reduce its vulnerability, hence suffered risks (UNISDR, 2015). Clearly, preparedness interventions may have different outcomes, given the characteristics of the places involved: to some extent, large cities behave – and perform – differently from rural or remote regions. Moreover, what also matters is quality of institutions, which may differ across a country (see Barone and Mocetti, 2014 for a comparative analysis about Italian earthquakes).

While previous works have mostly focused on vulnerability to natural hazards (given its implications in terms of possible mitigation strategies) (Cutter et al., 2003; Frigerio and De Amicis, 2016; Russo et al., 2017; Valensise et al., 2017), this work focuses on an empirical analysis of the territorial distribution of hazards, vulnerability and exposure across Italy, by exploring the features characterising their combination. Although it is hard to measure local risks, analysing the co-existence of hazard, exposure and vulnerability at a local level can still increase community-level awareness about risks. In particular, this is the ultimate goal of this work. By considering municipality-level data, urban–rural imbalances are likely to be also considered. In particular, Russo et al. (2017) claim that earthquakes and landslides tend to affect rural and "inner" municipalities (according to the definition of Barca et al., 2014) more than urbanised areas. Pagliacci (2017) found the opposite relationship when considering flood hazard, which tends to hit cities or urban areas. Nevertheless, the fact that a natural hazard might occur is just part of the story. Clearly, also local exposure and local vulnerability play a role; and they may vary greatly across a country or when either larger cities (or urban poles) or inner and remote areas are concerned. Understanding disaster risk represents the ultimate topic of this work as well.

Given this framework, and in addition to previous works (Frigerio and De Amicis, 2016; Pagliacci, 2017), two major novelties characterise this analysis: the adoption of a multi-hazard approach, by simultaneously considering earthquake, landslide and flood hazards; and a tentative analysis of the emerging risk as a combination of hazards, local exposure and local vulnerability. Due to the fact that this work is largely descriptive (being engaged with classification issues and mapping), testing some systematic hypotheses on resilience goes well beyond the scope of this work. Nevertheless, this chapter shows a strong policy focus and it aims to be of use to Italian decision makers. In general, the methodology framework proposed in the chapter may be applied to other countries that need to prioritise intervention plans against natural multi-hazards.

The chapter is structured as follows. Section 9.2 describes the case study (Italy and its long-lasting history of disasters) and the way earthquake, landslide and flood hazards can be assessed at the local (i.e., municipality) level. Section 9.3 is a methodological section, which firstly defines a Multi-Hazard Indicator (MHI) and the features of a cluster analysis, disentangling municipalities by type and intensity of hazard. Then, indicators of local exposure and vulnerability are also presented. Section 9.4 provides the main results, mapping them across Italy. In addition, Section 9.5 discusses the results under the light of well-consolidated territorial imbalances in the country (the urban-rural divide and the presence of inner areas). Section 9.6 concludes the work, suggesting possible future strands of this research.

9.2   THE CASE STUDY: NATURAL HAZARDS ACROSS ITALY

9.2.1   Data on Italian Hazards

In the *World Risk Report 2012* (Beck et al., 2012), Italy is listed as the fifth EU country in terms of probability of a disaster (and related human and economic losses), and also because of its particular location (Valensise et al., 2017). Although Italy is prone to natural hazards and it has suffered a long history of catastrophic events, only after the dramatic earthquake events of 2016 in Central Italy has the importance of implementing actions to reduce risks been brought back to the centre of general attention.

In the same year, the launch of the "Casa Italia" Plan – an extraordinary plan promoted by the Italian government, in line with the priorities of the Sendai Framework (UNISDR, 2015) – pointed out the importance of implementing "building back better" actions and building safer buildings (Pagliacci et al., 2017). Moving from the need for risk assessment, the plan has also encouraged the creation of an integrated information framework on the main hazards in Italy.

Thus, in August 2017, ISTAT (the Italian National Institute for Statistics) made available a dataset on hazards from earthquakes, volcanic eruptions, landslides and floods, on a municipality basis.[2] Municipality-level information is crucial to highlight local heterogeneity, and to strengthen the capacity of exposed local governments and communities to reduce their own vulnerability (Russo and Silvestri, 2017).

Given this updated dataset, for the purposes of the current analysis, only three types of hazards are considered: earthquakes, landslides and floods. Other hazards are ignored here for several reasons. Hurricanes and tornadoes do not actually occur in Italy. Wildfires and droughts, although they do affect the country, are not included in the ISTAT dataset, thus no available data can be analysed. Lastly, volcanic eruptions, although they occur, and are included in the dataset, are ignored as this hazard shows a tightly bound territorial concentration (e.g., Vesuvius and the Phlegrean Fields in Campania; the Etna area in Sicily), with a very high share of population, but with an overlapping seismic hazard.

The following sub-sections define each hazard, describing the methodology adopted by ISTAT to assess them (see Pagliacci, 2017 for further details).

9.2.2 Seismic Hazard

The intense seismic sequence that hit Central Italy in 2016–17 (the most powerful one since the earthquake in Irpinia in 1980) caused a tragic effect in terms of human losses (more than 300) and considerable damage to the economic, productive, artistic and social fabric. However, the wave of earthquakes that has affected Italy for more than 50 years is much longer and has spared no regions of the country (Chubb, 2002; Guidoboni, 2017; Sartori, 2017): Belice, in Western Sicily (1968); Friuli (1976), Irpinia over four regions in Centre-South Italy (1980), Umbria and the Marches (1997), L'Aquila (2009), Emilia (2012).

---

[2] Data have been retrieved from official sources – such as INGV (National Institute of Geophysics and Volcanology), ISPRA (Italian National Institute for Environmental Protection and Research) and ISTAT itself – and in compliance with rigorous statistical methodologies to guarantee homogeneity. The dataset is available at http://www.istat.it/it/ mappa-rischi.

Disasters in Italy firstly come from geological activity. Italy lies at the point of contact of two tectonic plates: the Eurasian and the African plate. Effects of this geological activity are clearly visible: volcanoes dot the fault line in the Southern part of Italy and large earthquakes are common throughout the whole country, with tragic consequences. Accordingly, the most seismically active zones are concentrated along the Apennine mountain range; in Calabria and Sicily regions; and in north-eastern areas of the country (Valensise et al., 2017).

In particular, seismic hazard can be estimated through Peak Ground Acceleration (PGA), which is the ground acceleration value measured during an earthquake. Here, maximum PGA, observed in each Italian municipality with respect to a grid of points (as measured by INGV in 2004), is considered as a proxy for seismic hazard. In fact, this value plays a role also in the Italian anti-seismic regulations: according to these regulations, four different seismic zones (from zone #1 to #4) are identified, with zone #1 (PGA > 0.25) representing the most seismic, hence dangerous, one and zone #4 (PGA < 0.05) the least dangerous one[3] (Civil Protection, 2015).

On the basis of this classification, in each municipality specific anti-seismic regulations and technical norms for building construction are adopted so that buildings should bear minor earthquakes without serious damage and major ones without collapsing (Civil Protection, 2015; Pagliacci and Russo, 2017).

9.2.3 Landslide Hazard

In Italy, mountain areas suffer from erosive phenomena and landslides (Consiglio Nazionale dei Geologi, 2014). About 500,000 out of 700,000 landslides in Europe actually occur in Italy, with sludge, debris flows and high-speed collapses (JRC, 2012; CNR-IRPI, 2015). Their consequences can be dramatic, such as in the case of the 1963 landslide over the basin of the Vajont dam. At the regional level, Trentino, Aosta Valley, Campania, Liguria and Tuscany are heavily affected by landslides.

Moving from the Inventory of Italian Landslides (ISPRA and Regions/Autonomous Provinces on 2007 data), the *Piani di Assetto Idrogeologico* (hydrogeological structure plans) assess landslide hazard in Italy, design specific soil protection interventions and draw up Civil Protection emergency plans (CNR-IRPI, 2015). Moreover, these plans single out five

---

[3] Since 2003 seismic classification, intervals of PGA, with a probability of exceeding the threshold equal to 10 per cent in 50 years, are assigned to each seismic area (Zone #1: PGA > 0.25; Zone #2: 0.15 < PGA < 0.25; Zone #3: 0.05 < PGA < 0.15; Zone #4: PGA < 0.05) (Civil Protection, 2015).

different hazard classes, where the application of different constraints and regulations on buildings occurs.

To assess landslide hazard, this work considers just the presence of three of them: areas with very high (P4) and high (P3) landslide hazards, as they are the ones with the greatest restrictions on urban planning and the erection of new buildings (Pagliacci, 2017), together with the areas of attention (labelled as PAA), for which there is information on possible hazard situations that have not yet been associated with a hazard class. Thus, this work considers the share of P4 + P3 + PAA sub-municipality areas at risk out of total municipality area. At-risk population is not considered here. In fact, the proportionality estimation method adopted could lead to inaccurate estimates[4] (Trigila et al., 2015).

9.2.4 Flood Hazard

Floods are usually caused by rivers, streams, lakes and the sea in coastal areas. The regions characterised by the highest values of flood hazard are Emilia-Romagna, Tuscany, Lombardy, Piedmont and Veneto. Floods are more and more frequent, because of extreme weather conditions (also due to climate change) and because of inadequate river and stream maintenance (CNR-IRPI, 2015).

As in the landslide hazard case, Italian River Basin Authorities (*Autorità di Bacino*) have drawn up detailed plans to perimeter the areas that are expected to be affected by floods, according to different probability scenarios (CNR-IRPI, 2015). On a national basis, ISPRA has created a mosaic of these areas, for three different scenarios (Trigila et al., 2015): low hazard for extreme event scenarios (P1); medium hazard for rare floods, with return time between 100 and 200 years (P2); high hazard for frequent floods, with return time between 20 and 50 years (P3).[5]

In this chapter, the share of at-risk areas out of total municipality area is considered. However, due to the fact that, in some regions, data are not available for each of the different scenarios, in order to get homogeneous results across the country, the widest at-risk area for each municipality is considered: in most cases, it refers to the P1 low-hazard scenario, but in some cases it might refer also to the P2 scenario (Trigila et al., 2015).

---

[4] At-risk population comes from the intersection, in a GIS environment, of at-risk areas with the ISTAT (2011) census tract data. As the exact location of population within each census tract is unknown, at-risk persons are estimated on a proportionality basis. However, estimates are inaccurate when focusing on scattered low-density rural sites (Trigila et al., 2015), which – on average – are the most affected by landslides (Pagliacci, 2017).

[5] Data are calculated by ISPRA every five years (latest data refer to 2015) and they are reported at municipality level by ISTAT.

9.3 METHODOLOGY

Since the 1990s, an extensive strand of literature has developed, tackling the problems of measuring risks, local resilience and social vulnerability to natural hazards (Briguglio, 1995; Cutter et al., 2003; Cardona, 2005; Beccari, 2016; Frigerio and De Amicis, 2016, Sartori, 2017; Valensise et al., 2017). Moreover, most of these works have also adopted a territorial approach.

In what follows, a local territorial focus is adopted. Firstly, multi-hazard heterogeneity with regard to the aforementioned main hazards is considered by means of a cluster analysis, at municipality level (7983 observations in total[6]). Secondly, a synthetic MHI accounts for the combination of hazards for each Italian municipality. Lastly, both exposure and local vulnerability are jointly considered in order to combine them with related hazard, framing a risk analysis.

9.3.1 Cluster Analysis

Cluster analysis tackles the issue of multiple hazards. As an unsupervised classification technique, cluster analysis or clustering aims to group a set of observations in such a way that observations in the same group are more similar to each other than to those in other groups. Here, observations are Italian municipalities and their similarity is computed on the basis of the following input variables: maximum PGA, as an indicator of seismic hazard; share (percentage) of the municipality area under landslide hazard; share (percentage) of the municipality area under flood hazard.

As these variables are expected to follow an inherently spatial distribution, even a non-spatial cluster analysis, as the one performed here, is expected to returns clusters that follow a spatial structure. More specifically, in order to perform non-spatial cluster analysis, input variables are preliminarily standardised and expressed in terms of z-scores. Then, a hierarchical approach is adopted (Kaufmann and Rousseeuw, 1990) using software R (R Core Team, 2015). The dissimilarity matrix of the input variables is computed by means of the Euclidean distance. Then, distances between clusters are assessed by means of Ward's method (Ward, 1963; Lance and Williams, 1966).

As the hierarchical clustering approach does not require any prior knowledge of the number of clusters to be extracted, it is necessary to choose the level (hence, the number of clusters) at which to stop the analysis. In this work, the output of the hierarchical cluster analysis is

---

[6] The number of municipalities refers to the 2016 administrative partition.

analysed by applying the Caliński–Harabasz Index, to identify the most suitable number of clusters to be selected (Caliński and Harabasz, 1974).

9.3.2 A Synthetic Multi-Hazard Indicator

In order to rank cluster analysis results, a synthetic MHI is computed, considering the same three indicators as inputs. The methodology follows a two-step approach. Firstly, normalisation (feature scaling) of input variables x_i is implemented:

$$x_i' = \frac{x_i - \min(x_i)}{\max(x_i) - \min(x_i)} \qquad i = 1,2,3 \tag{9.1}$$

In (9.1), i is any of the three hazards under consideration. Normalisation is needed as input variables are expressed in different measurements units.

Secondly, normalised data (x') are combined into the MHI, by taking the average of their squares:

$$\overline{x} = \frac{\sum\limits_{i=1}^{3} (x')^2}{3} \tag{9.2}$$

Actually, unlike the arithmetic mean, this indicator tends to weight more the presence of one single hazard with a high likelihood of occurring than the presence of more hazards, but with a lower likelihood.[7]

9.3.3 Exposure and Vulnerability

In addition to the assessment of hazards throughout the country, this analysis also maps exposure and vulnerability to hazards at municipality level. Although it is not possible to exactly estimate risks, according to UNDRO (1979), it is still possible to verify whether hazards, exposure and vulnerability move together or there are some counterbalancing effects at the local level. This analysis could at least represent a qualitative assessment of risk levels across Italy.

Nevertheless, some additional details on the adopted concepts are useful. Firstly, exposure should include the sum of all the at-risk elements.

---

[7] Let's take two examples. Municipality (a) shows extreme earthquake hazard but no landslide and flood hazards at all. Municipality (b) shows similar (but low-level) earthquake, landslide and flood hazards. If the average values had been taken, both municipalities would have had the same multi-hazard level (0.33). Instead, given (9.2), the MHI for municipality (b) is equal to 0.11 and it is lower than the MHI for municipality (a) (namely, 0.33).

However, it is hard to assess all possible values at risk. Here, only the following types of at-risk population and assets are considered, at municipality level:[8]

- total population (year 2015)
- number of residential buildings (year 2011)
- total employment (year 2015)
- total employment in manufacturing activities (Section C of the NACE Rev. 2) (year 2015)
- agricultural holdings with utilised agricultural area (year 2010).

As a strong major hypothesis, population and assets, within a given municipality, are expected to be exposed to natural hazards in the same way, an issue that will be discussed for further investigation.

As far as vulnerability is concerned, other works have already tackled this issue. For instance, Frigerio and De Amicis (2016) have insightfully assessed social vulnerability across Italian municipalities, applying Principal Component Analysis to a set of socio-economic and demographic factors. Their analysis identifies different spatial patterns across Italy, providing useful information for identifying the communities most likely to experience negative natural disaster impacts due to their socio-economic and demographic characteristics. Russo et al. (2017), focusing on earthquakes, also find that socio-economic vulnerability (computed by means of Principal Component Analysis and cluster analysis, on a set of 14 variables[9]) is greater, the more seismic a municipality is.

Here, an alternative indicator, namely, the Index of Social and Material Vulnerability (ISMV), made recently available by ISTAT (2018), is adopted. It provides a synthetic measure of the level of social and material vulnerability of each Italian municipality (ISTAT, 2018), combining together seven elementary indicators, which are intended to capture its key dimensions.[10]

---

[8] The data source is ISTAT (http://dati.istat.it, accessed 12 January 2018), with 2016 municipality partition.
[9] The variables cover geographical features and characteristics of the urban settlement; population and demographical features; characteristics of buildings (age of construction and number of dwellings); employment; agriculture and landscape.
[10] ISMV is grounded on the theoretical basis that vulnerability refers to the presence of uncertainty of one's social and economic conditions, although it might not necessarily occur in the short term (ISTAT, 2018). Accordingly, the input indicators – selected with a positive relationship with respect to social and material vulnerability – are: (i) percentage of illiterate population (25–64 years old); (ii) percentage of households with six and more components; (iii) percentage of single parent families; (iv) percentage of households with potential hardship, to indicate the share of families only composed of elderly people (65 years and older)

As far as exposure and vulnerability are concerned, differences will be analysed at cluster level and by means of Pearson correlation coefficients (with regard to MHI).

Moreover, the vulnerability issue calls into question an additional debate, namely, the one on rural and inner areas. Rural and remote areas (which in Italy mostly overlap, as observed by Bertolini and Pagliacci, 2017) had long been forgotten by national policymakers, although they have suffered from socio-economic weakness and negative demographic trends since the mass urbanisation process (Bertolini et al., 2008; Copus et al., 2015). Therefore, since 2014, Italian remote municipalities have been targeted by a specific "National Strategy for Inner Areas" (SNAI, in Italian), which disentangles/divides Italian municipalities into six types, according to service provision and their geographical remoteness[11] (Barca et al., 2014).

9.4   RESULTS

9.4.1   Mapping Hazards

Figure 9.1 shows the normalised values for each hazard indicator (earthquake, landslide and flood) together with the MHI values by municipality. The combination of the hazards under consideration here is generally highest across Central and Southern Italy (especially along the Apennines) as well as in Emilia-Romagna. Conversely, municipalities in North-Western Italy and in Sardinia are in the lowest-hazard quartile. When considering NUTS-2 level regions' average MHI values (computed as a simple average by municipality), additional details emerge. The regions showing the highest average MHI is Emilia-Romagna (0.26), followed by Molise (0.25) and Calabria (0.24). Conversely, South Tyrol, Sardinia, Piedmont and Trentino all face the lowest levels of hazard (MHI < 0.05) (Table 9.1).

In addition to the analysis of the territorial distribution of the MHI, more insightful results can be obtained by the application of cluster analysis. The analysis of the Caliński–Harabasz Index (Caliński and

---

with at least one 80-year-old component; (v) percentage of the population in the condition of serious crowding, given by the dwelling surface/inhabitants ratio; (vi) percentage of NEET (not in education, employment or training) young people (15–29 years old); (vii) percentage of households with potential economic disadvantage, indicating the share of families with children in which all members are unemployed, or have withdrawn from work (ISTAT, 2018).

[11] Inner areas are simply defined as those remote municipalities that lie far apart from those major urban municipalities that provide essential services (Barca et al., 2014). This national strategy aims to promote innovative projects within remote areas, also with the support of European Structural and Investment Funds.

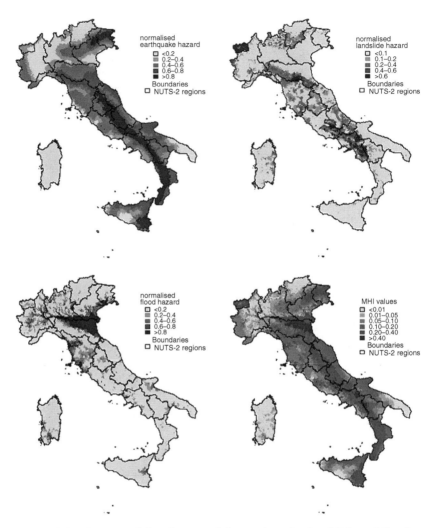

*Figure 9.1   Territorial distribution of the earthquake, landslide and flood
hazards (normalised values), and MHI*

Harabasz, 1974) suggests four clusters as the optimum number to be
selected. However, seven clusters – representing a local optimum – support
a more insightful interpretation of the results. Figure 9.2 maps them across
the country. Clusters are sorted by their average MHI value (computed
at municipality level). According to this sorting, we observe that, except
for a cluster showing almost no hazards at all (cluster #1), there are

Table 9.1   MHI, by region

	Average value	Standard deviation
North-West	*0.05*	*0.08*
Piedmont	0.04	0.05
Aosta Valley	0.23	0.09
Lombardy	0.05	0.08
Liguria	0.07	0.05
North-East	*0.15*	*0.13*
South Tyrol	0.01	0.01
Trentino	0.04	0.04
Veneto	0.13	0.10
Friuli-Venezia Giulia	0.19	0.08
Emilia-Romagna	0.26	0.14
Central Italy	*0.14*	*0.08*
Tuscany	0.13	0.08
Umbria	−0.16	0.07
the Marches	0.14	0.03
Latium	0.13	0.10
South	*0.19*	*0.12*
Abruzzo	0.19	0.10
Molise	0.25	0.10
Campania	0.21	0.13
Apulia	0.06	0.08
Basilicata	0.19	0.13
Calabria	0.24	0.08
The Islands	*0.07*	*0.08*
Sicily	0.12	0.09
Sardinia	0.01	0.02

three medium hazard clusters (with MHI < 0.2) and three higher-hazard clusters (MHI > 0.2). In both groups, hazard types are distinguished as follows: (i) earthquake hazard; (ii) flood hazard and (iii) earthquake and landslide hazards.

Table 9.2 returns average cluster values, also showing the number of municipalities within each group, distinguished also according to the six-level classification of areas provided by the National Strategy for Inner Areas (urban poles, inter-municipal poles, outlying municipalities, intermediate municipalities, peripheral municipalities, ultra-peripheral municipalities) (Barca et al., 2014). According to Table 9.2, 42 per cent of Italian municipalities face no hazards (cluster #1), while 19 per cent of municipalities are in one of the clusters with the highest hazard levels. The share is larger when considering inner areas (namely, intermediate,

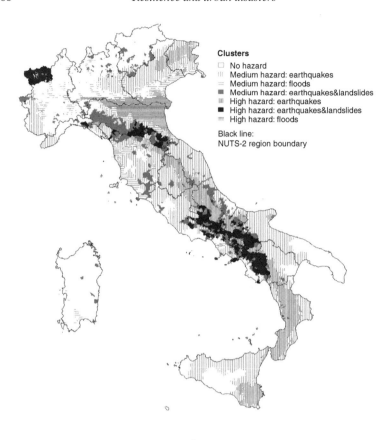

Figure 9.2   Territorial distribution of clusters

peripheral and ultra-peripheral municipalities): indeed, 63 per cent of the municipalities belonging to one of the high-hazard clusters (#5, #6 and #7) are inner municipalities (they also represent 12 per cent of the total number of Italian municipalities).[12]

---

[12]   Some further caveats have always to be considered when adopting multivariate statistical techniques. The case of the municipality of Norcia is particularly insightful. Despite being hit by several large earthquakes, in this classification it belongs to the "medium hazard: earthquakes&landslide". This occurs even if it shows a value for earthquake hazard above 0.9. Unfortunately, its value in terms of landslide hazard (about 0.25) is too high for it to be classified in cluster #5 and too low for it to be classified in cluster #6.

Table 9.2   Cluster features: hazard levels, MHI and other relevant characteristics

Cluster Name	Hazard normalised values			MHI	Number of municipalities (according to SNAI)						
	Maximum PGA (earthquakes)	Area under landslide hazard	Area under flood hazard		Total	Urban poles	Inter-municipal poles	Outlying	Inner areas		
									Intermediate	Peripheral	Ultra-peripheral
1 No hazard	0.150	0.049	0.056	0.017	3355	59	43	1653	860	606	134
2 Medium hazard: earthquakes	0.553	0.047	0.056	0.112	2068	79	41	892	581	381	94
3 Medium hazard: floods	0.234	0.023	0.540	0.133	487	37	5	328	101	15	1
4 Medium hazard: earthquakes & landslides	0.524	0.363	0.040	0.159	576	14	11	157	206	160	28
5 High hazard: earthquakes	0.889	0.057	0.021	0.268	691	15	9	148	282	205	32
6 High hazard: earthquakes & landslides	0.642	0.665	0.029	0.314	493	1	1	131	228	128	4
7 High hazard: floods	0.318	0.000	0.989	0.369	313	12	12	229	59	1	0

9.4.2   Comparing Multi-hazard with Exposure and Vulnerability

In addition to the analysis of multi-hazard territorial distribution, exposure and vulnerability are also important, as they can either enhance or limit risks at municipality level.

Total exposure by cluster (Table 9.3) is primarily driven by the number of municipalities each cluster comprises, but this is not the only possible driver. Cluster with no hazard (#1) is a good example. Although it comprises the largest number of municipalities, it hosts 20.8 million inhabitants, less than the population of cluster #2: the medium-hazard cluster prone to earthquakes hosts more than 22.8 million inhabitants (out of a population of about 60 million in Italy). Nevertheless, the latter cluster is not the most exposed when considering residential buildings or economic activities (5.7 million employees, of whom 1.2 million are employed in the manufacturing sector), but it still hosts the largest number of agricultural holdings (0.7 million).

In more general terms, when focusing on medium-hazard clusters, although they represent 39 per cent of the number of Italian municipalities, they host a larger share of population and employees (52 per cent of the total in both cases). In contrast, when focusing on the highest-hazard clusters, although they account for 18 per cent of the number of municipalities, they show a lower amount of exposed assets out of the national total (13 per cent of population and 11 per cent of employment). Their exposure is higher in terms of residential buildings (18 per cent) and of agricultural holdings (20 per cent).

When considering clusters and their economic specialisation, two additional patterns emerge. Cluster #7 (high hazard: floods) is the one with most manufacturing (31.3 per cent of manufacturing employment out of total employment), while cluster #6 is the most agricultural one, with eight agricultural holdings per thousand inhabitants. In both cases, they are high-hazard clusters (Table 9.3).

The analysis of vulnerability returns an even more worrying picture: the ISMV is positively correlated to MHI (Pearson's correlation coefficient is equal to 0.224; p-value = 0.000), so vulnerability is proved to be higher, the higher hazard is. Data by cluster confirms that: lower ISMV values characterise the no-hazard clusters. In addition to that, negative ISMV z-values (namely, lower levels of ISMV) characterise both clusters prone to floods (#3 and #7): both appear to be less vulnerable than the national average, as they comprise municipalities across flatlands, especially in Northern Italy (Table 9.4).

Table 9.3 Exposure, by cluster

Cluster name	Surface (km^2)	Population (2015)	Residential buildings (2011)	Employment (average 2015)	Employment in manufacture (average 2015)	Agricultural holdings (2010)
No hazard	103 070	20 851 694	4 240 618	5 958 330	1 281 454	694 158
Medium hazard: earthquakes	93 215	22 828 939	4 041 461	5 787 096	1 268 912	706 257
Medium hazard: floods	15 904	6 363 599	1 006 050	2 149 517	454 114	90 978
Medium hazard: earthquakes&landslides	22 993	2 600 248	686 843	556 932	130 211	120 104
High hazard: earthquakes	35 532	3 770 242	1 142 763	727 275	150 491	216 921
High hazard: earthquakes&landslides	17 955	1 471 073	481 539	250 593	53 479	118 308
High hazard: floods	13 404	2 779 756	588 424	860 133	269 363	69 838

Table 9.4   Vulnerability (ISMV), by cluster

	Cluster name	ISMV	
		Value	z-value
1	No hazard	98.25	−0.29
2	Medium hazard: earthquakes	99.72	0.27
3	Medium hazard: floods	98.14	−0.33
4	Medium hazard: earthquakes&landslides	99.49	0.19
5	High hazard: earthquakes	100.05	0.40
6	High hazard: earthquakes&landslides	100.25	0.47
7	High hazard: floods	98.57	−0.17

9.5   DISCUSSION AND POLICY IMPLICATIONS

In the attempt to shed new light on risks (hence, on the most appropriate DRR policies), multi-hazard levels have been analysed together with exposure and vulnerability. With regard to Italy, this analysis does not return encouraging findings. Exposure tends to be large among most of the high-hazard clusters and so does vulnerability. In particular, it seems that vulnerability is positively connected to hazard occurrence, with a potentially dramatic impact on risks.

The analysis of the territorial distribution of hazards across Italy (in terms of both MHI and clusters' features) suggests that no clear North-South divide occurs: the whole country suffers from natural multi-hazards, although the specific occurrence of each hazard is to some extent geographically clustered, because of specific geographic features (e.g., flatlands versus mountain areas). Also, the exposure side seems to play a minor role in the analysis of territorial divide, being fairly balanced among clusters.

Thus, the vulnerability issue seems to play the largest role (Sartori, 2017). In terms of policy implications, this issue calls into question the debate on inner areas, which has only recently gained greater attention (Barca et al., 2014). In addition to a generalised vulnerability to economic shocks (Barca et al., 2014; Bertolini and Pagliacci, 2017), this analysis confirms the idea that inner and rural areas are also particularly prone to natural events. Indeed, when analysing MHI values according to different types of municipalities (Table 9.5), it emerges that multi-hazard is high, both in urban poles (i.e., non-inner areas) and in intermediate and peripheral municipalities (inner areas). When dealing with hazards – and the related risks – these two types of municipalities have very different characteristics affecting them. On the one hand, larger cities represent

Table 9.5 Hazard, exposure and vulnerability, by inner area type

Inner areas	Hazard	Exposure (in million)					Vulnerability
	MHI	Population	Buildings	Employment	Employment manufacturing	Agricultural holdings	ISMV
Urban poles	0.13	21.74	2.30	7.24	0.90	0.21	99.87
Inter-municipal poles	0.12	3.04	0.46	0.76	0.18	0.06	100.76
Outlying areas	0.10	22.57	4.65	5.71	1.89	0.71	98.58
Intermediate	0.13	8.86	2.87	1.76	0.47	0.60	99.16
Peripheral	0.12	3.78	1.61	0.69	0.15	0.37	99.33
Ultra-peripheral	0.09	0.68	0.30	0.12	0.02	0.06	99.82

wide and complex socio-economic systems, which if hit by a natural hazard need huge restoration interventions. In those cases, preparedness can benefit from scale and spillover effects, as well as from larger public administrative organisations with more diversified competences. To this extent, it is possible to focus on 28 urban poles that are included in one of the high multi-hazard clusters (see Table 9.2): Gemona del Friuli, Cosenza, Foligno, Spoleto, Belluno, Avezzano, L'Aquila, Campobasso, Benevento, Reggio di Calabria, Messina, Ragusa, Siracusa, Catanzaro, Lamezia Terme (prone to earthquakes); Massa (prone to earthquakes and landslides); Casalmaggiore, Ravenna, Pisa, Adria, Rovigo, Cecina, Reggio nell'Emilia, Carpi, Mirandola, San Giovanni in Persiceto, Ferrara and Lugo (prone to floods). Among them, there are several NUTS-3-level capital cities, hosting more than 100,000 inhabitants and, in some cases, catastrophic events have already occurred in recent years (e.g., in L'Aquila).

Conversely, inner municipalities share a lower amount of exposed population and assets, which could lead to a reduction in total risks, although it does not make risks disappear. What is even more critical, in this case, is the fact that vulnerability could be particularly high. This has to do not only with ISMV but also with the small size of municipalities, located far away from urban poles providing services. In fact, 303 municipalities out of 939 inner municipalities located in one of the high-hazard clusters have less than 1000 inhabitants. They have no adequate infrastructure to plan and implement preparedness of individuals, organisations and communities. This makes it particularly hard (and challenging) to tackle a natural hazard and its impact on a very small community.

According to these findings, several policy implications may be discussed. This very preliminary analysis – which could benefit from further refinements in terms of adopted methodological tools and specification of hazard types, exposure and vulnerability – can nevertheless contribute to increase local communities' preparedness, pointing out the importance that both larger metropolitan areas and smaller remote municipalities should deserve consideration in the implementation of national-scale prevention plans. In this respect, the 'Casa Italia' Plan represents an interesting example.

Launched just after the 2016 series of large earthquakes that struck Central Italy, this plan is a 'comprehensive proposal aimed at protecting Italy's public buildings, homes and cultural sites over the next decades' (Pagliacci et al., 2017, p. 92). Aiming at realising effective measures for private buildings and dwellings and covering the whole of Italy, great attention to urban areas has been always stressed in the plan. However, in addition to these, inner areas also deserve fast interventions, because of their extreme socio-economic and demographic vulnerability, which tends to couple with a higher hazard level. As far as risks are concerned, both these elements seem to largely exceed the lower exposure that characterises remote municipalities. In a broader perspective, it is important that DRR policies (such as even the 'Casa Italia' Plan) are set up in such a way that they also involve the management and securing of the whole national territory as their ultimate goal. Moreover, the creation of multi-hazard territorial authorities could support Italian municipalities to integrate systemic plans to implement an effective preparedness at the local level.

9.6   CONCLUSIONS

A catastrophic disaster is not the inevitable consequence of a hazard event. Much has to do with exposure and vulnerability of local communities living in hazard-prone areas. Nevertheless, in order to enhance DRR policies, it is important to have a detailed awareness of the territorial distributions of hazards, exposure and vulnerability. This represents a key tool to implement effective actions to reduce vulnerability (UNISDR, 2015) and enhance resilience. In order to do this, a detailed municipality-level analysis has been carried out here, by taking advantage of the comprehensive ISTAT dataset (published in 2017) and by empirically applying the theoretical framework proposed by UNDRO (1979). The joint analysis of natural multi-hazard (through the computation of a cluster analysis), exposure and vulnerability at municipality level represents an important advancement in order to enhance local communities' preparedness for natural hazards and to make DRR policies more effective.

Although this analysis is only preliminary, its major novelty lies in the fact that it combines a Multi-Hazard Indicator at municipality level across Italy with exposure and vulnerability. In order to return a tool that is insightful for local stakeholders, further refinements are needed, especially in terms of risk assessment. Thus, future work will explicitly quantify local-level risks and define appropriate spatial granularity of data.

With regard to local level of risk, it would be necessary to distinguish a wider range of specific types of exposed assets (such as cultural heritage) and to consider alternative ways for computing their related vulnerability.

This also calls for a general question on the spatial granularity of information on each hazard, which may not be consistent with the data on population, economic activities and social infrastructures. Having to deal only with municipality-level aggregated data clearly makes any econometric analysis less accurate and hence less effective for policymakers too. A new generation of techniques from data science and data retrieval (such as those on the contracts of electricity services for residential and productive uses, or those on telephone/mobile services) would help in estimating specific population location in the municipality area and specific density of territorial use. The results of such analysis could substantially help the effectiveness of spatial multi-hazard, exposure and vulnerability analysis in the near future. From such an empirical effort, DRR in Italy (but also in other developed countries) can be properly enhanced. This could eventually strengthen resilience and a more sustainable development at the local level, by connecting top-down interventions with bottom-up and locally based participation processes.

REFERENCES

Barca, F., Casavola, P., and Lucatelli, S. (eds) (2014). A Strategy for Inner Areas in Italy: Definition, Objectives, Tools and Governance. Materiali Uval Series 31. Available at http://www.agenziacoesione.gov.it/opencms/export/sites/dps/it/docu mentazione/servizi/materiali_uval/Documenti/MUVAL_31_Aree_interne_ENG. pdf (accessed 30 March 2018).

Barone, G. and Mocetti, S. (2014). Natural disasters, growth and institutions: a tale of two earthquakes. *Journal of Urban Economics*, **84**, 52–66.

Beccari, B. (2016). A comparative analysis of disaster risk, vulnerability and resilience composite indicators. *PLOS Currents Disasters*, 14 March, Edition 1. doi: 10.1371/currents.dis.453df025e34b682e9737f95070f9b970

Beck, M.W., Shepard, C.C., Birkmann, J. et al. (2012). *World Risk Report 2012*. Alliance Development Works in Collaboration with UNU/EHS, the Nature Conservancy. Alliance Development Works, Bonn. Available at http://www.ehs.un u.edu/file/get/10487.pdf

Bertolini, P. and Pagliacci, F. (2017). Quality of life and territorial imbalances. A focus on Italian inner and rural areas. *Bio-based and Applied Economics*, **6**(2), 183–208.

Bertolini, P., Montanari, M., and Peragine, V. (2008). *Poverty and Social Exclusion in Rural Areas*. Brussels: European Commission.

Blaikie, P., Cannon, T., Davis, I., and Wisner, B. (1994). *At Risk: Natural Hazards, People's Vulnerability and Disasters*. London: Routledge.

Briguglio, L. (1995). Small island developing states and their economic vulnerabilities. *World Development*, **23**(9), 1615–32.

Brooks, N., Adger, W.N., and Kelly, P.M. (2005). The determinants of vulnerability and adaptive capacity at the national level and the implications for adaptation. *Global Environmental Change*, **15**, 151–63.

Caliński, T. and Harabasz, J. (1974). A dendrite method for cluster analysis. *Communications in Statistics*, **3**(1), 1–27.

Cardona, O.D. (2005). *Indicators for Disaster Risk and Risk Management*. Program for Latin America and the Caribbean: Summary Report. Manizales, Columbia: Instituto de Estudios Ambientales, Universidad Nacional de Columbia.

Cardona, O., van Aalst, M., Birkmann, J. et al. (2012). Determinants of risk: exposure and vulnerability. In C. Field, V. Barros, T. Stocker, D. Qin, D. Dokken, K. Ebi et al. (eds), *Managing the Risks of Extreme Events and Disasters to Advance Climate Change Adaptation*. Cambridge: Cambridge University Press, pp. 65–108.

Carrão, H., Naumann, G., and Barbosa, P. (2016). Mapping global patterns of drought risk: an empirical framework based on sub-national estimates of hazard, exposure and vulnerability. *Global Environmental Change*, **39**, 108–24.

Chubb, J. (2002). Three earthquakes: political response, reconstruction, and the institutions: Belice (1968), Friuli (1976), Campania (1980). In J. Dickie, J. Foot, and F.M. Snowden (eds), *Disastro! Disasters in Italy since 1860: Culture, Politics, Society*. New York: Palgrave Macmillan, pp. 186–233.

Civil Protection (2015). Seismic classification. Available at http://www.protezione civile.gov.it/jcms/en/classificazione.wp (accessed 11 January 2017).

CNR-IRPI (2015). *Rapporto Periodico sul Rischio posto alla Popolazione italiana da Frane e Inondazioni*. Year 2014. Available at http://polaris.irpi.cnr.it/wp-content/uploads/Report-annuale-2014.pdf (accessed 30 March 2018).

Consiglio Nazionale dei Geologi (2014). Comunicato Stampa del 13 settembre 2014. Available at http://www.cngeologi.it/2014/09/13/litalia-e-un-paese-morfologicame nte-fragile-perche-e-geologicamente-giovane/ (accessed 30 March 2018).

Copus, A., Melo, P.C., Kaup, S., Tagai, G., and Artelaris, P. (2015). Regional poverty mapping in Europe – challenges, advances, benefits and limitations. *Local Economy*, **30**(7), 742–64. doi: 10.1177/0269094215601958

Cutter, S., Boruff, B., and Shirley, W. (2003). Social vulnerability to environmental hazards. *Social Science Quarterly*, **84**(2), 242–61. doi:10.1111/1540-6237.8402002

Dao, H. and Peduzzi, P. (2003). Global Risk and Vulnerability Index Trends per Year (GRAVITY). Technical annex and multiple risk integration Phase IV. UNDP/BCPR, Geneva.

Esposito, F., Russo, M., Sargolini, M., Sartori, L., and Virgili, V. (eds) (2017). *Building Back Better: idee e percorsi per la costruzione di comunità resilienti*. Roma: Carocci editore (an English version of the abstracts of the contributions in this book is available at https://buildingbackbetterorg.wordpress.com).

Frigerio, I. and De Amicis, M. (2016). Mapping social vulnerability to natural hazards in Italy: a suitable tool for risk mitigation strategies. *Environmental Science & Policy*, **63**, 187–96. doi: doi.org/10.1016/j.envsci.2016.06.001

Guidoboni, E. (2017). Disastri e ricostruzioni nella storia d'Italia: l'azzardo sismico in un nodo storico non risolto. In F. Esposito, M. Russo, M. Sargolini, L. Sartori, and V. Virgili (eds), *Building Back Better: idee e percorsi per la costruzione di comunità resilienti*. Roma: Carocci editore, pp. 31–7.

ISTAT (2011). 15° Censimento Generale della Popolazione e delle Abitazioni. Available at http://dati.istat.it (accessed 12 Janaury 2018).

ISTAT (2018). 8milacensus. Una selezione di indicatori per ogni comune d'Italia. Available at http://ottomilacensus.istat.it/documentazione/ (accessed 12 January 2018).

JRC (2012). *Landslide Inventories in Europe and Policy Recommendations for their Interoperability and Harmonisation*. Report EUR 25666 EN. Luxembourg: Publications Office of the European Union.

Kaufman, L. and Rousseeuw, P. (1990). *Finding Groups in Data: An Introduction to Cluster Analysis*. Wiley Series in Probability and Mathematical Statistics. Hoboken, NJ: John Wiley & Sons.

Lance, G.N. and Williams, W.T. (1966). A generalized sorting strategy for computer classifications. *Nature*, **212**(5058), 218.

Pagliacci, F. (2017). La pericolosità da disastri naturali nell'Italia rurale. *AgriRegioniEuropa*, **13**(51), 16–21.

Pagliacci, F. and Russo, M. (2017). Earthquake hazard in Italy. Cluster analysis of socio-economic data to inform place-based policy measures, DEMB Working Paper Series no. 110. Università di Modena e Reggio Emilia, Modena.

Pagliacci, F., Russo, M., and Sartori, L. (2017). Social innovation and natural disasters: the "Casa Italia" Plan. *Sociologia Urbana e Rurale*, **113**, 87–102.

Peduzzi, P., Dao, H., Herold, C., and Mouton, F. (2009). Assessing global exposure and vulnerability towards natural hazards: the disaster risk index. *Natural Hazards and Earth System Sciences*, **9**, 1149–59.

R Core Team (2015). R: a language and environment for statistical computing. R Foundation for Statistical Computing, Vienna. Available at http://www.R-project.org/ (accessed 30 March 2018).

Russo, M. and Silvestri, P. (2017). Dati e strumenti di analisi per ricostruire meglio. In F. Esposito, M. Russo, M. Sargolini, L. Sartori, and V. Virgili (eds), *Building Back Better: idee e percorsi per la costruzione di comunità resilienti*. Roma: Carocci editore, pp. 154–61.

Russo, M., Pagliacci, F., and Righi, R. (2017). Does earthquake hazard couple with socio-economic vulnerability? Results from a municipality-level analysis in Italy. Paper presented at XXXVIII Conferenza Italiana di Scienze Regionali, Cagliari, Italy, 20–22 September. Available at https://www.aisre.it/images/aisre/596a236fec07 b7.76949695/Russo_Pagliacci_Righi.pdf (accessed 30 March 2018).

Sartori, L. (2017). Innovazione sociale tra vulnerabilità e resilienza delle comunità e dei territori. In F. Esposito, M. Russo, M. Sargolini, L. Sartori, and V. Virgili (eds), *Building Back Better: idee e percorsi per la costruzione di comunità resilienti*. Roma: Carocci editore, pp. 47–54.

Trigila, A., Iadanza, C., Bussettini, M., Lastoria, B., and Barbano, A. (2015). *Dissesto idrogeologico in Italia: pericolosità e indicatori di rischio*. ISPRA, Rapporti 233/2015.

UNDRO (United Nations Disaster Relief Office) (1979). *Natural Disasters and Vulnerability Analysis*. Report of Expert Group Meeting, 9–12 July, Geneva.

UNISDR (United Nations International Strategy for Disaster Risk Reduction) (2015). Sendai Framework for Disaster Risk Reduction, 2015–2030. Geneva: United Nations.

Valensise, G., Tarabusi, G., Guidoboni, E., and Ferrari, G. (2017). The forgotten vulnerability: a geology- and history-based approach for ranking the seismic risk of earthquake-prone communities of the Italian Apennines. *International Journal of Disaster Risk Reduction*, **25**, 289–300. doi: 10.1016/j.ijdrr.2017.09.014

Ward, J.H. (1963). Hierarchical grouping to optimize an objective function. *Journal of American Statistical Association*, **58**, 236–44.

10. Urban disasters crisis management scenario design and crisis management simulation

Karol Fabián, Lucia Rýsová and Michal Dobrík

10.1 CRISIS MANAGEMENT SCENARIO SIMULATION IN SUPPORT OF DISASTER PREPAREDNESS

Crisis simulations and crisis scenario design are preferred methods that may be employed to teach decision makers on how to act in time of crisis, or to understand the dynamics of crisis management. Another function of crisis simulations is to help planing for crisis management. It reveals weaknesses in existing plans, gaps in resource planning, improves coordination among operational elements of the plan, achieves higher levels of individual performance in carrying out disaster plans, gains public recognition of community emergency operations and assures the effective implementation of emergency plans and procedures (Kleiboer, 1997). Design of useful crisis management scenarios must have the form, role and content relevant to the problem at hand. Four decisions are important for scenario design: time setting; environmental setting; level of detail and knowledge; experience and sophistication of the players involved (Walker et al., 2011). The simulation software cannot be genneraly effective by itself, it must be set in the context of a particular organization, individual knowledge and preparedness. Computational modeling is expanding in the natural and social sciences, becoming increasingly prominent as a result of the spread of computational approaches, such as non-theory-driven simulations, computational methods of inference and the role of cognitive processes in computational model building (Nersessian et al., 2017). To be able to challenge responsible authorities and teams with scenarios as close as possible to reality, we need tools that support training and preparedness to tackle natural and human-made disasters with complex systems and procedures (Kazanský and Melková, 2015; Simoes-Marques et al., 2017). An effectively implemented crisis management scenario based on simulation software, which is described next, will increase the resilience performance of a state or organizations in crisis (Weick and Sutcliffe, 2007).

10.1.1   Crisis Management Center Infrastructure

Emergency Enterprise Manager KRIMA (EEM KRIMA) is the basic program tool of the Crisis Management Center (CMC) at Matej Bel University in the Slovak Republic (Atos, 2012). It is a crisis management digital system supporting various types of users and their requirements concerning prevention, solution and reconstruction. EEM KRIMA has been designed as a web application; it is not different from any other web sites. No special requirements have been set for users. The system is designed so that the individual user faces no restrictions during the process of crisis resolution. It supports the management of security and crisis situations, specifically "high risk" security incidents in urban environments. This is done in four steps, as shown in Figure 10.1, resulting in the final workflow of the crisis management scenario for the crisis situation in a particular organization or state.

1. The system administrator/designer creates a workflow within the environment.
2. Right after publishing, the workflow can be seen in the production environment, where it is used to handle incidents.
3. The system administrator/designer creates templates for incident or threat reporting; templates help the user in the process of incident reporting and they enable them to sort incidents and create groups.
4. In the production environment, available templates are used by users to report individual incidents.

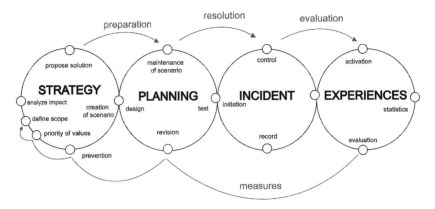

Figure 10.1   Overview of crisis scenario design and tuning

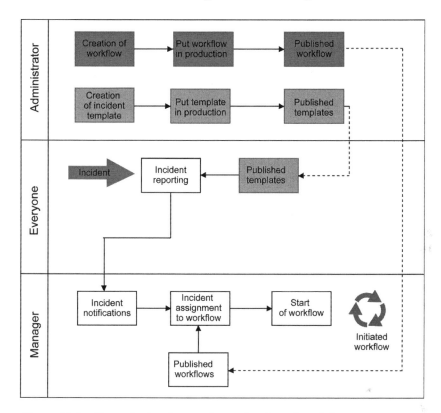

Figure 10.2   From the incident to the production of workflow

5. The manager assigns the reported incident to a crisis plan and launches the processing of incident workflow (Figure 10.2).

In the case of a failure of the central system, the crisis management software can be launched from any computer or external flash disc. The system is based on an Apache web server, which supports a multi-platform solution. EEM KRIMA supports all databases compatible with the SQL ANSI standard. The MS Sharepoint database was installed in order to store multimedia databases to support incident detection, identification, reporting and solution. The system logs important events automatically to enable the revision of objects and crisis situations in later stages. Ways to log in can be set in the configuration settings of the database server. Users with login rights and predefined privileges can only work in the system according to their role within the designed security measures. The layered architecture of the EEM consists of the object layer, containing predefined

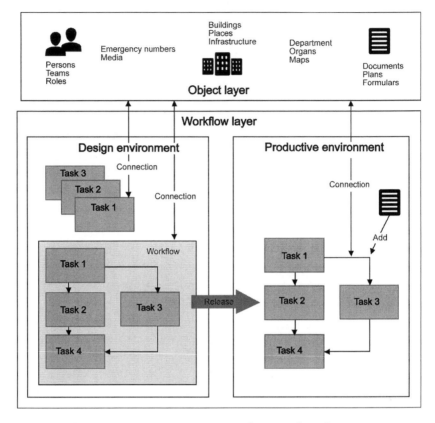

Figure 10.3   Crisis management scenario design and production

groups of objects, and the workflow layer, divided into design and productive environments (Figure 10.3).

Creation and management of workflow run in a graphic environment; there is no need to program anymore. Due to unlimited options of configuration and parameterization of the application, it is possible to create templates for various crisis situations, incidents and workflows. The system also has a number of predefined templates of well-known crisis situations. A user can be assigned to several user groups, which enable access to various functions of the system. The following user groups can access the system: system administrator, manager, reporter, designer, content manager and task manager. To launch a client computer, it is only necessary to call the URL application over a web browser. The system then creates a register of designed tasks and workflows. To make them available, it is necessary to publish them in an operating environment; this process is closely connected with versioning of workflows. There is also the possibility to automatically print out a crisis manual for every published workflow. The crisis manual can be printed for a particular workflow or in groups for several workflows. It contains basic information about the workflow and the crisis situation, a list of individual tasks with details, responsible persons, documents, maps and so on.

The system also supports a simulation mode. This mode is very similar to the real one. The simulation mode is configured to send notifications to created simulation accounts; not to responsible persons or management of an organization. This prevents the crisis management system from creating false alarms. The system can be linked with the public key infrastructure (PKI) of an organization. PKI can be used to log into the system or access protected content. In this way, we can achieve a very high security level. The system enables us to add new languages, and switch between them while editing. There is also the possibility to add signs to languages. The chosen language can be set as predefined. While control of "ready to adopt" processes is not finished, escalation notification is sent only to selected users. The system supports both manual and automatic sending of e-mails and text messages. It also enables the creation of various types of reports. One can use report filters to filter data concerning the incident according to the character of the incident, workflow, position, classification, date and so on. Reports can be printed or exported to Excel. Four main design and tuning cycles, Strategy, Planning, Incident and Experiences (Figure 10.1), are implemented in the basic system.

Crisis situation reporting uses templates to categorize the incident. A reported incident can be supported either by an existing workflow or by creating a new one, if necessary. Risk factor is calculated according to the severity of the situation. "Part Reports – Schedule of tasks" shows a list of all tasks of a crisis with a schedule, responsible persons, description of activities and workflow. You can filter the list by date, incidents, place and so on. All unfinished tasks (after the deadline) are clearly marked. Responsible persons can be seen in the detail of the workflow or task. The user can also see all tasks in the user EEM KRIMA Inbox. The user can get the overview by selection of dates or filter open or closed tasks.

10.1.2   Communication Subsystem

The modular communication subsystem based on the "client–server" architecture principle is an integral part of the CMC. A user-friendly mobile solution available for several operating systems and end devices was also implemented. It provides protection of data transmissions and voice communication against various forms of unlawful interception, as the system could deal with possible criminal activity by a sophisticated hacker. The system enables the selection of a secure communication regime in the following forms – secure calls, conference calls, texting, messages containing image, video and sound content (multimedia messaging service) – according to the requirements of individual users. A mobile VoIP system supporting group cooperation provides a stable and secure system of closed group communication (conference calls) for end users over IP networks. It also enables the selection of a secure communication regime as secure calls, conference calls, texting, messages containing image, video and sound content (multimedia messaging service), according to the requirements of individual users.

The system also enables one to use either a mobile network operator or a static IP network in the Slovak Republic and abroad, in order to make communication more effective (GPRS, EDGE, UMTS, WiFi and so on). The communication system can switch logs of events with various levels of detail on or off and save them to the database for further use. In case the user is not logged in, there is off-line messaging support. The system of conference calls is in a half-duplex regime (Push To Talk or PTT). There is also a User Presence/availability status implemented as part of the standard solution. Resolution of accessibility is designed by colored icons (logged in, logged off, absent, do not disturb). The system uses its own PKI in order to ensure proper operation and functions.

Communication between the client and the server runs using an encrypted SIP channel. Connection and secure delivery of data and voice communications between users is through an encrypted RTP protocol. The user configures all user and security settings according to individual requirements and settings of the organization (access point, DNS name server, TCP ports and so on). From the very beginning, the conversation regime supports texting and multimedia messaging. In fact, the user can use both voice communications and texting.

10.2 CRISIS SCENARIO OF CATASTROPHIC INCIDENT RESULTING IN MASS CASUALTIES

This case study was designed, set up and presented at the request of the Ministry of the Interior of the Slovak Republic. It is based on a large number of existing legal documents, regulations and directives valid for accidents that result in extraordinary levels of damage or mass casualties (Fabián et al., 2016). All possible crisis situations and corresponding variants of crisis scenarios are not yet covered in detail. If we want to

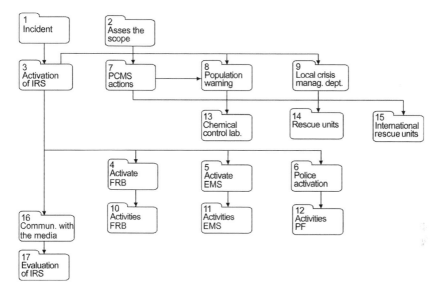

Figure 10.4   Crisis management scenario of catastrophic incidents resulting in mass casualties

implement the scenario in the real production environment for automated control of the crisis situation, each individual type of situation occuring in the urban enviroment must be elaborated in greater detail, including names, adresses and phone numbers of responsible persons from the crisis response teams at local and global levels. This case study shows the possibility of modeling and simulation using the EEM KRIMA system for the Department of Crisis Management of the Ministry of the Interior of the Slovak Republic. Tasks and activities are interleaved and in most cases they can be performed simultaneously, according to the crisis management scenario of the catastrophic incident (Figure 10.4). Units of the so-called Integrated Rescue System of the Slovak Republic (IRS), such as the Emergency Medical Service (EMS), Fire and Rescue Brigade (FRB) and the Police Force (PF), with all its components will be active in the crisis management scenario. Preparedness is a crucial ingredient in effective crisis management. The crisis scenario of a catastrophic incident resulting in mass casualties was designed with respect to existing legal documents for this type of event. It does not comprise elementary preparation elements for the involved organizations, as these topics are included in their basic everyday functioning.

Catastrophic incident (CI) is any incident that results in extraordinary levels of mass casualties and injured people, regardless of the real cause of the CI. In a situation like this, the priority should be given to early recovery and helping seriously injured people. In the case of the CI, the number of injured is usually so high that conditions at the site of intervention (in particular the ratio between the number of injured and IRS staff) do not allow immediate care for all injured.

One of the typical features of the catastrophic incident is that there is a lack of forces and resources particularly at the beginning of the IRS intervention. Therefore, it is necessary to pay attention to detailed organization and management of all IRS units, that is, the management of arrivals, departures to and from the intervention site. Considering the threat and the number of emergency response team members, the catastrophic incidents resulting in extraordinary levels of mass casualties and seriously injured can be divided into three basic types:

A. Catastrophic incidents where the actual conditions allow classifying injured persons according to the severity of their injury directly on the site or nearby, in the place where the injured persons are located. Performed by EMS without any apparent threat (e.g., significant part of traffic accidents).

B. Catastrophic incidents in which the injured persons need transport to a minimum safe distance, out of the reach of possible CI effects (e.g., explosion, possible structural failures and collapses, chemical or nuclear contamination and so on), which threaten both seriously injured persons and members of the rescue services. Classification of injured persons according to the severity of their injury and their transportation are generally performed by FRB, whose members transport injured people to the EMS.

C. Catastrophic incidents or hazardous material incidents determined by the presence of hazardous substances and materials. Emergency response teams must use the appropriate level of protection in this type of location. Only after reduced contamination are decontaminated persons handed over to the EMS.

10.2.1   Detailed Description of Crisis Management Scenario and Task Workflow

Task 1: Type and basic characteristics of catastrophic incident
It is the responsibilty of a crisis manager to decide which type of CI has occured. Catastrophic incidents resulting in extraordinary levels of mass casualties and injured can be divided into three types depending on the threat and the number of emeregency response team members, as

outlined above. The crisis manager is a member of the Permanent Crisis Management Service (PCMS) section, which takes the first call about the CI.

Task 2: Assessing the scope of the event

If the incident is beyond the capabilities and capacities of the regional response team, the PCMS section can ask for additional assistance from another region or the state, with notification to the Ministry of the Interior of the Slovak Republic.

If there is an incident (characterized by enormous numbers of dead and injured, the extent and location of the incident, the weather situation, the presence of hazardous substances and materials) that cannot be managed by local capacities and IRS resources, then it is necessary:

- to ensure delivery of information to the PCMS and, if necessary, request the assistance of chemical laboratories to distribute the information about the incident via electronic mass communication media and so on.
- to provide a public warning if necessary (e.g., transport of hazardous substances and the population can be at risk)
- to initiate the establishment of relevant territorial/or regional crisis management bodies (municipality, district, region)
- to coordinate the activities of individual IRS units and components in order to provide maximum assistance to the incident commander.

Task 3: Activation of resources

Operators of the PCMS headquarters provide services concerning the information on the CI resulting in mass casualties and injured. There is an emergency telephone number 1-1-2 which allows a caller to contact the local emergency service.

Task 4: Activation of Fire and Rescue Brigade

FRB units are activation of the FRB, which involves a sufficient number of apparatus consisting of cars, tankers, rescue trucks and so on, as well as firemen. Each individual task requires a decision about the number of necessary apparatus (cars and other machinery).

Task 5: Activation of Emergency Medical Service

Activation of the EMS is determined by the nature of the CI; a decision on the number of doctors and other medical specialists must be made. If necessary, medical air transport, ambulances and specialized medical facilities should be used. On some occasions, mortuary ambulance services and forensic units are used as well. Conventional means of public transport can be used for mass transportation of injured persons who do not require immediate medical attention.

Task 6: Activation of the Police Force

The Police Force must be activated in the case of the CI resulting in mass casualties and injured, for the purpose of the investigation. If necessary, this task also includes the activation of the police aviation service to provide air support.

Task 7: Permanent Crisis Management Service

If required, the PCMS calls the IRS for additional assistance. The PCMS crisis manager makes a request for assistance, which activates the response teams of the IRS within the framework of international assistance and humanitarian cooperation. In the case of a serious traffic accident, for example, transport of hazardous chemical substances and materials, the PCMS sends a request to the Civil Protection Controlling Chemical Laboratory, and ensures cooperation with other specialized facilities and organizations (hygiene facilities, specialized laboratories and so on). If the incident is beyond the capacities of the regional response teams of the IRS, then it is necessary to request additional assistance from another region (e.g., neighboring district). If the CI has happened near the state border, the PCMS can call to request additional assistance from another state. Based on actual requirements, the IRS will provide a public warning about the incident via electronic mass communication media (radio, television). If the CI goes across the state borders, and exceeds the territory of the Slovak Republic, the response teams of the neigboring state are provided with full information about the incident. Sometimes it is also necessary to inform relevant organizations and bodies (such as the European Union (EU), United Nations (UN), North Atlantic Treaty Organization (NATO) and so on) on a daily basis.

Task 8: Public warning

In the case of catastrophic incidents resulting in extraordinary levels of mass casualties and injured, it is necessary to inform the public. The crisis management team provides a public warning that the population may be at risk.

Task 9: Activation of local crisis management departments

This task initiates the establishment of crisis management bodies at municipal and district levels. The running scenario sends them the necessary information through dedicated channels activated by the running scenario. Right after the establishment of the local crisis management bodies, crisis management authorities are provided with a full information service, which is necessary for decision-making processes and local management. The Civil Protection Information Service provides relevant information about the state and course of individual rescue tasks; it also informs the public.

Task 10: Operation of the emergency call center of the FRB
The FRB emergency call center (emergency telephone number 1-5-0), as an integral part of the IRS, answers the calls, processes and evaluates the information on the CI. It also receives information from another operation center of the IRS. The FRB operation center upon receiving the information on the emergency sends the intervention unit and manages its actions and activities in the field; it also informs the IRS about the action immediately.

Task 11: Operation of the emergency call center of the EMS
The EMS emergency call center (emergency telephone number 1-5-5), as another integral part of the IRS, answers the calls, processes and evaluates the informations on the CI. It also receives information about the CI from other operation centers of the IRS. In addition, the EMS activates the appropriate level of traumatology plan (according to the number of seriously injured estimated by the first EMS members at the intervention site), ensures EMS units are sent from the nearest points, organizes reinforcement and means according to the number of injured people, and requests additional assistance from neighboring EMS operation centers. The center calls for medical facilities for transport of injured persons and verifies the current state of possible urgent admissions to hospitals. On request, it provides a supply of medication, medical materials and devices to the place of intervention and, if necessary, sends medical air transport. The center provides the PF Operational Center with the necessary personal data of all patients and their injuries.

Task 12: Operation of the police operation centers (central, regional and local levels)
Police operation centers at national, regional and local levels organize and ensure smooth traffic flow and, if necessary, take appropriate action to let ambulances or other IRS vehicles pass through. The police also close off the traffic in case of an accident. They can also close off the CI area if long-term investigation is required and unauthorized access is prohibited.

Task 13: Civil Protection sends chemical laboratory
In the case of a serious traffic accident involving hazardous substances and materials, the IRS sends a chemical laboratory to the site of the accident. The IRS manages its activities and ensures cooperation with other specialized facilities and organizations (hygiene, specialized laboratories and so on).

Task 14: Sending response teams from another region or district
If the incident is beyond the capabilities and capacies of the regional response team, the PCMS section requests additional assistance from another region or state, with notification to the Ministry of the Interior of the Slovak Republic.

Task 15: Deployment of IRS in terms of international assistance
If the incident is beyond the capacities of the regional response teams of the IRS, then it is necessary to request additional assistance from another region (e.g., neighboring district). If the CI has happened near the state border, the PCMS can call for additional assistance from another state. Based on the actual requirement, the IRS will provide a public warning about the incident via electronic mass communication media (radio, television). If the CI goes across state borders, that is, if it exceeds the territory of the Slovak Republic, the response teams of the neigboring state are provided with full information about the incident. Sometimes it is also necessary to inform relevant organizations and bodies (EU, UN, NATO and so on).

Task 16: Communication with the media
Working with mass media, notifying and informing the relatives of injured relatives and other victims is an important part of the intervention and it is an obligatory task of the IRS. As time passes, pressure from the public and the media to provide information usually increases and does not cease even after the intervention has ended.

Task 17: Evaluation of the impact of IRS components
The identification of victims enables legal declaration of death, which is done by issuing a death certificate. The provision of essential trauma care to injured people is not only important during the intervention on the CI site. The number of people who need such care usually soars after the CI, mainly due to the nature of the situation (relatives of seriously wounded people or dead people and survivors). These CI implications cannot usually be resolved by the time of the intervention. Therefore, it is necessary to initiate essential trauma care at the level of operational management entities.

10.3   CRISIS SCENARIO OF SWINE FLU PANDEMIC AND CRISIS MANAGEMENT PROCESS

Influenza is one of the oldest diseases common to humans and animals. Annual flu epidemics are caused by the frequent evolution of the viral genome. The constant changes of influenza virus genes means that the human immune system may not recognize the flu viruses and the person exposed to these viruses can get sick again. From time to time a major change of flu virus occurs. People do not have the immunity to protect themselves against the new virus and thus an epidemic starts to spread quickly, potentially causing a global pandemic situation. Flu is the most common human infectious disease, affecting 10 percent of the world's population each year. In a pandemic period, 40 to 50 percent of people are infected in the world. There are three levels of disease incidence within the epidemic process. The first one is a sporadic occurrence, where the morbidity does not exceed the usual incidence at a given time in a given territory. The second one is the epidemic incidence, in which the morbidity clearly exceeds the prevalence of the infection. The third one is a pandemic occurrence with an unusually large epidemic, which could cause millions of deaths.

Pandemic waves of flu in the past have caused millions of deaths (e.g., the Spanish flu, or 1918 flu pandemic, resulted in the deaths of 50 to 100 million people), so there must be careful preparation of an effective crisis management scenario for a flu pandemic, based on the most current scientific research. It is now clear that only immediate action such as the killing of infected poultry, birds and pigs has saved mankind from a new large-scale flu pandemic. This is based on the recommendations of the World Health Organization (WHO) and the Food and Agriculture Organization. There are huge financial losses for lost sales and replacement of poultry.

The mild scenario of the flu outbreak would count on 1.4 million deaths and a 1 percent loss from the global economy's GDP (or gross world product) (US$ 330 billion). In contrast, a serious flu outbreak would amount to 142 million deaths worlwide and a 12.6 percent decline in global GDP (US$ 4.4 trillion). The following crisis management scenario for a flu pandemic is based on a complex analysis of a number of legal documents and laws of the Slovak Republic, the WHO and the EU (Uhrínová, 2017). It is complex from the point of view of the state, while not yet covering all tasks that must be performed at the local level by authorities in the case of a flu pandemic. As already mentioned in the previous case study, preparedness is crucial in effective crisis management. The crisis scenario of a swine flu pandemic, which can cause millions of deaths, was designed

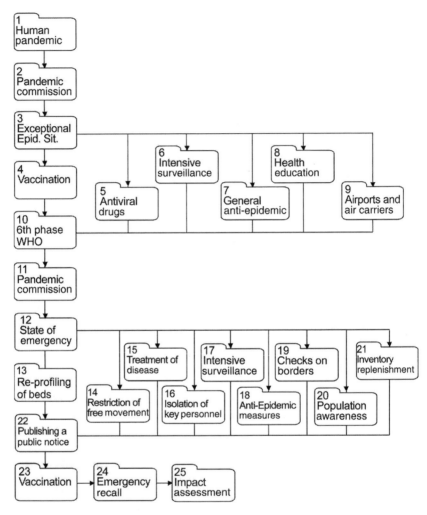

Figure 10.5   Crisis management scenario of swine flu pandemic

with respect to existing crisis management legal documents for this type of disease (Figure 10.5). It does not comprise all necessary preparation elements for the state and the involved organizations. Again, this topic is included in their basic everyday functions and is therefore not part of the described crisis scenario simulation.

10.3.1   Detailed description of crisis management scenario and task workflow

Task 1: Human flu pandemic
Crisis management scenario with the occurrence of Type A flu, a new dangerous subtype. The conditions for declaration of the 5th phase of the six phases of the revised WHO Pandemic Alert Scale have been met. Potential occurrence was reported within the WHO European Region, including the Slovak Republic. There is a progressive adaptation of the virus to humans, but not yet to the full pandemic extent.

Task 2: Session of Pandemic Commission
The Central Task Force and the Security Council of the Slovak Republic discuss the meeting of Pandemic Commission of the Slovak government, the Central Crisis Staff of the Slovak Republic and the Security Council of the Slovak Republic. They have to reconsider the conclusions of the meeting of the Pandemic Commission of the Slovak government, and agree on further actions – including updating and coordinations during the pandemic period. The Pandemic Commission's operations center provides information on the conclusions of the meeting to the relevant pandemic centers operating at national and regional levels. The crisis manager has to check whether specific persons other than those preprogrammed by the EEM KRIMA system have been called to the meeting. The members of the Security Council are the contact points in the crisis scenario, namely, the Prime Minister of the Slovak Republic and the Ministers of Defense, Interior, Finance, Foreign Affairs, Health, Justice, Transport, Construction and Economy of the Slovak Republic. Besides these, there are also several other persons involved – the secretary of the Security Council of the Slovak Republic and the main hygienist of the Slovak Republic. These people are contacted automatically at the start of the crisis management, in the form of an e-mail notification.

Task 3: Declaration of an exceptional epidemiological situation
The declaration of an exceptional epidemiological situation (EES) in the areas of flu outbreak, the occurrence of the rapid spread of a new subtype of Type A flu in the region of the Slovak Republic. The regional hygienist has a central position; he decides to declare the EES and commands the implementation of extraordinary measures. The regional hygienist announces his decision to members of the Regional Anti-Epidemic Commission at the Regional Authority of Public Health (RAPH). At the same time, the regional hygienist contacts the district operation centers of EMS. If the regional hygienists conclude that it will be necessary to declare

the EES, the RAPH starts its professional crisis management operation in the region. The crisis manager confirms the EES statement in the form of an option – YES or NO. At the same time, a document containing the report of the flu pandemic according to the Decree of the Ministry of Health of the Slovak Republic gives details on the prevention and control of communicable diseases. Additionally, objects to be notified by the EEM KRIMA system are sent in the form of short text messages (SMS) on mobile phones to district offices and the EMS district operation center. It is also necessary to ensure feedback is given.

Task 4: Vaccination
Vaccination is one of the most important tasks because the vaccine and its availability can save and protect lives, and maintain the functioning of the critical infrastructure of the state. The basic measure is to order a vaccine against the flu pandemic strain. The order is issued by the Minister of Health of the Slovak Republic, who acts based on an issued approval of the government of the Slovak Republic. After the vaccine is delivered to the Slovak Republic, distribution will take place. This will be managed by the Ministry of the Interior of the Slovak Republic. Application of the vaccine should be in accordance with a detailed plan, which instructs each ministry to establish a list of persons that are necessary for the maintenance of the state, and therefore will be vaccinated in the first round. At the same time, persons at risk are also vaccinated in accordance with the detailed schedule, the inventory of which is enclosed in the document. Vaccination is carried out through cooperation with doctors and medical specialists of the first contact. The crisis manager confirms in the running EEM KRIMA crisis scenario whether the vaccine has been ordered.

Task 5: Management of the administration of antiviral drugs
The administration of the specific antiviral drugs is an essential part of the treatment of flu. They are immediately administered to ill people and to all persons with clinical signs at the focal points of laboratory confirmed flu. At the same time, the Ministry of Health of the Slovak Republic, together with the State Reserves Administration, shall provide enough antiviral drugs and their distribution. Approved groups of staff and individuals have to follow the guidelines concerning chemoprophylaxis. To ensure that sufficient antiviral drugs are available, over the counter sale in pharmacies will be forbidden. Appropriate measures will be taken to prevent breaches of this ban – surveillance and possible sanctions against infringers. The crisis manager will also confirm if the sale of antiviral drugs is limited. Within the framework of the task, the information is provided for the

administration of antivirals in the 5th phase of the flu pandemic of the Plan for Infectious Diseases in the Slovak Republic.

Task 6: Intensive surveillance
Step 1 of intensive surveillance will be replaced by step 2 at a certain point. The task represents an active search to find ill people. Subsequently, a report is filed in accordance with corresponding laws. Within this task a document must be attached to a scenario informing about the current status of the pandemic. It is important to provide not only oral but also intravenous administration of antiviral drugs because ill people are sometimes unable to swallow. An essential part of surveillance is to ensure laboratory investigations of samples taken from ill people. As a result of the significant increase in the number of samples tested, it is necessary to increase the capacity of laboratories and to ensure that there is enough testing volume available. Within the framework of the task, selected laboratories for the given regions perform a diagnosis according to the Expert Guidelines of the Ministry of Health of the Slovak Republic to carry out re-profiling and change of the bed fund usage within the healthcare facilities and other measures. At the same time, the results are reported to the corresponding bodies of the EU and the WHO, particularly via the National Reference Laboratory for Influenza to the WHO Reference Laboratory for the Region of Europe in the City of London.

Task 7: General anti-epidemic measures
General anti-epidemic measures (step 1), like Task 6, will continue with the second step. The RAPH and other district authorities have competences to issue appropriate measures. There are practical tasks in the form of isolation and treatment of ill people. At the same time, contact with them is restricted. An appropriate monitoring unit investigates the flu outbreak. Principles of medical hygiene measures are requested. The Ministry of Health of the Slovak Republic in cooperation with the Slovak State Reserve Administration shall provide sufficient personal protective equipment, nursing aids, special devices (respirators and so on) and their subsequent distribution according to the current needs. The individual ministries issue measures for the fulfillment of anti-epidemic measures within their sphere of competence, including the representative offices of the Slovak Republic abroad. The crisis manager indicates if the necessary actions have been fulfilled in the running scenario in the EEM KRIMA system.

Task 8: Intensification of health education
Intensification of health education is focused mainly on the public. The Ministry of Health of the Slovak Republic activates its call centers which

are used to contact the public. At the same time, if necessary, the ministry will alert its staff. Furthermore, within the framework of the given task, the Ministry of Health of the Slovak Republic, in cooperation with the RAPH, informs the public via electronic mass media about the symptoms of the flu disease, the way it is transmitted and the possibilities of its prevention and health protection. The ministry informs the public about the epidemiological situation or issues further guidance.

Task 9: Airports and air carriers control
Control of airports and air carriers refers to the implementation of measures against the spread of flu disease. It takes place at airports in the Slovak Republic and all air carriers operating within the Slovak Republic. Responsibility lies with the Ministry of the Interior of the Slovak Republic as it is responsible for the protection of state borders. It cooperates with the Ministry of Transport, Construction and Regional Development of the Slovak Republic.

Task 10: 6th phase of the flu pandemic
The Chief Hygienist of the Slovak Republic announces the declaration of the 6th phase of the flu pandemic (according to the WHO). The incidence of the disease will be reported to the WHO, Centers for Disease Control and Prevention (CDC), European Centre for Disease Prevention and Control (ECDC) and others. This task is performed if there is an epidemic in the Slovak Republic (infectedness of the Slovak population is about 35 percent) with high morbidity (10 percent). The task is to instruct the EEM KRIMA to send a notification to the Chief Hygienist of the Slovak Republic.

Task 11: Meeting of the Pandemic Commission
The Pandemic Commission, the Central Crisis Staff and the Security Council of the Slovak Republic perform activities similar to those under Task 2, with the provision of inspections carried out under the auspices of the RAPH. Similar to Task 2, the crisis manager checks whether specific persons other than those contacted by the EEM KRIMA system have been called to the meeting. The institutions responsible for inspections are also confirmed.

Task 12: State of emergency in the Slovak Republic
State of emergency in the Slovak Republic, refers to the situation when the government is empowered to perform actions that are usually not permitted. The life and health of citizens is in danger as a result of the flu pandemic. The crisis manager assigns the duration of the state of emergency to the task.

Task 13: Re-profiling of beds
Re-profiling of beds means changing usage of beds. In the case of pandemic influenza, all hospital beds are dedicated to the pandemic with the exception of oncological and psychiatric beds in accordance with the Expert Guidelines of the Ministry of Health of the Slovak Republic for the bed fund in healthcare facilities.

Task 14: Restriction of movement
A "curfew" or restriction of movement when people are required to stay indoors at a specified time. At the same time, a measure is adopted, the extent of which is directly dependent on the epidemiological situation, ordered by a health authority at the local, regional or national level. Measures at the local level are accepted by directors of organizations or by responsible staff, such as hospital directors, school principals, city and municipal authorities. The Ministry of Education, Science, Sport and Research of the Slovak Republic is responsible for this area. Another example is home-based social services, which must also isolate ill people, as ordered by the public health authority. This area is under the responsibility of the Ministry of Labor, Social Affairs and the Family of the Slovak Republic.

Task 15: Treatment of disease and strengthening services
The administration of antivirals to ill people continues according to the document attached to the task in the EEM KRIMA crisis management scenario. Healthcare facilities continue through isolation of patients with flu from other patients, restriction of new patient admissions, limitation of surgeries, visiting bans at the hospitals and exclusion of ill personnel.

Task 16: Isolation of key personnel
To ensure the functioning of the state, key personnel have to be isolated away from the sources of the flu infection. For this reason, the Chief Hygienist of the Slovak Republic will issue an instruction to isolate workers whose performance and activities are necessary to maintain the functionality of all strategic sectors, components responsible for monitoring and control of the flu pandemic. The emergency supply is ensured by the Ministry of Economy of the Slovak Republic, which also carries out emergency supplies in case of quarantine measures. The crisis manager checks whether these positions are isolated by selecting the option YES or NO in the running scenario.

Task 17: Intensive surveillance

Intensive surveillance (step 2) replaces Task 6, further intensifying the analysis. The crisis manager checks whether or not the respective institutions have executed and implemented the instruction.

Task 18: General anti-epidemic measures

General anti-epidemic measures (step 2) continue to act, as in Task 7. However, there is an order to wear protective masks on public transport and in places where there is close contact between large numbers of people. Concurrently, the transport of bio-hazardous waste and the burial of a large number of dead people is ensured. These take place within the framework of the relevant territorial classification, according to the attached document for the task. The crisis manager indicates in the task whether or not the removal has been done and whether a recommendation has been issued.

Task 19: Border control, airport security control

It is necessary to step up the measures from Task 9. Not only are border control and airport security control underway, air traffic is also strongly limited. Each individual person infected is prevented from entering or exiting the state. The task is carried out in cooperation with the Ministry of Transport, Construction and Regional Development of the Slovak Republic, the Ministry of Defense of the Slovak Republic and the Ministry of the Interior of the Slovak Republic. The crisis manager confirms traffic security in the corresponding step in the EEM KRIMA scenario.

Task 20: Population awareness

Population awareness is very similar to Task 8; it establishes call centers and dedicated information lines in hospitals as well as all RAPHs.

Task 21: Inventory replenishment

Inventory replenishment refers to the continuous replenishment of inventory, personal protective equipment, nursing aids, medication, medical material and special devices.

Task 22: Publishing a public notice

A public notice is published focused on a search for healthcare volunteers. This search is for healthcare volunteers who will help the emergency response teams during the flu pandemic. If necessary, transitional care hospitals are established in order to care for critically ill patients.

Task 23: Vaccination of other people
Vaccination of other people takes place and antivirals against flu are administered to people who cannot be vaccinated due to allergy contraindications to the vaccine. Monitoring of the safety and efficiency of flu vaccination is carried out. The crisis manager monitors whether or not the vaccines are distributed and the people are subsequently vaccinated.

Task 24: Emergency recall
Emergency recall takes place. The WHO revokes the state of the pandemic and the government of the Slovak Republic recalls the state of emergency. After this step there is no immediate danger to the life and health of people due to the spread of the flu pandemic. At the same time, all measures are taken in connection with the state of emergency and the Constitutional Act. The crisis manager confirms that the crisis has been recalled.

Task 25: Pandemic Impact Assessment
Pandemic Impact Assessment within the Slovak Republic documents the effectivness of measures related to the end of the crisis and the end of the flu pandemic. There follows an evaluation of the precautions taken and preparation for any further pandemic waves.

10.4   CRISIS SCENARIO OF A RANSOMWARE ATTACK ON CRITICAL INFRASTRUCTURE AND CRISIS MANAGEMENT

National and business infrastructure, often referred to as critical infrastructure, has always been a potential target from the ancient to the modern world. Industrialization created new targets, for example, energy supply, telecommunications, financial system and so on. Only very few things in this modern industrialized world can function without energy, transportation, healthcare or communications. Life as we know it today would no longer be possible if there was no energy industry or if we had to face a long-term power outage. The sectors and industries in Table 10.1 are widely considered to be critical infrastructure, according to the Organization for Security and Co-operation in Europe (OSCE, 2013).

This is the main reason why states must take responsibility for the above-mentioned sectors and implement various measures in order to guarantee protection for all industries. The contemporary geopolitical situation is very complicated with all its hybrid wars. Global cyberspace is a perfect playground for virtual terrorism (Fabián et al., 2017).

Today, the term "ransomware" is used to describe certain groups of

Table 10.1   Critical infrastructure sectors and industries

Sectors	Industries
Energy	Electricity
	Natural gas
	Oil
Information and communiction technology	Telecommunications (including satellites)
	Broadcasting systems
	Software, hardware and networks (including the Internet)
Traffic and transportation	Shipping
	Aviation
	Rail transport
	Road traffic and transport
	Logistic
Heathcare	Healthcare
	Medication and vaccines
	Laboratories
Water supply	Dams
	Storages
	Treatment and distribution networks
Finance and insurance	Banks
	Stock exchanges
	Insurance companies
	Financial services
Goverment and administration	Goverments
	Parliaments
	Legal institutions
	Emergency services
Nutrition and agriculture	Food trade
	Agriculture
Media and cultural assets	Radio
	Press
	Symbolic/iconic buildings

malware that force users to pay a ransom (or fee), usually in a so-called cryptocurrency (e.g., digital currency bitcoin). Payment should guarantee that the user will regain access to the infected device. Ransomware attacks have enormous potential to cause serious problems for critical infrastructure of states, institutions and individuals today, and in the near future the danger may even be greater. Ransomware groups responsible for identifying targets do not hesitate to target institutions where lives can be put in danger. Careful preparation in order to avoid or, once it happens, minimize corresponding damage is a must for responsible states or organizations. First, we summarize all known types of ransomware attacks and their behavior. Second, we recommend tools and methods to minimize the damage caused by the attack by creating a ransomware crisis management scenario. This scenario can be adapted by states and/ or institutions according to different IT architectures, using backup media and restore procedures and planning. When carefully debugged in the simulation setup, it can than be run in the case of an attack in real time.

The increasing number of ransomware attacks from cyberspace is getting more and more attention as the danger of immediate closing of business for the attacked organizations rises dramatically. High-level encryptions used by the current versions of ransomware make it almost impossible for them to be decrypted in real time and the probability of production going live again for the attacked organization is thus low. Estimated revenue up to US$ 1 billion in 2016 makes this type of cybercrime activity very popular within the hackers' community. The ransomware attack in 2017 on healthcare facilities and critical transport infrastructure with the customized NSA code WannaCry infected more than 300,000 computers worldwide. A known weakness of the Windows 7 operating system was an open door for the WannaCry worm.

10.4.1   Ransomware as a Business Model

Since 2013, ransomware has been a serious problem for Windows users. Also, the rapid rise of ransomware incidents on mobile devices and the most popular mobile platform, Android (Lipovský et al., 2016), is just another logical outcome of the previous successes of this underground community on the Windows platform. Various smart devices using OS Android and a growing number of devices connected on the Internet of Things (IOT) can also be attacked, for example, Smart TVs. Mac OS and Linux are not resistant against ransomware attacks. Several functional samples of ransomware code have also appeared on these platforms.

Malware infection causes serious problems to institutions, and individuals as well. During the first three months of 2016 an organized group of hackers obtained $US 209 million from various institutions and individuals. There was a real presumption that revenues from these activities exceeded US$ 1 billion at the end of 2016. Considering the published case of the attack on the Los Angeles hospital, the profit of hackers was US$ 17,000, paid in bitcoins. Hackers attacked the hospital, blocked all e-mail services, access to medical records, results of lab tests, encrypted complete medical records, disrupted the work of medical labs, pharmacies and also caused temporary closure of the radiation and oncology departments. Patients had to be transferred to other hospitals, because this hospital had no capability and capacity to admit them. After ten days, the hospital decided to pay the ransom.

Ransomware and social engineering, through which ransomware infects "victims", are up to 72 percent of the total package of malware according to the Isaca Cybersecurity Snapshot 2016. A link in an e-mail (31 percent) and attachment in an e-mail (28 percent) are the most common methods of ransomware penetrating organizations according to Oesterman Research Inc. (2016). In 2016, almost 97 percent of phishing e-mails were infected by ransomware. Other common ways of infiltration are the so-called "drive-by-downloading" (a user visits compromised web-pages and unintentionally downloads malware onto a computer) and malvertising (injecting malware-laden advertisements into legitimate online advertising web-pages and networks). Those methods usually misuse well-known vulnerabilities of the web browser or plug-ins, for example, the Flash Player plug-in. There are also other traditional ways of malware spreading techniques, for example, downloading of infected freeware and modified illegal versions of commercial programs or infected external storage devices (e.g., USB).

Contemporary ransomware, unlike its very first versions such as Windows Cryptolocker, uses strong cryptography; this means that the infected user has no chance to regain access to the infected device without the decryption key. The government of the United States, together with the FBI and other relevant US governmental bodies, released an official directive on the prevention and response to ransomware attacks – Presidential Policy Directive (PPD-41) United States Cyber Incident Coordination. Specialized units of Europol, the Dutch police and several companies dealing with cyber security decided to fight ransomware in Europe. An initiative entitled "No More Ransom!" is the direct result of this cooperation (https://www.nomoreransom.org). At the time of writing of this chapter there were more than 200 known types of ransomware in the world. The most well-known ransomware includes CryptoLocker, CryptoWall, CTBlocker, Locky, TeslaCrypt, TorrentLocker, KeRanger, Petya, Mischa, Simplocker, Chimera, Jigsaw and many others. There are also various mutations of ransomware codes today. The continuous, massive emergence of new mutations of ransomware codes complicates effective prevention. This is even despite installation and frequently updated security software.

After successful installation, most ransomware logs on to the management server (Command and Control Center) and then forward basic data about the infected device. Almost 3 percent of victims have paid a ransom. An increasing number of infected devices results in enormous profits for organized groups of criminals. These groups share their profits according to precisely defined rules. Profit is shared between the authors of malware codes and the distributors of malware through web-pages, infected links in e-mails or infected attachments in e-mails, with the majority of the profit going to the authors of malware codes. Using contemporary cloud terminology, such a business model can be called "Ransomware as a Service" (RaaS). However, every user is able to prevent ransomware attacks.

10.4.2 Crisis Management for an Unprecedented Ransomware Attack on Critical Infrastructure

Prevention is the most important part of incident preparation against ransomware attack. Elimination is the best solution of every crisis situation. It means that a backup plan and update of operating systems should be a permanent part of a user's life. It is also necessary to perform routine backups of files of the workstations and then to disconnect the backup device from the operating system after backing up. Even though ransomware can block all storage devices, including the USB, the user is able to retrieve the data from the disconnected backup device in this way. The user can restore the infected files and minimize damage (Figure 10.6).

Regular training of employees potentially the target of cyber attack is an inseparable part of complex prevention. Testing of e-mail attachments (which could be infected and then represent a certain real threat for user or users, particularly .pdf files or e-mail attachments .bat, .cmd, .exe, .scr, .js, .vbs) in dedicated sandboxes without allowing the infected software to harm the institution's network is today an everyday practice. If the institution does not use sandbox testing, then it is appropriate and highly recommended not to send those e-mails to users because they can be infected. Malware targets users using RDP (Remote Desktop Protocol), so the user should keep the RDP disabled. It is also necessary to avoid suspicious files and run programs from AppData/LocalAppData because it can protect the system against various malware mutations. Shared folders represent another serious threat for institutions. Ransomware can encrypt all files stored on computers and network drives. Regarding prevention, it is necessary to pay attention to user rights and to restrict access to the data structures of single users who do not necessarily need it. Backup systems should be disconnected from the operating system; otherwise the infection can occur and the malware will also encrypt the backup devices, thus the user will not be able to retrieve files from backup.

Windows ScriptHost is a frequent tool of ransomware infection. Activation is recommended only for users who need it. These users should be made aware of the increased risk of ransomware infection. Automatic run should be replaced by using, for example, "Open with . . .", according to the type of file.

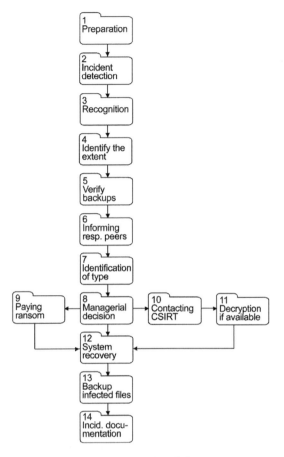

Figure 10.6 Crisis management scenario of the ransomware attack on critical infrastructures

10.4.3 Detailed Description of Crisis Management Scenario Tasks and Workflow

Task 1: Preparation for the incident
Incident preparation is an important part of the solution to the crisis situations. It contains predefined items.

- *List of incident-related systems.* The list consists of both logic and physical systems, including their DNS reports, operational systems, IP addresses and so on. It contains all network devices and infrastructure parts which can be attacked, including communication routes and nodes.

- *List of persons responsible for systems.* The list consists of contacts with the specification of who and when to inform. It reflects the organizational structure of the workplace and institution. Departments of law, energy, fire protection and labor safety are also of great importance. Each individual contact must have their own backup definition.

- *List of institutions which must be informed (according to severity).* The provider of communication services, CSIRT.SK as a governmental institution dealing with monitoring of cyber incidents and warning against actual cyber threats, the police, media and other relevant institutions must be in the list.

- *List of possible incidents, prioritization.* The list contains individual incidents. The type of incident determines the potential impact of the incident on the institution; it can influence confidence, institutional integrity and data availability. Data concerning the time and resources necessary to restore the organization's activities are of great importance too. The list includes the following incidents and can be renewed as needed: DoS and DDoS incidents, botnets, malware, phishing, scaring, identity theft, social engineering, worms, key loggers, ransomware, Trojan horses, spyware and adware. The list must be permanently updated because of the changing environment of cyberspace.

- *Definition of escalation procedures.* Each individual incident has its own specific escalation procedures; this part will be subject to further survey and research. KRIMA enables us to control workflow and implementation of procedures in real time and generates permanent automatic information to responsible persons, and damaged institutions or persons.

- *Monitoring and update of systems.* Monitoring of information about published threats on the CSIRT portal, control of system files integrity in preparation for possible threat, control of configuration files, log control and proactive search for suspicious activities are very important.

Task 2: Incident detection and disconnecting all devices from the network
This runs either by automatic warning from monitoring and control systems (e.g., lost connectivity alarm, temporary unavailability of service) or inadequate parameters (e.g., CPU utilization, packet loss, extension of network response, attack on wireless network and so on). To report an incident, one can use the predefined EEM KRIMA on-line form,

telephone, e-mail or other appropriate means. The system administrator finds out suspicious activity through routine control of logs and spot checks of monitoring systems. The emergence of unknown files on the server, changed configuration of files, network communication on ports from unknown IP addresses, changed intensity of network traffic and so on can be considered as incidents. Internal and external users of systems can report unavailability of services, publishing of confidential data on the Internet and so on. Electronic spamming from internal systems of the institution can be reported by an automatic anti-spam service. Other relevant sources of incident reporting are the reports of lawyers of the damaged institutions, for example, because of multimedia file sharing. To stop encryption, immediately disconnect the infected device from the network. If the device (infected device) uses wireless connectivity (Wi-Fi, Bluetooth), it is necessary to disable the appropriate adapter. It is also necessary to disconnect all external storage devices (USB, external hard drive). It is not recommended to delete any files, even if they are considered to be suspicious files, because this could complicate or completely disable the data recovery process.

On the basis of the results of the previous analyses, one can design a solution and workflow. Right after this, it is necessary to check the effectiveness of the adopted solution and modify it (if necessary) in order to achieve the desired results, for example, to block the IP addresses of an attacker at the level of either network (IP access list) or server (host firewall), to replace damaged system files from installation media or the Internet. If a particular service was misused for an attack, it is necessary to switch it off or reduce access to a limited number of users. If passwords were cracked, then it is necessary to change them all and initiate the process of a secure communication in order to access the systems.

Task 3: Recognition of the type of incident
The responsible persons have to avoid actions that can complicate the situation. The sudden switch off of all servers or routers, that is, changes of configuration, can do more damage and later complicate the solution of the incident and reconstruction of functions.

The reported incident must be evaluated in terms of its severity. The important parameters can be identified as follows:

- Identification of systems, that is, services which are under attack, badly damaged or unavailable.
- Identification of systems, that is, services which can be affected by malfunctioning of systems which are under attack.
- Duration of incident, types of leaked data, estimated extent of the problem and the time to fix it.

- Necessary human, material and financial resources.
- Identification of possible external subjects which can be/are part of the incident.
- Call together all members of the team (crisis management team) or use predefined escalation procedures.
- Distribution of tasks to individual members of the crisis management team.
- Given the nature of the incident, it is necessary to make a decision about the content and extent of information at risk in order to eliminate any negative factors occurring during the process of solution.

Task 4: Identify the extent of infection to critical infrastructure
Collection of data and report evidence. All information about the incident, parts of logs, memory content, running processes, suspicious files and other relevant information are archived in a safe place in order to analyze them, operate them and use them in possible civil or criminal law cases. On the basis of the information gained, one can identify the cause of the incident. It is necessary to control the integrity of the file systems and control the content of the server file systems in order to detect suspicious changes. It is necessary to analyze network communication directed to the attacked system, including IP addresses and ports. There should also be a search for other attacked systems communicating with the IP addresses of the attacker. Addresses are assigned to real branches of institutions.

Task 5: Verify the existence of backups
The existence and the status of the backup data fundamentally influences further processes of the solution. If a backup exists, it is necessary to compare it with the list of encrypted files and folders. If the backup has not been done automatically, and the user has not backed up the last versions of the affected files and folders, there is a high risk that the restoration of the files will not be completed.

Task 6: Informing responsible peers in the organization and/or state
After analysing the severity of the incident, it is advisable to contact the relevant security authority within the organization or state. Depending on the organizational structure, there may be several relevant information security units.

Task 7: Identification of type and version of malware (ransomware)
This step is very important in the case of the existence of backups because precise identification of the ransomware infection can help the user to rescue the systems and adopt effective measures in order to prevent another

infection. In some cases, the type and version of ransomware is published in the alarm message, which directly communicates with the user that the computer was infected (e.g., CryptoLocker). In other cases, it is necessary to identify the ransomware according to the alarm message or methods of payment. It is possible to use some available identification tools on the Internet; they work on the basis of analysing samples of the encrypted files. One such tool is available on the web-page of the above-mentioned initiative "No More Ransom!". Another tool called "ID Ransomware" is able to identify 264 types and versions of ransomware (https://id-ransomware. malwarehunterteam.com/). Other similar identification tools can be found on web-pages of several companies, which provide antivirus solutions.

Task 8: Managerial decision for next steps
Pay or do not pay ransom? If the external technical support does not help, the infected user has only two options left. First, the user does not pay a fee (ransom) and loses all the encrypted data. Second, the user pays the ransom in order to regain access to all files, and hopes that the attackers give him the key to decrypt his locked data. However, paying the ransom does not mean that the attackers will give the user a functional decryption key that will really work. One in five users who actually paid the ransom were unable to retrieve the infected data, according to Kaspersky Lab (2016). The well-known case of the attacked hospital in the United States demonstrates that paying the ransom does not mean that the user is able to regain all encrypted data and files. Sometimes attackers demand another payment in order to unlock all other files. There is also a high probability that the attackers will send another malware together with the decryption key. It is evident that if the "victims" pay a fee, they de facto agree with this "business model" and so support the development of new malware. An important recommendation of the IT community, therefore, is do not pay a ransom, even at the cost of data loss. Very important data, such as pertaining to health, should be backed up without compromise.

Task 9: Paying ransom
Paying ransome is not advised. In the most recent massive ransomware energy distribution infrastructure attack in Uraine in June 2017, decryption was not possible. Altought critical infrastructure was very well secured, the malware was imported and installed by an infected business partner of the power distribution company.

Task 10: Contacting CSIRT and/or other organizations for decryption
If the organization is not able to find a ransomware decryptor in order to unlock files, or a ransomware decryptor is available but the user is not able

to unlock the infected files and folders, or the user is not able to precisely identify the type and version of ransomware, then it is necessary to try to contact the technical support of a company providing antivirus solutions or a computer incidents unit (Computer Security Incident Response Team – CSIRT, https://www.csirt.gov.sk). There are many specialists working in these centers and units who have up to date information on how to deal with these types of computer security incidents. However, in many cases they are not able to decrypt and unlock the infected files. This is because some types and versions of ransomware use the RSA encryption algorithm with 2048-bit keys, which is virtually unbreakable.

Task 11: Decryption if available
Decrypting, if there is no backup or if the backup does not completely cover all encrypted files, is necessary to find out if the identified type and version of ransomware gives the user the possibility to decrypt infected files and folders. The web-page of "No More Ransom!" offers quite a long list of so-called "ransomware decryptors", that is, tools used to unlock files locked by ransomware. Other ransomware decryptors can be found on the web-pages of companies providing antivirus solutions, for example, ESET, which has published tools called "Crysis" (http://support.eset.com/ kb6274), and TeslaCrypt (http://support.eset.com/kb6051).

Task 12: System recovery from or without backup
Disaster recovery or business continuity procedures start to run. Damaged data must be reconstructed from backup media. These well-known procedures are implemented at all critical infrastructure computer systems.

Task 13: Backup infected files for future identification
Backup encrypted data if the user decides not to pay a ransom. It is highly recommended to backup all encrypted data because there is a non-zero chance that the ransomware decryptor for a specific type and version of ransomware will be developed in the near future.

Task 14: Incident documentation and evaluation
The evaluation and documentation phase of the incident and the incident solution itself consist of the following steps. A summary of the information/knowledge gained concerning the cause and adopted procedures should be generated. This information is provided to the management of the organization, relevant third parties and the media if necessary. Measures are adopted to eliminate repetition of the incident, including training courses for system administrators and users. Based on the results of previous analyses, a new solution and corrected workflow are designed.

Right after that it is necessary to check out the effectiveness of the adopted solution and modify it (if necessary) in order to achieve the desired results. If a particular service was misused for an attack, then it is necessary to switch it off or reduce access to a limited number of users. If the passwords were cracked, then it is necessary to change them all and initiate the process of a secure communication in order to access the systems.

10.5 CONCLUSION

The EEM KRIMA simulation software implemented and operated at the Crisis Management Center of Matej Bel University is dedicated to the design, simulation and production of crisis management scenarios. The system has been outlined in detail in the chapter. The disaster crisis situations described have enormous potential to cause serious problems for states, organizations and individuals, if not properly managed. Crisis management using automated digital crisis scenarios is a proven solution to these problems. Careful preparation of modeling scenarios in order to avoid, or once it happens, minimize damage and save lives is a must of today. We chose and then described three crisis management examples with a very distinct impact. A catastrophic incident such as a traffic accident resulting in mass casualties, a global swine flu pandemic and ransomware attacks on critical infrastructure have enormous potential to cause very serious problems for communities. Today, their potential is even rising. When carefully debugged in simulation setups, these case study scenarios of the described catastrophic incidents, flu pandemic and ransomware attacks can run in real time.

REFERENCES

Atos (2012). *Atos IT Solutions and Services: KRIMA User's Manual*, Vol. 1, Bratislava, Slovakia, pp. 1–91.
Fabián, K., Kollár, D., and Francu, D. (2016). Simulačný systém pre tvorbu scenárov krízového manažmentu a prípadová štúdia: nehoda s hromadným postihnutím osôb. In *Proceedings of Crisis Scenarios in the Training System of Crisis Managers at Police Academies*, Academy of Police Forces, Bratislava, Slovakia, pp. 118–22. ISBN 978-80-8054-662-5.
Fabián, K., Kottman, P., and Dobrík, M. (2017). Ransomware crisis management and crisis scenario simulation. In *Proceedings of the 15th International Multidisciplinary Scientific Geoconference (SGEM)*, Sofia, Bulgaria, pp. 533–40. ISBN 978 619 7408 01 0.
Kaspersky Lab (2016). Consumer security risk survey 2016, https://media. kasperskycontenthub.com/wp-content/uploads/sites/45/2018/03/08233604/ B2C_survey_2016_report.pdf (accessed 10 February 2018).

Kazanský, R. and Melková, M. (2015). Information technologies and their usage in crisis management as a tool to increase the quality of educational process. In *Proceedings of the 15th International Multidisciplinary Scientific Geoconference (SGEM)*, Vol. 3, Sofia, Bulgaria, pp. 917–24. ISBN 978-619-7105-41-4. ISSN 1314-2704.

Kleiboer, M. (1997). Simulation methodology for crisis management support, *Journal of Contingencies and Crisis Management*, **5**(4), December, 198–206.

Lipovský, R., Štefanko, L., and Braniša, G. (2016). Rise of android ransomware, ESET, Bratislava, Slovakia, https://www.welivesecurity.com/wp-content/uploads/2016/02/Rise_of_Android_Ransomware.pdf (accessed 1 March 2018).

Nersessian, N.J. and MacLeod, M.A.J. (2017). Models and simulations. In L. Magnani and T. Bertolotti (eds), *Springer Handbook of Model-based Science,* Switzerland: Springer, pp. 119–32. doi: 10.1007/978-3-319-30526-4 5

Oesterman Research Inc. (2016). Best practices for dealing with phishing and ransomware, Oesterman Research White Paper, August, https://www.osterman research.com/home/white-papers/ (accessed 5 March 2018).

OSCE (2013). Good Practices Guide on Non-nuclear Critical Energy Infrastructure Protection from Terrorist Attacks Focusing on Threats Emanating from Cyberspace, Action against Terrorism Unit, Transnational Threats Department, Organization for Security and Co-operation in Europe, *Vienna, Austria. ISBN 978-92-9235-022-2.*

Simoes-Marques, M.J., Bica, J., and Correia, A. (2017). Modeling and simulation in support of disaster preparedness. In *Proceedings of the International Conference (AHFE)*, *Advances in Intelligent Systems and Computing*, Vol. 592, Los Angeles, July, pp. 121–32.

Uhrínová, B. (2017). Krízový manažment: Simulácia krízového scenára pre prípad pandémie chrípky, Master's Thesis, UMB Banská, Bystrica Bystrica, Slovakia.

Walker, W.E., Giddings, J., and Armstrong, S. (2011). Training and learning for crisis management using a virtual simulation-gaming environment, *Cognition, Technology & Work*, **13**(3), 163–73. doi: 10.1007/s10111-011-0176-6

Weick, K.E. and Sutcliffe, K.M. (2007). *Managing the Unexpected: Resilient Performance in an Age of Uncertainty*, San Francisco, CA: Jossey-Bass.

11. Emerging urban dynamics and labor market change: an agent-based simulation of recovery from a disaster

A. Yair Grinberger and Daniel Felsenstein*

11.1 INTRODUCTION

A large-scale disaster has an immediate destructive effect on the urban environment. Tangible and readily observable impacts highlight the devastation to urban stocks such as roads, critical infrastructure, housing, offices and industrial plants. Urban flows are also disrupted but they have received much less attention. These relate to the movement of workers, households, information and capital in the aftermath of a disaster. Stocks and flows are of course dynamically related. For example, the movement of people is facilitated by highways and the movement of financial capital by high speed cables infrastructure. A key flow relates to the operation of the labor market. A large-scale shock reduces capital stocks and alters the demographic composition. The abrupt destruction of capital exerts a downward force on wages initially driven by a reduction in marginal productivity. While damage to stock is dramatic, visible and easily simulated, flow effects are harder to capture. Wage rigidities can slow down the actual decline in wages and matching and search frictions can cause job vacancies to remain unoccupied. Empirical evidence of recent disasters suggests that destruction to capital stock does not always elicit the anticipated flow response in terms of reduction of wages or employment (Deryugina et al., 2014; Groen et al., 2015; Fabling et al., 2016). Urban recovery from a

* Acknowledgements: Thanks to Peleg Samuels for instructive comments on earlier drafts of this chapter. This work was funded under research agreement #3-12548, Ministry of Science, Technology and Space, the Japan-Israel Bilateral Research Fund as part of the research program 'Increasing Urban Resilience to Large Scale Disasters: The Development of a Dynamic Integrated Model for Disaster Management and Socio-Economic Analysis (DIM2SEA)'.

disaster is therefore dependent on the non-symmetrical interdependencies between stocks and flows.

The objective of this chapter is to capture these interdependencies using an agent-based (AB) model that simulates urban dynamics post-disaster. To the best of our knowledge the post-disaster labor market has not hitherto been treated in this way. AB models conceptualize the dynamics of a system as emerging from the behavior of its most atomistic components and from their interactions with the environment and with each other. This bottom-up approach simplifies the analysis of complex systems behavior by highlighting three fundamental entities: (1) agents and their attributes; (2) the environment and its attributes; and (3) decision rules guiding the behavior of agents. The current model builds on previous work (Grinberger and Felsenstein, 2016) and identifies building-block agents as city residents (individuals and households). While AB models have been applied in disaster studies (Chaturvedi et al., 2005) they have not been spatially explicit and have generally been set in hypothetical rather than real-world environments. Conversely, spatially explicit models of urban dynamics have not addressed catastrophic urban change (Ettema, 2011; Lemoy et al., 2017). The current model builds on previous work that looked at the distributional effects of urban disasters but was absent an explicit labor market model (Grinberger and Felsenstein, 2016).

This chapter proceeds as follows. We outline the components of the AB model in the following section, highlighting the labor market sub-model. The data and parameter values used for calibrating the model are then presented and the case study area for the simulation is described. Simulation outputs at the micro (building) level are subsequently analyzed with a view to understanding the contribution of labor market process to formulating emerging urban dynamics in the aftermath of a disaster. The chapter concludes with some observations relating to the interdependencies between stock and flows in generating urban recovery.

11.2　AGENT-BASED SIMULATION OF THE LABOR MARKET

Figure 11.1 depicts the urban system as comprising three distinct markets: the housing market; the land-use market; and the labor market. Agents such as individuals, households and workers operate in these markets directly through bottom-up impacts on other agents and their environment (represented by capital stock). Elements of the environments such as buildings and job are defined as immobile quasi-agents. They do not initiate actions like regular agents but are still sensitive to environmental

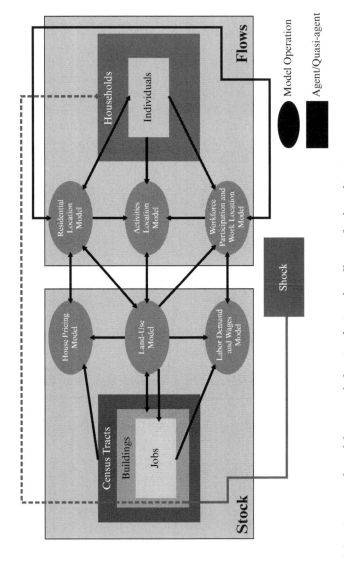

Figure 11.1   An agent-based framework for simulating the effects of urban disasters

changes taking place in their vicinity via a set of top-down rules of influence (in contrast with the bottom-up activity of agents). Accordingly, each
subsystem simulated in Figure 11.1 includes an agent-oriented bottom-up
behavior model and a stock-oriented top-down model of environmental
effects. We introduce a physical shock, representing an earthquake into
this system. This generates damage to buildings and the road network and
thus directly affects agents and their behavior. Through the dynamics of
the model, indirect and lasting changes may also emerge. The Appendix
presents the general procedures of the system. Previous work (Grinberger
and Felsenstein, 2016; Grinberger et al., 2017) discusses specific definitions
of elements unrelated to the labor market. Our discussion here focuses on
the labor market component of the AB framework and only briefly surveys
other sub-models.

11.2.1 Housing Market Dynamics

Household decisions within the housing market are based on pre-defined
probabilities. At each iteration (representing a temporal unit of one day)
households decide whether to move from their current place of residence
to a new location within the study area or outside. The decision to move
to a new location is based on an income constraint (assuming the agent is
employed) and household preference with respect to commuting distances
and neighborhood socio-demographic homogeneity. The model computes
attractiveness scores for different locations based on the mixture of these
two factors. These are then assessed in relation to agent preference values
(computed on the basis of current location conditions) and the households
choose the first sufficiently attractive asset allocated. If a relocating
household fails to find a suitable location after a pre-defined number of
attempts, it out-migrates. Members of out-migrating households can keep
their jobs within the area. Otherwise, these jobs become unoccupied. The
model also considers in-migration, where the number of new households
created at each iteration is set stochastically, based on the number of unoccupied assets.

 Change in the size of population represents change in the demand for
housing. We couple this with changes to the number of residential units
(i.e., supply of housing) and to the number of non-residential functions
(representing service level) to generate change in census-tract-level housing average values per m^2. These changes trickle down to the level of the
individual building where the value of a building and its related monthly
rent are computed based on the tract-level housing values and building
accessibility to services. Hence, price levels vary between tracts and within
them creating heterogeneous local housing markets.

11.2.2   Land-use Dynamics

At each iteration, individual agents perform different activities within the study area. The number of activities is stochastically determined according to agent mobility and employment profile. For example, children, disabled populations, agents with no access to vehicles and unemployed agents undertake fewer activities. The location of each activity is set according to floor-space volume (larger buildings are more attractive), the nature of the buildings environment (i.e., the share of unoccupied buildings) and the road-network distance from the previous activity, starting from home. These components are correspondingly the product of three behavioral assumptions: preference for scale; risk evasiveness; and distance minimization. The primary activity of locally employed agents is set as their workplace. The shortest road-network routes are computed for each sequence of activities. To minimize computing demand, a routine is computed for each agent which changes only at specific instances for example, when the agent changes residence or workplace, when land-use or the road-network change or when a disaster occurs.

Land-use change is related to flows of populations with households moving away from residential buildings and leaving them unoccupied and with households moving into buildings and making them residential. We also define a top-down environmental-sensitivity-based procedure to account for changes to the commercial building stock. This procedure relies on the assumptions that larger buildings require more commuters to be sustainable and that traffic loads on roads near buildings are a proxy for commuter flows. A correlation should therefore exist between traffic flows and commercial floor-space volumes. For each building, a correlation is computed based on the relative location (within the entire population of buildings) of building floor-space volume and its nearby average traffic load value over the previous 30 days. When the correlation is low enough, non-commercial buildings become commercial and commercial buildings become unoccupied. When a building changes land-use, all agents employed in the building lose their jobs. Residents of the building randomly decide between out-migrating and relocating locally and new jobs are created based on building floor-space volume and the job density parameter (see Appendix). Public-use buildings never change their use even after reconstruction following a disaster and remain unoccupied during the rebuilding stage.

11.2.3 The Labor Market

The labor market is conceived as comprised of tradeable and perfectly mobile labor and a spatially rigid product market.[1] In this world, jobs represent the stock or labor demand side and their wage levels represent firm reactions to local market conditions. Agents supply labor and are free to move between jobs including those located outside the study area. Given the small size of the study area (see below), we assume any agent seeking to commute will manage to find a job.

The top-down sub-model in this context deals with setting wages attached to unoccupied jobs. We introduce a parameter termed the 'local clearing wage' which is akin to the level of wage firms would offer under a closed equilibrium setting. It is based on an intra-temporal linear approximation of the marginal product of labor derived from a Cobb-Douglas production function (equation 11.1).

$$\log\left(\frac{W_t}{W_{t-1}}\right) = \alpha \cdot \log\left(\frac{K_t}{K_{t-1}}\right) + (\beta - 1) \cdot \log\left(\frac{L_t}{L_{t-1}}\right) \rightarrow W_t$$

$$= W_{t-1} \cdot \frac{K_t^{\alpha}}{K_{t-1}^{\alpha} \cdot \left(\frac{L_{d,t}}{L_{d,t-1}}\right)^{1-\beta}} \qquad (11.1)$$

where W_t represents clearing wage levels, K_t capital stock levels, $L_{d,t}$ the demand for labor at time t, and α and β are Cobb-Douglas parameters.

Floor-space volume represents capital stock and the share of occupied jobs represents the demand for labor from all jobs. Changes to the value of this latter parameter trickle down to the level of the individual unoccupied job (the model assumes firms are unable to adjust wages of occupied jobs) where its value shifts with the change in clearance wage levels.

Individual agents react to these changing wage levels and their actions form the supply side. Based on these changes, agents may decide to join the workforce and the larger the increase in the clearing wage, the more agents are attracted. Unemployed agents constantly look for an open position that satisfies their requirements. We compute the attractiveness of a specific workplace as a function of the wage offered and the commuting distance required from the agent:

---

[1]   This structure is chosen purely for agent-based simulation tractability. See Grinberger and Samuels (2018) for an alternative structure simulated numerically.

$$S_{i,j} = \alpha \cdot \frac{d(h_i, b_j)}{\max\{d(k, b_j): k \in B\}} + (1-\alpha) \cdot \frac{w_j - \min\{w_k \forall k \in J\}}{\max\{w_k: k \in J\} - \min\{w_k: k \in J\}}$$

$$(11.2)$$

where $S_{i,j}$ is the attractiveness score of an unoccupied job j for agent i, α is used to weight the different components, h_i is agent i's residential location, b_j is job j's location, w_j is the wage offered by job j, $d(x,y)$ is the network distance between locations x and y, B is the entire buildings set, J is the set of unoccupied jobs.

This specific formulation is driven by the assumptions that judgments are relative and that agents substitute wages with commuting distance. In such a case, agents are willing to accept a cut in wages if this allows them to reduce their commute. Agents' preference scores are computed according to their previous workplace characteristics or randomly, if they were never employed. Agents are not assumed to have perfect information and their capabilities are constrained to considering only seven unoccupied jobs at each iteration. When failing to find a job, an agent may decide to commute out of the area or leave the labor force. This decision is random and becomes more probable the longer the agent's job-search. If an agent decides to commute, its income is defined by the expected wage from previous employment or randomly. Finding a position within the study area alters not only the agent's earnings but also those of its household.

11.3   DATA, DEFINITIONS AND CONTEXT OF THE CASE STUDY

Model implementation relates to a hypothetical earthquake in the Jerusalem city center. This is a small (1.45 km²), well-defined, mixed land-use area incorporating both residential and commercial land-uses, a large enclosed street market (Machane Yehuda) and government offices (Figure 11.2). The majority of floor-space in the area is commercial (505,000 m²) followed by public (420,000 m²) and residential (243,000 m²). In terms of buildings counts, most of the structures are residential use (717) followed by public (179) and commercial (119). The area is served by two major public transportation arteries (Jaffa and King George Streets) (Figure 11.2).

National 2008 census data records a resident population of the study area of 22,243 individuals comprising 8665 households and 39,069 jobs. Information on individual buildings, including land-use, number of floors and floor-space are derived from data supplied by the Israeli Land Survey but no such micro-level data is available for population and the

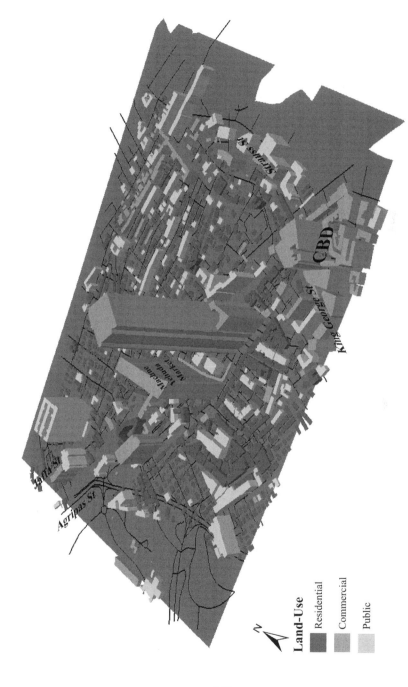

Figure 11.2   The study area: height represents floor-space volume

Land-Use

Residential

Commercial

Public

labor market. Hence, we utilize a disaggregation procedure algorithm (Grinberger and Felsenstein, 2017) which produces synthetic representations of individuals, households and their traits, and allocates them to buildings. The resulting dataset may not be accurate at the level of the single observation but still conforms to Statistical Areas (i.e., census tracts) totals. The allocation of jobs is synthetic in that the number of jobs in a building is computed using a land-use specific jobs per meter (i.e., job density, see Appendix) parameter. Wages are randomly drawn for these jobs from a normal distribution defined by the average wage and standard deviation parameters (see Appendix). We assign agents to jobs in a way that minimizes the differences between agent earnings and wages from jobs. We assume an initial state of full employment and job occupancy. All jobs not assigned to agents are assumed to be occupied by commuters. The resulting share of jobs occupied by non-residents defines the value of another model parameter used to determine whether non-residents would occupy new jobs when they are created (*In-comm*, see Appendix).

We simulate the scenario 25 times, allowing for an initial run-in period of 30 days in which no land-use changes are allowed. Throughout the rest of the simulation no regulation of land-use change is enforced except for public use. We let the model run another 30 days before activating the earthquake model at t = 60 in order to let the system reorganize at least in terms of the land-use system (wages may still vary at the end of this period). As many changes happen at t = 30, it is better to consider this point in time as the true starting point of the simulation. We simulate the earthquake as a single shock spreading outwards from a randomly located epicenter to avoid spatially biasing the results. The shock can lead to the collapse of buildings, and building height and distance from the epicenter determine collapse probabilities. A building collapse forces residents to relocate and makes agents employed within it unemployed. It also blocks the proximate roads nearby (i.e., those starting/ending in the junction nearest to the building) until the building is restored. Restoration periods are proportional to floor-space volumes. The simulations run for three years after the earthquake (i.e., 1155 iterations).

11.4 RESULTS

11.4.1 Macro-level Patterns

For a macro perspective on emerging urban dynamics we observe indicators of the ability of the urban system to achieve stability post-disaster over the long term (Table 11.1). This is accomplished by identifying the

Table 11.1 *Frequency and duration with which various measures achieve equilibrium and the related changes in their values*

Category	Variable	Share of simulations reaching an equilibrium (%)	Days until equilibrium (average)	Initial value	Rate of total change – simulations reaching stable state (%)	Rate of change – simulations not reaching equilibrium (%)
Building stock	Residential buildings	100.00	118.68	562.31	−2.38	–
	Commercial buildings	100.00	396.88	270.41	−33.09	–
Labor market	Total number of jobs	88.00	146.41	37081.44	−33.11	−35.77
	Occupancy rate	100.00	0.00	99.51%	–	–
	Local occupancy rate	88.00	28.95	13.67%	−17.44	−21.24
	Clearance wage	100.00	108.48	7138.08	−2.74	–
	Average wage – occupied by resident	96.00	0.00	5354.43	−0.93	4.76
	Average wage – occupied by commuter	100.00	0.00	7237.20	1.65	–
Population	Households	100.00	206.48	6411.84	72.27	–
	Agents	100.00	223.36	16834.73	122.55	–
	Workforce participation rate	100.00	80.68	60.87%	−12.95	–
	Unemployment rate	36.00	926.33	0.75%	261.10	130.96
	Local employment rate	88.00	279.05	49.74%	−71.44	−75.15
	Average earnings	100.00	78.12	5199.32	16.41	–
	Average earnings – locally employed	100.00	0.00	5353.23	−1.00	–
	Average earning – employed outside	100.00	88.60	5046.43	23.51	–

last significant change to have been registered for a given measure in each simulation and calculating the extent of this change. To reduce sensitivity to temporary and minor changes, for each iteration we compute the average value over the subsequent 30 iterations (i.e., the moving average). A significant change is identified when the difference between two subsequent moving average values is greater than 0.1 percent. An equilibrium state is identified if the last significant change is registered at least 60 days prior to the end of the simulation. Table 11.1 details the frequency of achieving stability over all simulations for each measure, average duration and average rate of change relative to the last pre-shock moving average value (i.e., at t = 30), when equilibrium was achieved and when it was not.

Table 11.1 implies that the urban system tends to reach a stable equilibrium with most measures attaining some sort of stability. This new state, however, is not similar to pre-shock conditions (i.e., conditions at t = 59). This is evident in the status of the stock. While residential stock succeeds in maintaining its size, commercial stock loses almost a third of all buildings. Since residential stock suffers from a shock but rebounds quite fast, it seems that its recovery is not related to the reconstruction of damaged buildings but to the conversion of previously commercial structures to residential use. The commercial building stock requires much more time to stabilize, suggesting a lingering effect of the shock.

Housing and commercial stock-level changes directly influence the labor market. As residential functions produce less jobs than commercial functions, the number of jobs rapidly decreases and stabilizes shortly after the residential stock has reached an equilibrium. In the two simulations in which a stable state was not achieved this situation only intensifies, suggesting that the shock is of sufficient magnitude to derail the urban system for the time period under consideration. It is reasonable to expect that if longer periods were simulated a stable state would be attained in all simulations. Occupancy rates and wages of occupied jobs (by residents and commuters) do not change, however, due to the rigidity of the labor market. Firms, as defined in the model, cannot fire employees or adjust wages and thus the values of these measures are dominated by the jobs that survive the shock. What does change is the value of the clearance wage parameter. This stabilizes quite quickly to a lower-level value in most cases. Given that occupancy rates do not change, this change is primarily driven by change in floor-space. Hence, it is not surprising to see that recovery periods are very similar for both the residential stock and this parameter. Interestingly, change in the total floor-space translates into a relatively constrained decrease in the parameter value.

Constrained as it is, this change is large enough to affect the labor force. Population size increases significantly with the number of agents more than doubling, that is, potential workers enter the area, due to more living spaces becoming available. These new residents face lower wage levels and reduced demand for labor. Consequently, they are forced to find alternative solutions such as dropping out of the workforce (decreasing participation rates) or commuting to locations outside the study area (decreasing local employment rates). As some of the new population in-migrate while retaining their original workplaces outside the area, the latter effect is much stronger. Workers choose a commuting option in the absence of a labor market solution that meets their earning requirements. Given the higher level of average offered wages outside the area, this pushes up both overall average income and out-commuters' average income.

Note that unemployment rarely reaches equilibrium within the given recovery frame and the effect is more constrained when it does not stabilize (Table 11.1). This is largely a technical outcome resulting from this parameter's initial moving average value and the manner by which equilibrium is identified here. Since the initial value is 0.75 percent, the identification process becomes very sensitive to small changes. From about day 650 when the system tends to settle down (Figure 11.3), a change of about 0.1 percent in unemployment rates (equivalent to an increase/decrease of less than one agent) is sufficient for a significant change to be identified. When the sensitivity of the procedure is decreased so that stable states are identified using a 0.5 percent threshold, the unemployment measure reaches

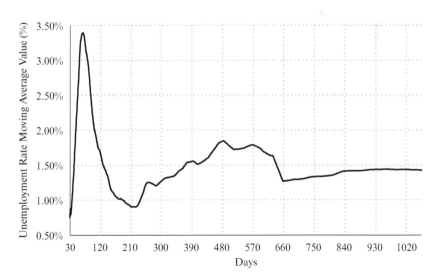

Figure 11.3 *Average change in the moving average value for unemployment (over a time frame of 30 iterations)*

equilibrium in 88.00 percent of the simulations, after 556.23 iterations on average, and the level of change is greater in simulations that do not achieve stability.

In sum, the macro-level results depict a relatively negative picture for the study area. It is subject to large-scale and permanent change that alters its fundamental nature. From a mixed-use area affluent in commercial activity it changes into a functionally suburban-type neighborhood with a residential population but little non-residential and employment activities and with much commuting to out of area places of employment by higher income earners.

11.4.2   Micro-level Results

The macro-level results smokescreen important micro-level spatial dynamics. AB modeling facilitates the investigation of building-level (micro) changes driving labor market change. In the results below we present snapshots of these dynamics at specific temporal junctions such as prior to the shock (t = 59), two months into recovery (t = 120), t = 250 and t = 750. When land-use is presented (Figure 11.4), each building is shaded according to its most frequent use across the simulations. For other measures, discrete building-level values are converted into continuous surfaces using ESRI's ArcGIS's Kernel Density tool,[2] in order to clearly illustrate emergent patterns.

Figure 11.4 presents changes in land-use patterns. Each time period beyond t = 0 presents only those buildings that change land-use relative to their initial use. The initial dynamics of the model lead to many small commercial uses emerging in the study area. This is an effect unrelated to the disaster and driven by the fact that no land-use regulation is enforced in the model, thus creating a first round of reorganization over the time period t = 30 to t = 60. Most changes, however, happen shortly after day 30, indicating that the land-use system re-stabilizes. The earthquake makes this new arrangement untenable and by t = 120 close inspection reveals that some of these new venues return to their initial use. In addition, other commercial uses, including those within the central business district (CBD), become residential by this point. These buildings are characterized by larger floor-space volumes. This trend intensifies over time, with more commercial venues vanishing, including the Machane Yehuda market. This continues until most surviving commercial uses locate in one cluster

---

[2]   Cell size was defined to be 25 meters, search radius 100 meters, and output values taken as the expected values according to the calculation (in contrast to the default option of the Kernel tool which is density values).

t = 0

t = 59

t = 120

t = 250

t = 750

t = 1000

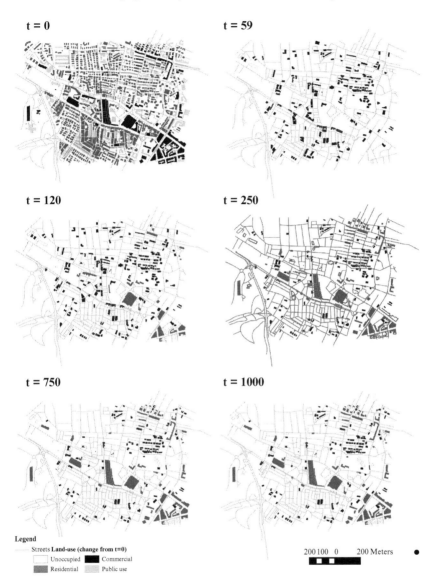

Legend

Streets **Land-use (change from t=0)**

Unoccupied   Commercial

Residential   Public use

200 100   0   200 Meters

Figure 11.4   Changes in land-use distribution at different time periods (only buildings that changed their initial land-use are presented at each time frame)

at the eastern part of the area, north of Jaffa Street. This cluster is the only venue capable of attracting sufficient visitors to cause mobility patterns to stabilize. These changes occur between the periods t = 120 and t = 250. They also explain the aggregate-level results such as the increase in population size and the longer recovery periods required by commercial stock.

Land-use change represents a physical change that also animates the number of jobs. In this way, stocks and flows in the urban environment are dynamically linked. The number of jobs stabilizes before the t = 250 period and jobs become more evenly distributed with the disappearance of the large commercial functions (Figure 11.5a). The composition of the labor market is more related to the flows of individuals and is thus more flexible and volatile. It remains dynamic even after the dynamics of stocks have settled down. This is true for the spatial distribution of the rates of job occupancy and local job occupancy (Figures 11.5b and 11.5c). The patterns these measures represent do not correlate with the distribution of jobs either spatially or temporally. Clusters of employment develop in the north-west and south-west corners of the area with the former character-ized by high local occupancy rates which continue to change significantly long after land-uses reach equilibrium. These emerging job clusters reflect the effect of commuting. They emerge in neighborhoods that retain their residential nature yet become more accessible to employment opportuni-ties across all time periods.

Figure 11.6 shows urban dynamics driven by supply-side changes in the labor market. The number of agents in the area is highly dependent on the supply of housing. It may seem that the largest change in housing supply occurs before the earthquake with a large office complex located between the CBD and the Machane Yehuda market changing to residential. Yet this result is biased by the size of this building – this change is registered so early only in one case, but since the building is able to house many households this acts to push the average number of residents up. This change becomes more common after the earthquake (recorded on eight other simulations by t = 120 and on a total of 11 by t = 250), along with the emergence of residential land-uses in the market and CBD, as evident in Figure 11.4. No notable changes can be identified after t = 250 (Figure 11.6a). Average incomes, however, show a certain level of rigidity while also presenting a dynamic nature. On the one hand, the main clusters of high earning agents remain stable throughout the simulation. On the other hand, they do not retain their original magnitude but spread spatially over time (Figure 11.6b). It is possible to attribute this to the limited tolerance high income households have for proximity to households of lower economic status. This tends to generate wealthier households in the clusters. High income and tolerant households are more likely to disperse from clusters,

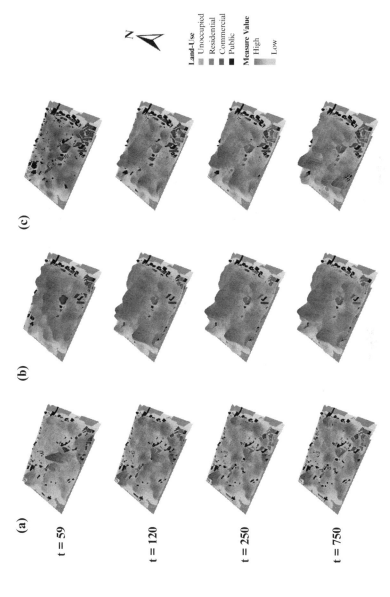

Figure 11.5 Changes in the spatial distribution of (a) jobs, (b) occupancy rates, and (c) share of jobs occupied by residents, over various time periods

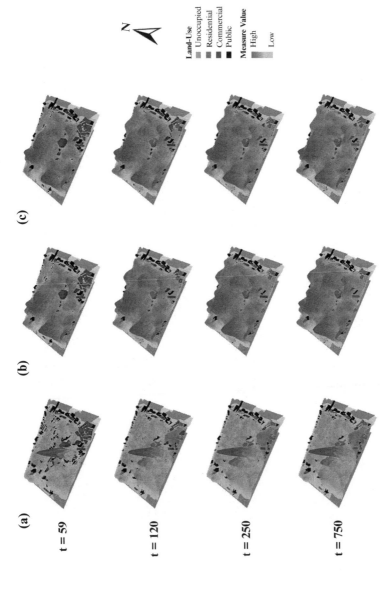

Figure 11.6   Changes in the spatial distributions of (a) agents, (b) average agent income, and (c) average locally employed agent income, over various time periods

especially when this reduces commuting. If this happens they will transform the nature of their local environment, facilitating the further dispersal of high income households. The 'invasion' of new and existing wealthier households into other neighborhoods drives housing prices up, limiting the ability of lower income households to cope with the new market conditions. These clusters continue to evolve beyond t = 250. Interestingly, the change in income of locally employed agents only partially follows this pattern. In this case, initial clusters retain much of their attraction power (Figure 11.6c). This can be related to their original location which remains accessible to commercial activities despite the changes to the distribution of land-uses. The outcome is that agents residing in these locations are in an optimal position to occupy the jobs created there.

11.5   CONCLUSIONS

Disasters such as earthquakes physically affect the urban fabric. They also generate a second wave of shocks that have a long-term effect on flows of residents, workers, activities and financial capital. Previous work has illustrated how this second wave can materialize into a spatial and functional reorganization of the system (Grinberger et al., 2017). The results presented in this chapter reflect these patterns. The pre-disaster dispersal of commercial activity remains viable and increasingly re-groups post-disaster as larger commercial concentrations become less sustainable. Earlier work also found these urban dynamics have negative distributional effects on lower income households (Grinberger and Felsenstein, 2016). Ostensibly, labor market dynamics might have been expected to increase the economic competitiveness of the lower income earners. However, the results reported in the chapter seem to replicate emerging social dynamics previously observed. While average incomes rise despite a decrease in the clearance wage parameter, the in-migration of wealthier households who disperse across the city creates new clusters of affluent populations.

Incorporating labor market processes into the understanding of urban dynamics highlights the fact that over the long term the area does not stabilize on a new state. Rather, it changes its function relative to the outside world and evolves into a type of residential suburb in which most working residents commute. This is due not only to lower levels of demand for labor but also to available jobs becoming less attractive to residents as evidenced by falling local job occupancy rates. This implies that agents are not forced to commute but choose to do so. The micro-level analysis reveals that the only locations still attractive to local workers are those located within residential neighborhoods. This is because they represent locations offering sufficient accessibility-related benefits to overcome wage-related considerations. The state of the road network and its recovery rate therefore represent an important component, facilitating or constraining urban recovery outcomes.

This chapter has shown the interdependence between urban stock and flows in post-disaster recovery. These relations are not, however, symmetrical and direct damage is not solely determined by the extent of physical destruction. In our case study, residential patterns reorganize within the area attracting even more population and most of the labor out-migrates. This is of course related to the way the labor market is articulated. Labor supply is perfectly mobile but firms and jobs are assumed to be rigid and constrained by existing contractual obligations. They do not adjust prices to remain competitive. Residential functions, however, have a flexible pricing mechanism that adjusts to demand in the market. Hence, outcomes are to a great extent dependent on the flexibility of stocks in adjusting to changing flows. While these working assumptions can be questioned, they highlight the importance of identifying the rigid components of the system requiring assistance, such as low income households or locally based firms. Informed analysis of urban dynamics through the prism of stocks and flows can assist policy makers in formulating locally tailored responses in the wake of a disaster.

REFERENCES

Chaturvedi, A., S. Mehta, D. Dolk and R. Ayer (2005), 'Agent-based simulation for computational experimentation: developing an artificial labor market', *European Journal of Operational Research*, **166** (3), 694–716.

Deryugina, T., L. Kawano and S. Levitt (2014), 'The economic impact of Hurricane Katrina on its victims: evidence from individual tax returns', No. w20713, National Bureau of Economic Research.

Ettema, D. (2011), 'A Multi-agent model of urban processes: modeling relocation processes and price setting in housing markets', *Computers, Environment and Urban Systems*, **35**, 1–11.

Fabling, R., A. Grimes and L. Timar (2016), 'Labour market dynamics following a regional disaster', Working Paper 16-07, Motu Economic and Public Policy Research, accessed 7 March 2018 at https://ssrn.com/abstract=2781769.

Grinberger, A.Y. and D. Felsenstein (2016), 'Dynamic agent-based simulation of welfare effects of urban disasters', *Computers, Environment and Urban Systems*, **59**, 129–41.

Grinberger, A.Y. and D. Felsenstein (2017), 'Using big (synthetic) data for identifying local housing market attributes', in Laurie Schintler and Zhenhua Chen (eds), *Big Data for Regional Science*, London and New York: Routledge, pp. 109–20.

Grinberger, A.Y. and P. Samuels (2018), 'Modeling the labor market in the aftermath of a disaster: two perspectives', *International Journal of Disaster Risk Reduction*, **31**, 419–34.

Groen, J.A., M.J. Kutzbach and A.E. Polivka (2015), 'Storms and jobs: the effect of Hurricane Katrina on individuals' employment and earnings over the long term', No. 15-21R, Center for Economic Studies, US Census Bureau

Grinberger, A.Y., M. Lichter and D. Felsenstein (2017), 'Dynamic agent based simulation of an urban disaster using synthetic big data', in Piyushimita Thakuria, Nebiyou Tilahun and Moira Zellner (eds), *Seeing Cities through Big Data: Research, Methods and Applications in Urban Informatics*, Cham: Springer, pp. 349–82.

Lemoy, R., C. Raux and P. Jensen (2017), 'Exploring the polycentric city with multi-worker households: an agent based microeconomic model', *Computers, Environment and Urban Systems*, **62**, 64–73.

APPENDIX: FORMALIZATION OF THE AGENT-BASED FRAMEWORK

This appendix details the procedures behind the behavior of different components of the AB model. These procedures rely on a number of parameters that are outlined along with their values in Table 11A.1.

Table 11A.1   Model parameters

Parameter	Type	Sub-model(s)	Description	Value in case study	Source
Out_prob	float	Residential location	Chance of household migrating out of the study area; ranges from 0 to 1	0.000029	Central Bureau of Statistics (CBS), 2016 data
In_comm	float	Residential location, land-use	Chance of a job being occupied by a worker residing outside the study area; ranges from 0 to 1	Set after the initialization of the simulation to be the share of jobs occupied by in-commuters out of all jobs	Endogenous
job_dens$_{residential}$	float	Land-use	Number of jobs per m^2, for residential uses	0.00047	Computed by integrating floor-space and job numbers per spatial unit data*
job_dens$_{commercial}$	Float	Land-use	Number of jobs per m^2, for commercial uses	0.03151	
job_dens$_{public}$	float	Land-use	Number of jobs per m^2, for public uses	0.04795	
a_wage	float	Land-use, Wages	Clearance wage	7177.493	Endogenous, based on input data
σ_{a_wage}	float	Land-use, wages	SD value for clearance wage	1624.297	Endogenous, based on input data
SL	float	Workplace location	Median length of job search	30	Arbitrary

Source: * CBS 2016 data.

BOX 11A.1   HOUSEHOLD BEHAVIOR RULES

h:= a household
if random(0,1) < *out-prob*: {
      delete *h*
      delete members of *h*
      stochastically determine whether jobs occupied by members of the household
           become unoccupied, in accordance to *In-comm*
}
else if random(0,1) < census-tract-level relocation probability {
      candidates:= {empty or residential buildings}∩{buildings where rent is lower
           than a third of *h*'s income}∩{buildings with free assets}∩{undamaged
           buildings}
      pref:= attractiveness score for *h*'s current home
      do min(100,length(candidates)) times {
           c:= random element of candidates
           score:= attractiveness score for *c*
           if score >=pref: {
                 h moves to *c*
                 stop iteration
           }
      }
      if no suitable candidate was found {
           delete *h*
           delete members of *h*
           stochastically determine whether jobs occupied by members of *h*
               become unoccupied, in accordance to *In-comm*
      }
}

BOX 11A.2   ACTIVITY LOCATION DECISION PROCEDURE

```
i = agent
a_num:= computed number of activities for i
loc:= i's home
path = empty list
do a_num times {
        if i is employed locally and this is the first activity {
                append the list of roads on-route between i's home and workplace to path
                loc:= i's workplace
        }
        else {
                pref:= random number between 0 and 1
                candidates:= {occupied buildings}∩{buildings accessible from loc}∩
                        {buildings for which attractiveness score <pref}
                if # candidates > 0: {
                        b:= random element of candidates
                        append the list of roads on-route between loc and b to path
                        loc:= b
                }
        }
}
append the list of roads on-route between loc and i's home to path
```

BOX 11A.3   PROCESSES ACTIVATED WHEN A BUILDING CHANGES ITS LAND-USE

```
n_lu:= new land-use for the building
for h ∈ {households residing in the building} {
        if random[0,1] < 0.5 {move out}
        else {relocate}
}
for i ∈ {agent employed within the building} {
        make i unemployed and set income to 0
}
```
create new jobs in the building in accordance with floor-space and $job\_dens_{n\_lu}$
stochastically draw wage levels for all jobs from a normal distribution based on a_wage and σ_{a_wage}
stochastically determine whether new jobs are occupied by a non-resident, in accordance to *In-comm*
set the new land-use for the building.

BOX 11A.4   WAGE MODEL PROCEDURES

compute the new a_wage parameter value
update wage levels for unoccupied jobs based on the change in a_wage
wf_chance:= 0.5*(the ratio between old and new a_wage levels)
candidates:= {adult and elderly agents not part of the workforce}
do #unoccupied jobs times {
      if random(0,1) < wf_chance {
          i:= random element of candidates with preferences to adults
          add *i* to the workforce
      }
      if #candidates=0 {stop}
}

BOX 11A.5   WORKPLACE LOCATION MODEL PROCEDURES

ujobs:= unoccupied jobs
do 7 times {
      j:= random element from ujobs
      $S_{j,i}$:= attractiveness score of job *j* for agent *i*
      P_i:= agent *i*'s preferences score
      if $P_j >$ =S_i {
          set *i*'s workplace to be *j*
          update *i*'s income and expected income in accordance with *j*'s offered
          wage
          P_i:= S_j
          stop
      }
}
if *i* is still unemployed {
      increase *i*'s search duration by 1
      S_i := *i*'s search duration
      if $1-e^{Si/SL} >$ random(0,1) {
          set *i* to commute outside of the area
          set *i*'s income in accordance with its expected income
      }
      else if $1-e^{Si/SL} >$ random(0,1) {
          remove *i* from the workforce
      }
}

Index

hierarchical cluster analysis 126,
128–30, 182
hospitality 31, 41, 44, 48
hurricane 10–11, 31, 51, 179

incident detection 201, 225
industry 4, 31–6, 41–5, 49, 76, 84, 88,
95–6, 98, 106–11, 118, 123, 165,
219
inequality 156–8
informality 170
inner areas 178, 185, 187, 189,
192–4
input-output analysis 76
intensive surveillance 215, 218
Internet of Things (IoT) 221
Italy 10–11, 176–80, 183–7, 190, 192,
194–6
Istanbul 95–6, 98–111, 117, 122–3

Japan 4, 10–14, 51–5, 58, 60, 62–5,
70–71, 74–84, 88–91, 163, 232

landslides 51, 175, 177, 179–81, 188–9,
191–2, 194

malware
and malware infection 220–23, 225,
227–8
manufacturing 35, 45, 89, 184, 190,
193
mass casualties 204–8, 230
mitigation 3, 22–3, 119, 163, 176–7
mountain areas 180, 192
municipality 143–4, 160–63, 168,
170–71, 177–86, 190, 195–6,
207

natural disasters/events 4, 6–7, 10–16,
21, 23, 33, 54–5, 109, 121, 175–7,
192
New Zealand 30–33, 35, 44, 48

overlapping seismic hazard 179

policy 3–8, 18–21, 25, 48–9, 55, 63, 71,
96, 109, 117, 137, 155–60, 164,
171, 178, 192–5, 222, 250
preparedness 7, 15, 97, 175–7, 194–5,
199, 205, 211

Presidential Policy Directive (PPD-
41) United States Cyber Incident
Coordination 222
prevention 7, 15, 21, 23, 55, 71, 175–7,
194, 200, 214, 216, 222–3
probability of a disaster 176, 178
profitability 31–4, 36–7, 40–41, 44–9
public warning 207–8, 210

Ramsey growth model 58
ransomware
and ransomware attack 219–25,
227–30
reconstruction 15, 21, 49, 53–4, 62, 71,
88, 90–92, 175–6, 200, 226, 236,
242
recovery 2, 4, 16–18, 22–3, 31–2, 37,
44, 49, 52, 54, 62, 71, 76–9, 91–2,
96, 101, 120, 175–6, 206, 226,
232–3, 242–4, 246, 250
remoteness 185
restoration 5, 51–5, 58–60, 63–4, 66,
68–71, 194, 227, 240
risk assessment 19–25, 163, 179, 195
risk governance 163, 175

scale 6, 10, 23, 30, 57, 63–4, 70, 74,
97, 105, 107, 120, 155–6, 159–60,
164–6, 170–72, 194, 213, 236
scenario
and scenario building 3, 19–20, 24–5,
107, 181, 199–200, 202, 204–21,
224, 230, 240
seismic hazard 179–80, 182
simulation software 199, 230
socio-economic conditions 176
social innovation 175–6
subsidy 35–6
supply chain 32–3
survival
and surviving 31–2, 37–49, 44–5, 48,
244
SWOT analysis 96, 98, 102–3, 105–9,
115
SWOT-TOWS analysis 109
see also TOWS matrix

task workflow 206, 213
territorial distribution 177, 185–6, 188,
190, 192, 195